JUDAISM'S TRUTH ANSWERS THE MISSIONARIES

JUDAISM'S TRUTH ANSWERS THE MISSIONARIES

BETH MOSHE

Bloch Publishing Company • New York

Library of Congress Cataloging-in-Publication Data

Moshe, Beth.
  Judaism's truth answers the missionaries.

  Bibliography: p.
  Includes indexes.
    1. Christianity—Controversial literature.
2. Judaism—Apologetic works.   3. Jesus Christ—Jewish interpretations.   I. Title.
BM590.M68   1987   296.3   87-15184
ISBN 0-8197-0520-9
ISBN 0-8197-0515-2 (pbk.)

Dedicated to Beloved Parents
Gittel and Moshe
And Others Like Them
Who Lived As Lights
Reflecting God's Love

With Special Love and Thanks
To My Sister
Esther - Estelle
An Angel of Help and Goodness

And to
The Six Million Holocaust Souls
And Our Other Jewish Martyrs

CONTENTS

1

Introduction

BOOK FOR JEWS. This book is a Jews for Judaism guide, written primarily to counter the thrust of the Christian missionary directed to the Jew. It is aimed at the mind and heart of the Jew who has an interest in or an attraction to Christianity. Every person of Jewish heritage who is a convert to Christianity or is contemplating conversion should read this book—now. In addition, it is meant to be read by Jews steadfast and devoted to Judaism, who nevertheless have wondered about Jesus. Jews who want to have answers, when sadly confronted with a loved one who would desert his heritage, will find this book a must for study, use, and their bookshelf. Although it is written for Jews, Christians who would like to know Biblical Judaism as Jews understand it will also find this book of interest. They will see that Christianity's Messiah and Judaism's Messiah have nothing in common, nothing at all!

PRO-JUDAISM. The book's presentation is pro-Judaism, an affirmation of the truth of Judaism for Jews. It is not intended to prove Christianity wrong, but rather Judaism right. The confirmation of Judaism's enduring validity as of God will be shown through the pages of the Hebrew Bible as well as Christianity's New Testament. The search through the Holy Scriptures of both religions will serve to reinforce Judaism, without necessarily disproving Christianity.

CHRISTIANITY AND HEBREW BIBLE. Christianity has based itself on the Hebrew Scriptures. If it did not, if it were a completely detached religion which did not validate itself on the claimed fulfillment of Judaism's Bible, we Jews would have little to say about it. If it

1

were a detached religion, we would have no legitimate means to confront it. But, Christianity is built upon Judaism's foundation and, therefore, is made vulnerable to Judaism's interpretation of its own Holy Book.

JEWS KNOW THE HEBREW BIBLE BEST. Judaism is a faith built on solid Hebrew Biblical knowledge. Jews have always lived attached to every word, every sentence, every nuance in the Scriptures. Study of God's word has been a holy activity for devout Jews throughout the ages, even to the detriment of earning a living. This is common knowledge concerning our dedication to God. It can be said that no one knows our holy revelation better than those to whom it was addressed, namely ourselves. Our martyred pious ancestors clung to Judaism due to firm conviction based on Biblical evidence, not only because of honor to heritage and respect to people.

PROOF-TEXTS ARE WRONG. Our Hebrew Bible has nothing to say about Jesus, not one thing. Christianity's use of our Bible is both their strength and their flaw. It is their strength because the Hebrew Bible is the word of God. It is their flaw because they misinterpret and misappropriate our Scriptures to support their claims. The New Testament is theirs, not ours, to contemplate. But, when Christianity claims fulfillment of, and yet obliterates, the Hebrew Bible's message, Judaism has a right, even a duty, to demonstrate the error. In this book we have organized Judaism's responses to the alleged proof-texts with which the missionary assails the Jew.

JUDAISM'S FAITH BASED ON BIBLICAL REASON. Jews are not blind or stiff-necked, as charged by Christianity. Indeed, we have faith in God, Judaism's revealed God. We have belief, belief in our Torah which imparts the laws of God. Christianity's message is fully comprehended. However, it is seen as full of fallacies. Christianity's faith cannot be accepted by any Jew who is even slightly knowledgeable of the Hebrew Scriptures and who uses his reasoning ability. As God created our minds, He expects us to use our reasoning together with our faith. Faith is not a substitute for reason, but a development from it and alongside it.

JUDAISM'S HOLINESS. Although we believe Christianity lacks the Biblical verification claimed, they do strive after God. In this regard, they possess our respect. Judaism should also be treated with respect by Christians, as Judaism's holiness is revealed in the Bible which they revere. This, Christianity should teach, even though they believe we are wrong. Proselytizing activities directed to Jews, who already worship God, should cease. But, unfortunately, the Christian message has been to validate itself while simultaneously invalidating Judaism. Instead of tolerating Judaism in co-existence, the missionary refuses to allow for Judaism's survival. It seems he must have the demise of Judaism in order to obtain the religious security he needs. In fact, the missionary values the Jewish convert above all others, because in one fell swoop he believes he catches the soul, fortifies his own conception of salvation, and deals a blow to Judaism.

JEWS ARE BLAMED. Hand in hand with the determined destruction of Judaism, which is rooted in the New Testament, is found a hatred of Jews. This has traveled from the Scriptures, to the pulpit, into the hearts of Christians. The budding Church parted itself from the Synagogue by severely abusing it. Jews were blamed for the killing of the Son of God, even though the Romans killed Jesus in crucifixion. Jews were blamed even though the Christian belief is that Jesus' death was predetermined and expected. Jews were blamed even though those around Jesus, including his family, disciples, and multitudes were all Jews. Jews were blamed even though Jesus remained a Jew unto his last breath on the Roman cross. Jews were blamed even though Jesus pleaded for no blame to be placed on his people. Jews were blamed even though Christianity claims to be a religion of love, not hate. The result of this blame has been two thousand years of sorrow for Jews and shame for Christians.

TAUGHT HATRED OF JEWS. Paul shaped the Church in a manner which stripped away all links to Judaism and cursed it at the same time. The New Testament says Judaism is bad and abandoned by God, while Christianity is good and beloved. It says the law of Moses is not valid and the Covenant is dead for the Jews. Instead, the Church's laws and the New Covenant take their place. In sum, God loves Christians and has no love for Jews. This is what Christianity has taught and Christians, including the clergy, have used to batter and bloody the Jew during two thousand years of persecution. We have suffered, through the Church's hatred of Jews and Judaism, all manner of humiliation, ostracism, hardship, degradation, misery, torture, and murder, culminating in Auschwitz and the Holocaust in Christian Europe.

CHRISTIANITY OWES JUDAISM KINDNESS. Christianity's evil effect on Jews should be admitted and condemned by all good Christian people. Christianity bears a responsibility to examine and correct their teaching concerning Judaism, which has been the root cause of great harm to the Jewish human being. As their words have caused persecution, so their words must end persecution and their actions bespeak of Jesus' teaching of love. For too long the words of Jesus have been Christianity's own accuser from *Matthew 7:18,20 (Luke 6:43-44)*, *"A good tree cannot bring forth evil fruit . . . Wherefore by their fruits ye shall know them."* Furthermore, ironically, the following seems befitting the people of Israel, rather than Christians, namely *Matthew 5:11*, *"Blessed are ye, when men shall revile you, and persecute you, and shall say all manner of evil against you falsely, for my sake."* How very, very ironic.

JESUS SAID JUDAISM IS GOOD. While Paul advanced separation from Judaism, Jesus announced Judaism's greatness. The same New Testament debases and extols Judaism. We have gathered in this book those portions of the New Testament which show Jesus was a practicing, believing Jew who taught faithfulness to his religion's Torah. He affirmed it was the way to God and eternal life. He and his family all observed the Jewish customs, holidays, and Saturday Sabbath in synagogue. Jesus said personal salvation is obtained in Judaism. Christianity has announced a new way to salvation, through belief in Jesus' vicarious atonement for sins and resurrection from death. But, this development does not invalidate Jesus' own words in Christianity's own Book. Jews need not investigate Christianity's claim, for the New Testament itself proclaims Judaism's eternal truth.

JESUS' GOD IS JUDAISM'S GOD. In no place in the New Testament did Jesus claim to be God, or God incarnate, or part of a Trinity, or in any way a special substance of God. This idea of Christianity has no basis in Jesus' pronouncements. We have gathered all pertinent verses in the New Testament to demonstrate that Jesus' God is the God of the Jewish people as we know Him, no other. As startling as this may be to Jews and Christians, when searched with an open mind, the New Testament of Christianity shows that Jesus lived and died a Jew who believed in Judaism, the God of Judaism, and the everlasting nature of Judaism.

CHRISTIANITY IS CHRISTOLOGIC. Even though Jesus the Jew in the New Testament believed in the Jewish religion, it is obvious that Christianity does not. Christianity is not the religion of Jesus, but the religion about Jesus. In this book, we are not inquiring into why the separation occurred or analyzing the various layers found in the New Testament. The contradictions and conflicts exist in the New Testament for all to see. But, the Book is theirs and is Christologically interpreted, with a resulting new religion in Paul's terms. What Jesus desired or thought is of no consequence at this point in Christianity's history.

NO BASIS IN HEBREW BIBLE. What we present in this book is evidence that, contrary to Christianity's claim, there is no confirmation of Christology in the Hebrew Scriptures, none whatsoever. Missionaries use proof-texts to advance their position that Christianity is the fulfillment of Hebrew Scripture. The so-called proof-texts are used to confirm their beliefs. In this book we demonstrate that these verses from our Hebrew Bible are not proof-texts at all for the message of Christianity. They are all erroneously utilized. We have organized them and explained them, commenting on their fallacies as presented by the missionary. Not one alleged proof-text has any merit in proving Christianity. They are faulted in many ways. They are taken out of context, twisted in meaning, forced in connection, mistranslated, misquoted, or a combination of these formidable defects. In addition, many of the events related in the New Testament were clearly written to fit or created to fit the Hebrew Bible's verses. We need not ascertain whether the event really occurred or not. The New Testament openly states that it was "done that it may be fulfilled." Such a fulfillment is obviously valueless as a proof. Biblical prophesy says nothing of Christology, and Christology has no legitimate basis in the Hebrew Bible.

HEBREW SCRIPTURES VALIDATE JUDAISM. What we do find in the Hebrew Bible are verses which show that personal salvation and life eternal is obtained through Judaism. The missionary is unwilling to see this, for if he did his whole mission of soul salvation for the Jew would crumble. But, the Holy Bible is replete with passages which prove personal salvation is secured through Judaism. Moreover, Jesus also said this in the New Testament itself. God is shown in the Holy Bible to have a special relationship, a Covenant, with the people of Judaism which is perfect, unbreakable, and eternal.

HEBREW MESSIAH IS NOT CHRIST. The Bible describes the Messiah and the Messianic Era. The Hebrew Messiah and the Christ of Christianity have absolutely nothing in common. Jesus did not fulfill the Messianic expectations for the Messiah at all. Christianity's Christ is supposed to have a second coming to accomplish the expectations. However, there is nothing in the Hebrew Scriptures about a second coming. Jesus' followers waited for his immediate return, during their lifetime, to accomplish his supposed Messianic role. This, of course, did not happen, and Christianity has had to explain this nonoccurrence in their own terms. But, their explanation still leaves the Hebrew Messiah awaited.

JUDAO-CHRISTIANITY IS AN IMPOSSIBILITY. Some missionaries to the Jews use the "Jews for Jesus" subterfuge to attract Jews to Christianity. A synthesis between Judaism and Christianity is an impossibility however. A person can be a devoted Jew or a devoted Christian, each of whom sincerely seeks God, but he can never be a Judeo-Christian. Wearing a yarmulka or tallit, lighting Friday night Sabbath candles, or reading prayers in Hebrew does not make a Jew, not if the message of the cross is believed. There is a seeking of justice, goodness, peace, and love under the guidance of God our Father in both religions. Nevertheless, there cannot be a blending of belief and observance because there are fundamental differences which are inherent, unalterable, and important between Judaism and Christianity. Our beliefs are incompatable. A Jew cannot accept Jesus as the Messiah or the only Son of God, and certainly he cannot accept Jesus as God the Son of the Trinity. For, if he does, he no longer is a Jew, but a convert to Christianity. Those Jews who emotionally refuse to be labeled apostates and assert they aren't leaving Judaism when they embrace the cross are both confused and in error. Many Christian leaders agree that Jews for Jesus is a misnomer which perverts our two faiths.

OUTLINED HERE ARE OUR FUNDAMENTAL DIFFERENCES.

MONOTHEISM OR TRINITARIANISM. Judaism is strictly monotheistic, with God being "one" and not divisible or being of multi-essence. Although Judaism meditates on God's being, He is left unknowable. Except for the assertion of His "oneness" and belief that God has no bodily form, being uniquely spiritual, Judaism leaves the understanding of God's basic nature to God alone. Yes, God is humanized so that He is brought nearer to man's understanding, but He is never corporeal. On the other hand, Christianity worships a triune God, in God the Father (as in Judaism), God the Son (God incarnate as Jesus Christ), and God the Holy Ghost (Spirit of God). Truly, we share Him, but He is who He is to each.

PERSONAL OR VICARIOUS ATONEMENT. Judaism's and Christianity's atonement methods differ dramatically and are in opposition to each other. Judaism is optimistic about man's efforts being capable of earning God's approval. Man is considered able to fulfill God's desires for man's conduct. Just as God made man with faults, with a capacity for sin, He also made man with a pure nature. God planned that man must choose life through good conduct or death through bad conduct. God planned it this way. Righteousness is within mankind's reach. To follow God's Torah and make life's moments holy is sufficient for atonement. Effort is what is required, not perfection of achievement. Each human being is responsible for his own personal salvation in Judaism. On the other hand, Christianity teaches vicarious atonement, belief that man is unable to attain God's approval through good deeds and needs help beyond himself. Mankind is considered hopelessly sinful through "original sin." However, salvation is obtained by belief that Jesus Christ made vicarious atonement for man's sinfulness through his sacrificial death. His resurrection offers hope of salvation to all believing Christians. Efforts to goodness are auxiliary to belief and not essential for salvation.

SINFULNESS OR ORIGINAL SIN. Sin, the transgression against God, is a deeply divergent idea in our religions. Judaism says man's soul is pure and transgression is the result of weakness and inclination to wrong-doing, rather than basic depravity and incapacity for righteousness. Our free will choice to follow God's laws maintains our harmony with God. Following our good impulses allows man to rule over sin. On the other hand, Christianity teaches that man has the profound guilt of original sin from which he cannot escape by himself. He is blemished with a corrupt nature which good behavior cannot overcome. He needs an intercessor, Jesus Christ, to take away his sinfulness.

WORLDLY SEEKING OR WORLDLY DENIAL. Seeking happiness, as necessary to appreciate the majesty of God's creation, is encouraged in Judaism. The bodily desires are God-given, to be used in purity. The human vessel, created by God, is to be piously employed and appreciated. On the other hand, Christianity asks for a passing through this life in denial of the flesh in order to obtain piety. The body's desires are evils to be suppressed and overcome.

LAWS OF MOSES OR LAWS OF NEW COVENANT. The Holy Torah's laws are the path to righteousness for Jews, for they guide man in doing God's will. God and man meet in the performance of the laws. The Torah brings holiness to every part of our life and is spiritually fulfilling because of the sacredness of duty to God. The immutable Covenant is connected to the duties of Torah observance, which are a certain bond to God for the Jew. On the other hand, Christianity denies the value of the laws and instead substitutes its own laws which must be fulfilled. It presumes that Judaism's Torah is of no value and that Christianity possesses a New Covenant, which replaces the original.

CAN JEWS BE FOR JESUS THE JEW? We have shown why Jews cannot be for Jesus the Christ of Christianity. How about being for Jesus the Jew? Jews cannot be for Jesus as a prophet, because

Hebrew prophets justified their pronouncements on God's Holy Torah. Jesus, in contrast, used his personal authority for justification of his teachings. Also, Jews cannot be for Jesus as an inspired rabbi, because rabbis expound and preserve the laws, while Jesus did not. Perhaps Jews might be for Jesus' teachings of goodness and morality. But, if so, we would simply be admiring Judaism's own ethical background in which Jesus was deeply rooted. In short, Jesus has no place in Jewish belief in any context!

2

Jesus the Jew—Introduction

It isn't Jews who should see Jesus as the Christ of Christianity, but Christians who should be made aware of his Jewishness! That Jesus was a devoted Jew is openly narrated over and over again in the New Testament. Jesus' deep fidelity to Judaism's God, belief in the Hebrew Scriptures, and observance of the Jewish religion are abundantly described. As a dedicated Jewish man he taught Jews, and Jews exclusively, to do God's will, which he found in the Torah. What he expounded to the multitudes came from his Jewish heritage. He was a religious person, within the mainstream of Judaism, who understood the Torah's eternal nature and value. Jesus was born a Jew, spoke as a Jew, lived as a Jew, prayed as a Jew, and died still a devout Jew. He never discarded or debased Judaism, but extolled it. Nor did he found a new religion to replace Judaism. Jesus was not an apostate, nor did he teach others to leave Judaism. So, if being Jewish was good enough for Jesus, why shouldn't all Jews feel the same!

Yes, all of this can be discovered in the New Testament. Under all the layers and among all the strands which comprise the Christian Book can be found the Jewish Jesus, before Christianity made him their own.

Jews have no need to search the New Testament to verify Judaism. The Hebrew Bible, God's holy word, stands complete for us. It is interesting to know that Christianity agrees that the Hebrew Bible (the Old Testament as they call it) is God's Holy Book. They combine it with the New Testament into one Holy Bible for Christians. So, while Christians must probe our Scriptures for passages which lend credence to their beliefs, Jews have no such reciprocal need. Nevertheless, although we have no need to seek reinforcement of Judaism outside the

9

Hebrew Scriptures, it is astonishing to locate such reinforcement, to discover it does exist, in the New Testament itself!

Judaism's advocates fully understand that the New Testament is about Christianity's Christ. The Christian Scriptures present a new religion based on Jesus being the Messiah or Christ, the only begotten Son of God, the second part of a triune God. Christianity says he came to earth to be sacrificed for the sins of mankind so that those who believe this can be saved and have eternal life. That essentially is the Christian belief. But, this same New Testament which relates the story of the Christian Savior also details Jesus as a man who lived and died a faithful Jew. This same Jesus, in the underlying strands in the New Testament, belongs fully to Judaism. By selective extraction from the New Testament, of what Jewish advocates could call reverse proof-texts, it can be demonstrated that the Jewish religion has a sacred essence. In these verses are shown the eternal bond between God and His Chosen People, the Jews. And these Biblical quotes, which express the truth of our Jewish beliefs, are from Christianity's New Testament itself.

The reverse proof-texts have clarity and simplicity. The verses' traditional meanings cannot be misinterpreted. The language is taken from the King James Version of the New Testament and correctly presented. Even though a selected reverse proof-text may lie side by side with a verse of Christologic import, the one does not negate the other. What is meant is what you read in direct terms.

Selected extraction of reverse proof-texts is not intended to disprove Christianity. What is presented is pro-Judaism, not anti-Christianity. Judaism's advocates, quoting reverse proof-texts, do not want or expect to diminish the Christian's belief in his religion. However, we do hope and intend to make firm the Jew's belief in his own God and God-given religion. The Jew's attachment to Judaism will be strengthened, when he sees that Judaism "has it and never lost it," even as seen in the New Testament. That the Jewish religion has always been a pathway to God and a means for life everlasting is plainly acknowledged by the words of Jesus the Jew, Jeshua ben Joseph, himself.

Of course, that the New Testament contains ample validation of Judaism's eternal truths must be very surprising to most Jewish people, who have no reason to open its pages. It is not a book to be read, but a book of dread for Jews throughout our long sufferings. Through the pages of the New Testament, Judaism is vilified and condemned, Jews are defamed and despised, and the cross is made to impale God's Chosen People. It brought hope of salvation to the Christian, but only severe persecution and misery to the Jew. It is a book teaching hate for the Jew, and as such it remains. Therefore, it surely should be shocking for most Jews to learn that in its pages are also found words of confirmation that Judaism is of God eternally.

No doubt, it also should be surprising to most Christians, who read their Holy Book with Christian orientation, that reverse proof-texts can be gathered to support Judaism. These strands of early origin can be found between the strands of preaching the new "good news." Christians may not think the pro-Judaism passages are important. They can be ignored by those seeking the salvation of the New Testament. Furthermore, the Christian may not even realize the verses are a vindication of Judaism.

Christianity, however, must explain away these verses because they are incompatable with scriptural vituperations against the Jew and Judaism. It cannot be that pronouncements of Judaism's ineffectual nature and demise and Christianity's power and succession exist in the same Holy Book with open declarations of Judaism being God-bestowed and eternal. Or can this be? Can it be that the New Testament affirms the validity of Judaism as a way to God eternally? The Christian Scriptures promote Judaism's obliteration. Can it be that the same Christian Bible is, as well, Judaism's supporter? Read and see.

3

His Family and Lack of Holy Awe

Jesus, whose birth name was Jeshua ben Joseph, was the firstborn in a large family of blood brothers and sisters. His mother Mary or Miriam, therefore, was not an eternal virgin. Joseph, his father, was known by people to be Jesus' father of heritage and a carpenter. Four brothers' names are given, and he had at least three sisters. The word "brethren" designates his blood brothers, not his disciples. His family was not far from him during his life. We are given no information about Jesus from age twelve until about age thirty, when his public ministry began which lasted only one to three years.

Matthew 1:25 (Luke 2:7), ". . . till she had brought forth her firstborn son: and he called his name Jesus."

John 6:42 (John 1:45) (Luke 4:22), ". . . Is not this Jesus, the son of Joseph, whose father and mother we know? . . ."

Matthew 13:55-56 (Mark 6:3), "Is not this the carpenter's son (carpenter)? is not his mother called Mary? and his brethren James, and Joses, and Simon, and Judas (Juda)? And his sisters, are they not all with us? . . ."

John 2:12, ". . . he, and his mother, and his brethren, and his disciples . . ."

Luke 8:19-20 (Matthew 12:46-47) (Mark 3:31-32), "Then came to him his mother and his brethren, and could not come at him for the press. And it was told him by certain which said, Thy mother and thy brethren stand without, desiring to see thee."

Now that we have shown you Jesus' family background, let's progress to the following inquiry of importance. Shouldn't a truly startling revelation, of a nature beyond anything imaginable, of a heavenly dimension, be forever influencing the life of the human being who received and is affected by this revelation? Surely, yes. Why, then, is the relationship of Jesus and Mary so lacking in awe and reverence?

Luke 1:26-35 relates a remarkable story of Mary and the angel Gabriel. Mary is told by the angel that without knowing a man, but with God's intervention alone, she would conceive and give birth to a child. This child, she is told, is to be the Messiah. Is this not a dumbfounding scene:—angel—talking—virgin birth—Messiah child? *In Luke 2:7, 11* the birth occurs with Joseph there. Shepherds are told by an angel that it is the Messiah who is born and is lying in a manger. The story in *Matthew 2:1-2, 11* has the wise men of the east following a star to find the newborn King of the Jews, the Messiah. They find him in a house (not a manger) with Mary and worship him. Even Elizabeth, Mary's cousin, knew of the supposed miraculous event. For in *Luke 1:42-43* we read, *". . . Blessed art thou (Mary) among women, and blessed is the fruit of thy womb. And whence is this to me, that the mother of my Lord should come to me?"* Joseph also knew of the New Testament's miracle because in *Matthew 1:20-21* an angel appeared to him in a dream telling him.

Certainly, therefore, Mary and those around her were aware of the mind-boggling occurrence. She understood the startling miracle which was told her because she exclaims in *Luke 1:48-49, ". . . for, behold, from henceforth all generations shall call me blessed. For he that is mighty (God) hath done to me great things . . ."* Think. Shouldn't her relationship to Jesus have been one of sublime mutual respect and awe in light of all this amazing background? Shouldn't Jesus' whole family have been his first followers? Yet, they were not. If there were truth to this extraordinary story of his birth, there would necessarily be a tremendous continual reverence between Jesus and Mary. Yet, there was not. The New Testament reports quite the contrary, which brings a heavy cloud of doubt to the entire supposed miraculous event. Let's present here how far from sublimely reverent their relationship was, indeed how disrespectful.

Matthew 12:46-50 (Mark 3:31-35) (Luke 8:19-21), "While he yet talked to the people, behold, his mother and his brethren stood without, desiring to speak with him. Then one said unto him, Behold, thy mother and thy brethren stand without desiring to speak with thee. But he answered and said unto him that told him, Who is my mother? and who are my brethren? And he stretched forth his hand toward his disciples, and said, Behold my mother and my brethren! For whosoever shall do the will of my Father which is in heaven, the same is my brother, and sister, and mother."

COMMENT: His mother came to talk to him, but he did not go to her. For any son this would be disrespectful. For Jesus, whose mother reportedly bore him through the unique intervention of God, this is astonishingly disrespectful. Moreover, Jesus did not speak of his mother in a loving manner, but curtly brushed her aside, together with his brothers. Jesus certainly could have made the point, that all who do God's will are important, without being disrespectful and disparaging his mother. How could he speak of his mother, Mary, in such a manner if she were the holy virgin mother of Christianity?

Luke 11:27-28, ". . . a certain woman . . . said unto him, Blessed is the womb that bare thee, and the paps which thou hast sucked. But he said, Yea, rather, blessed are they that hear the word of God, and keep it."
COMMENT: Here he reiterates his belief that those who do God's will are the blessed of this world. This is pure Judaism. This is Jesus the Jew talking. But, in regard to our point here, in addition to his lack of respect for Mary, he evidently denies the supposed blessed state of his mother. Thus he denies the exclamation of Mary in *Luke 1:48,* wherein she says all generations shall call her blessed. Where is the expected reverence?

John 2:4, "Jesus saith unto her, Woman, what have I to do with thee? . . ."
COMMENT: This passage is also indicative of the shocking attitude of Jesus to Mary. She is his mother, yet he coldly calls her "woman" and separates himself from her. In fact, never in the New Testament does Jesus use any endearing term for his mother. Not only is there a lack of reverence, but there also is a strange lack of simple affection.

John 19:26-27, "When Jesus therefore saw his mother, and the disciple standing by, whom he loved, he saith unto his mother, Woman, behold thy son! Then saith he to the disciple, Behold thy mother! And from that hour that disciple took her unto his own home."
COMMENT: Here we have John's description of Jesus' crucifixion, where Jesus is dying and sees his mother near him. Remember, these are the last words Jesus spoke to Mary. And remember that she is Christianity's holy mother of the miracle-birth Messiah, the Son of God. Wouldn't you think something more appropriate would have been said, such as "We will be in heaven together?" Wouldn't you suppose that words expressing eternity would have been in his parting thoughts to his mother? Yet, no such words are directed to her. Instead, he uses those words for the criminal who was being crucified with him by the Romans in *Luke 23:43.* What is reported here is that Jesus loved his disciple so much he gave his mother to him and him to his mother. What a strange turn. Notice, it is the disciple, not his mother, "whom

he loved." We can only guess why he had to assign her care to someone when she had at least seven other children of her own, any one of whom should have been responsible for her care.

Luke 2:43,45-46, 48-50, "And when they had fulfilled the days, as they returned, the child Jesus tarried behind in Jerusalem; . . . And when they found him not, they turned back again to Jerusalem, seeking him. . . . after three days they found him in the temple, . . . both hearing them, and asking them questions. . . . and his mother said unto him, Son, why hast thou thus dealt with us? behold, thy father and I have sought thee sorrowing. And he said unto them, How is it that ye sought me? wist ye not that I must be about my Father's business? And they understood not the saying which he spake unto them."
COMMENT: First and foremost we here see Mary did not understand Jesus' alleged mission. It is clear from this that Mary had not been forever affected by Christianity's miraculous birth. She "understood not." We see here that Mary and Joseph both do not understand that Jesus must do God's work, as he is the Messiah. If the scene with the angel Gabriel were true, his parents would fully comprehend Jesus' special nature and mission. But, they do not.

We must offer another thought about these verses concerning Jesus' attitude towards his parents. His behavior is so ill-befitting a caring son to a holy mother, don't you think? How could Jesus give his parents such worry? How could he cause sorrow to his mother who supposedly gave birth to him in a miraculous way, touched by God alone? Wouldn't his reverence for her prompt him to treat her with supreme consideration? Indeed, how could Christianity's Jesus, who taught love, be so inconsiderate at all, even if his mother were not a holy being? Surely, there is an absence of any heavenly relationship indicated here. In fact, the scene seems like one so often occurring to us simple human beings with children who forget to inform us of their whereabouts, add more white hairs to our heads, and then explain they thought we knew where they were.

What has been described is a complete lack of spiritual reverence of Jesus for his mother Mary. This irreverence casts great suspicion on the veracity of Christianity's remarkable story of Jesus' birth. Now, let's look into verses which show the absence of awe for Jesus by those close to him. This should complete the picture of doubt being presented concerning Jesus' miraculous birth.

Mark 3:21, "And when his friends heard of it, they went out to lay hold on him: for they said, He is beside himself."
COMMENT: It seems that those who were close to him, his friends, thought him crazy, not holy. Don't you believe they would have heard

of his miraculous birth and that he was the expected Messiah from his parents, his family, or from Jesus himself? Obviously, they know nothing of his alleged mission as the Messiah. They know nothing of his miraculous birth. In addition, they actually believe Jesus is mad.

John 7:3,5, "His brethren therefore said unto him, Depart hence, and go into Judea, that thy disciples also may see the works that thou doest. For neither did his brethren believe in him."
COMMENT: His "brethren" are his blood brothers, not his cousins, friends, or disciples. His brothers, during his ministry at this point, are reported to have no belief in him. Isn't this surprising? For if the story of the miraculous birth and announcement of Messiah child were true, Jesus' home would have been filled with its wonderous awe. Yet, his brothers did not "believe in him." This presents a formidable obstacle to accepting the Christian story as fact. It is clear that when James was in contact with Jesus here he did not believe Jesus to be God's appointed Messiah. So we can deduce that he was not aware of Christianity's miraculous event. We cannot visualize such a lack of knowledge in a family of so momentous an occurrence. No secrecy was ever declared. Therefore, again, we are given reason to doubt. *Galatians 1:19* does not contradict this because it deals with James at a later time, after the crucifixion, when other factors were involved.

Mark 6:4 (Matthew 13:57) (Luke 4:24) (John 4:44), "But Jesus said unto them, A prophet is not without honor, but in his own country, and among his own kin, and in his own house."
COMMENT: We read here that Jesus himself said his family gives him no respect. They lack understanding and give him no honor. This is implicit denial of the truth of the supposed miraculous birth and the attending Messianic announcement. We do not doubt that the miraculous birth could have occurred, for surely God can do anything. Nevertheless, we are stating that we do not have New Testament corroboration. There is no appropriate action and reaction in the lives of the people involved. Jesus, Mary, family, and others interact inappropriately. They are seemingly oblivious of the startling revelation of Christianity. There is no awe or reverence where it surely should exist, which completely destroys the credibility of the virgin birth story as well as the announcement of Jesus' Messianic appointment!

4

His Ethical Teachings Are Judaism's

Virtually nothing in the moral teachings of Jesus is unique, for all, in one way or another, stem from Jewish thought! Parallels are found in the Hebrew Bible, Apocrypha, Midrash, and Talmud. Some are exact phraseology, one to the other. Other writings convey similar meanings. The pinnacle of moral teaching in the New Testament is undoubtedly Jesus' Sermon On the Mount, *Matthew 5, 6, and 7.* This grand selection from the New Testament is almost entirely paralleled in Hebrew writings, either previous, then current, or after. The later Jewish writings were based on Jewish oral sources from which Jesus also must have drawn his sayings. This is obvious because there is no possibility that Judaism's religious men would use the New Testament for ideas of ethics.

The Lord's Prayer in *Matthew 6:(7-8)9-13* is phrase by phrase a compilation of Hebrew thought in Bible, prayers, and Talmud. Look at the following remarkable comparison which makes our point.

NO VAIN REPETITIONS. *Ecclesiastes 5:2, ". . . for God is in heaven, and thou upon the earth: therefore let thy words be few."*

OUR FATHER WHICH ART IN HEAVEN. *Isaiah 63:16, "Doubtless thou art our Father, . . . thou, O Lord, art our Father, our redeemer thy name is from everlasting."*

HALLOWED BE THY NAME. *Kaddish prayer, "Exalted and hallowed be God's great name in this world of His creation."*

THY KINGDOM COME. THY WILL BE DONE IN EARTH AS IT IS IN HEAVEN. *Kaddish prayer, "May His will be fulfilled and His sovereignty revealed speedily and in our day."* Also see *Daniel 2:44, "the God of heaven (shall) set up a kingdom, which shall never be destroyed . . ."* Also see *Micah 4:7, ". . . And the Lord shall reign*

over them in mount Zion from henceforth, even for ever."
GIVE US THIS DAY OUR DAILY BREAD. *Proverbs 30:8, ". . .
feed me with food convenient for me (Hebrew original 'with mine allot-
ted bread'):"*
AND FORGIVE US OUR DEBTS, AS WE FORGIVE OUR
DEBTORS. *Exodus 22:25, "If thou lend money to any of my people
that is poor by thee, thou shalt not be to him as an usurer (Hebrew
original 'creditor') . . ."* Also see *Jeremiah 31:34, ". . . for I will forgive their iniquity . . ."*
AND LEAD US NOT INTO TEMPTATION, BUT DELIVER US
FROM EVIL; *Berakot 60b, ". . . bring me not into sin, or into iniquity, or into temptation . . . and deliver me from evil."*
FOR THINE IS THE KINGDOM, AND THE POWER, AND THE
GLORY, FOR EVER. *I Chronicles 29:11, "Thine, O Lord, is the
greatness, and the power, and the glory, and the victory, and the majesty: . . . thine is the kingdom . . ."*

The Beatitude format is found in the Secrets of Enoch, a Pharisaic
apocryphal work of the first century B.C.E. We see the following ideas
of blessedness. Blessed is he who—blesses all the Lord's work—keeps
the father's foundations—raises the fallen—implants peace and love—
speaks humbly—enters only good houses—brings gifts with faith
before the Lord's face for forgiveness of sin. And it is said the just
who escape the great judgment are blessed.

Now let's display the parallels to the Beatitudes of the Sermon On
the Mount from *Matthew 5:3-10.*
5:3 BLESSED ARE THE POOR. *Psalm 34:18, "The Lord . . . saveth
such as be of a contrite spirit."*
5:4 BLESSED ARE THEY THAT MOURN. *Isaiah 61:2, ". . . to
comfort all that mourn,"*
5:5 BLESSED ARE THE MEEK. *Psalm 37:11, "But the meek shall
inherit the earth . . ."*
5:6 BLESSED ARE THEY WHICH DO HUNGER AND THIRST
FOR RIGHTEOUSNESS. *Deuteronomy 16:20, "That which is alto-
gether just shalt thou follow, that thou mayest live . . ."*
5:7 BLESSED ARE THE MERCIFUL. *Shabbat 151b, "He who has
mercy on his fellow creatures obtains mercy for himself."*
5:8 BLESSED ARE THE PURE IN HEART. *Psalm 24:3-4, "Who
shall ascend into the hill of the Lord? . . . He that hath clean hands,
and a pure heart . . ."*
5:9 BLESSED ARE THE PEACEMAKERS. *Psalm 34:14, ". . . do
good; seek peace, and pursue it."*
5:10 BLESSED ARE THEY . . . PERSECUTED FOR RIGHT-
EOUSNESS' SAKE. *Isaiah 51:7-8, "Harken unto me, ye that know*

righteousness, the people in whose heart is my law; fear ye not the reproach of men, neither be ye afraid of their revilings. . . . my salvation (shall be) from generation to generation."

Let's here correct a wrong impression presented in the New Testament about the Hebrew tradition of treating one's enemies. In *Matthew 5:43-44* read, *"You have heard that it hath been said, Thou shalt love thy neighbor, and hate thine enemy. But I say unto you, Love your enemies . . ."* From this you would believe that this "hate" is found in the Hebrew Scriptures or oral sayings, but it is not. Hate of our enemies is nowhere taught. Instead, we have *Proverbs 25:21, "If thine enemy be hungry, give him bread to eat; and if he be thirsty, give him water to drink:"*

The term "Judao-Christian ethics" is used by Christians who know that the basis of much ethical teaching in the New Testament is derived from the Jewish common source. Of course, the Ten Commandments are from *Exodus 20:1-17* and *Deuteronomy 5:6-21* and are God's laws given to Moses on Mount Sinai. We are admonished not to kill, commit adultery, steal, lie, or covet. Here is a sampling of more verses from the Hebrew Scriptures which demonstrate its high morality.

Exodus 23:4, "If thou meet thine enemy's ox or his ass going astray, thou shalt surely bring it back to him again."

Exodus 23:7, "Keep thee far from a false matter; and the innocent and righteous slay thou not."

Exodus 23:9, "Also thou shalt not oppress a stranger: for ye . . . were strangers in the land of Egypt."

Leviticus 19:14, "Thou shalt not curse the deaf, nor put a stumbling block before the blind . . ."

Leviticus 19:15, "Ye shall do no unrighteousness in judgment: . . . in righteousness shalt thou judge thy neighbor."

Leviticus 19:17, "Thou shalt not hate thy brother in thine heart. . ."

Leviticus 19:18, "Thou shalt not avenge, nor bear any grudge against the children of thy people, but thou shalt love thy neighbor as thyself . . ."

Leviticus 19:34, "But the stranger that dwelleth with you shall be unto you as one born among you, and thou shalt love him as thyself . . ."

Now we will present a sampling of Jewish writings of high ethical stature found in books other than the Bible. Our great rabbis Hillel, Shammai, Akiba, Meir, Eliezar, Tarphon, etc., make the pages of the Talmud and Midrash shine with the beauty of holiness. Rabbi Hillel, for example, was a saintly, learned moralist of the first century B.C.E., whose level of excellence in righteous teaching is unexcelled in Judaism. He may have been Jesus' guide in many matters. It is said that Rabbi Hillel when asked by a Gentile to explain the principles of Judaism while standing on one foot replied, "Do not do unto your neighbor what you would not have him do unto you; this is the whole of the law, the rest is commentary." This summation of Judaism's laws might well have come from the mouth of Jesus, don't you think?

The Pirke Aboth (Sayings of the Fathers) tractate in the Mishnah is a compilation of writings entirely devoted to ethical teachings. It alone is a storehouse of religious moral values. But, let's list some other writings here.

T. Berachoth III 11 and Berachoth 29b (short prayer) ". . . Do thy will in heaven and on earth give comfort to them that fear thee, and do what is right in thy sight." and *". . . May it be thy will, O our God, to give to every one his needs and to every being sufficient for his lack."*

Ben Sira 28:2-5, "Forgive thy neighbor's sin and then, when thou prayest, thy sins will be forgiven; man cherisheth anger against man, and doth he seek healing (forgiveness) from the Lord?"

Aboth II 4, "Judge not thy neighbor till thou art come into his place."

Sota I 7, "With what measure ye mete it shall be measured unto you."

Sota 48b, "He who has a morsel of bread in his vessel and yet says, 'What shall I eat tomorrow?' is of little faith."

Baba Bathra 9b, "He who giveth alms in secret is greater than Moses our master."

Baba Bathra 11a, ". . . My fathers laid up treasure for this world; I have laid up treasure for the world to come."

Baba Bathra 15b, "If he (the reprover) say to him, Take the mote from thine eyes, the other replies, Take the beam from thine eyes."

Baba Bathra 49b, (on oaths) "A righteous yea and a righteous nay."

T. Pear 4:9, "Alms giving and good works outweigh all the other commandments."

Tanhuma, Shemini 12, "How doth it affect the Holy One, blessed be He, whether a man slay a beast according to halakha (law) or not . . . or whether a man eat food clean or unclean? . . . the commandments were not given save as a means to purify mankind."

Massekheth Kallah, "He who deliberately looks on a woman is as though he had a connection with her."

Even "turning the other cheek" is not unique to Jesus. It also has its place within Judaism, although not to the exclusion of self-protection to ward off danger. In summary, it means "do not return evil for evil," which is a principle of Judaism. Indeed, the source is

Hebrew Scripture *Lamentations 3:30, "He giveth his cheek to him that smiteth him . . ."*

Shabbat 88b, "They who are insulted yet insult not again, who hear themselves reproached yet answer not again, who act out of love and rejoice in afflictions . . ."

What we have gathered here is only a small selection of the very many beautiful teachings of Judaism, which must have influenced Jesus learning in the synagogue. Read Judaism's ethical teachings and you can feel the essential nature of Jesus the Jew. Perhaps, you by now can appreciate why Jewish people spend their whole lives studying the holy books of Judaism, extracting the wisdom of the sages who wrote the words which give life and understanding to God's Biblical work.

5

Laws Are Observed

Jesus asserted that the law of Moses should be observed, even as instructed by the Pharisees. He was circumcised, as a sign of the Covenant between God and the children of Abraham. Mary was a faithful Jewish woman who performed the ritual of mikvah for cleansing of Jewish women. As an infant he was taken to Jerusalem and presented to the Lord God, with sacrifice offered according to the law. As a youngster Jesus went to the Temple in Jerusalem, listened to the religious Jewish teachings, and asked questions about Judaism. As Jews do, he recited the blessing over bread. Rituals by Temple priests and gifts given at the Temple altar were recognized as proper religious duties. Tithing and fasting were accepted Jewish functions by him. Jesus observed the Saturday Sabbath by attending synagogue, where he learned, taught, and read the Hebrew Scriptures. The synagogue was then, as now, a place of prayer as well as religious education. Pharisees and other men learned in Judaism went there regularly to speak and listen. Jesus spoke Aramaic, a Semitic language very similar to Hebrew, and knew the Hebrew Scriptures well. He taught daily in the Temple and also preached outdoors the Hebrew gospel of the Kingdom of God. Multitudes of people, all of them Jews, heard. The sanctity of the Jerusalem Temple was highly respected by Jesus, who believed it was a house of prayer for all. Of course, he was familiar with and participated in the Jewish holidays. Succoth and Passover are specially recorded.

Everything we have outlined above is found in the pages of the New Testament. All of this reveals Jesus the Jew. Now, let's look at the passages which present his Jewishness. While reading, ask this:— Why would Jesus be immersed in the laws and customs of Judaism if his alleged mission was to extinguish them?

Luke 2:21, "And when eight days were accomplished for circumcising of the child, his name was called Jesus . . ."

Luke 2:22, "And when the days of her (Mary's) purification (mikvah—ritual cleansing) according to the law of Moses were accomplished . . ."

Luke 2:22-24,27,39, ". . . they (his parents) brought him to Jerusalem, to present him to the Lord:—As it is written in the law of the Lord, Every male that openeth the womb shall be called holy to the Lord;—And to offer a sacrifice according to that which is said in the law of the Lord, A pair of turtledoves, or two young pigeons . . . and when the parents brought in the child Jesus, to do for him after the custom of the law . . . And when they had performed all things according to the law of the Lord . . ."

Luke 2:46-47, (as a young boy) ". . . after three days they found him in the temple, sitting in the midst of the doctors both hearing them, and asking them questions."

Luke 24:30, ". . . he took bread, and blessed it, and brake, and gave to them."

Mark 1:44 (Matthew 8:4) (Luke 5:14), ". . . show thyself to the (temple) priest, and offer for thy cleansing those things which Moses commanded for a testimony unto them."

Luke 17:14, "Go show yourselves unto the priests . . ."

Matthew 5:23-24, "Therefore if thou bring thy gift to the altar, and there rememberest that thy brother hath ought against thee; Leave there thy gift before the altar and go thy way; first be reconciled to thy brother, and then come and offer thy gift."

Matthew 6:16, "Moreover when ye fast . . ."

Matthew 23:23 (Luke 11:42), ". . . ye pay tithe of mint and anise and cummen (herbs), and have omitted the weightier matters of the law, judgment, mercy, and faith: these ought ye to have done, and not to leave the other undone."

Mark 1:21 (Luke 4:31), ". . . and straightway on the sabbath day he entered into the synagogue, and taught."

Mark 3:1 (Matthew 12:9) (Luke 6:6), "And he entered again into the synagogue . . ."

Mark 6:2 (Matthew 13:54), "And when the sabbath day was come, he began to teach in the synagogue . . ."

Matthew 9:35, "And Jesus went about all the cities and villages, teaching in their synagogues . . ."

Matthew 4:23 (Mark 1:39), "And Jesus went about all Galilee, teaching in their synagogues, and preaching the gospel of the kingdom . . ."

Luke 13:10, "And he was teaching in one of the synagogues on the sabbath."

Luke 4:16, ". . . and, as his custom was, he went into the synagogue on the sabbath day, and stood up for to read."

Matthew 21:23 (Mark 11:27) (Luke 20:1), "And when he was come into the temple, the chief priests and elders of the people came unto him as he was teaching (preaching the gospel) . . ."

John 8:2, "And early in the morning he came again into the temple, and all the people came unto him; and he sat down, and taught them."

Luke 21:37-38, "And in the day time he was teaching in the temple; . . . And all the people came early in the morning to him in the temple, for to hear him."

Luke 19:47, "And he taught daily in the temple. . . ."

Mark 11:17 (Matthew 21:13) (Luke 19:46), "And he taught (in the temple), saying unto them, Is it not written, My house shall be called of all nations the house of prayer? . . ."

Mark 11:15-16 (Matthew 21:12) (Luke 19:45), "And they came to Jerusalem; and Jesus went into the temple (of God), and began to cast out them that sold and bought in the temple, and overthrew the tables of the moneychangers, and the seats of them that sold doves; And would not suffer that any man should carry any vessel through the temple."

John 7:10, ". . . then went he also up unto the feast (of tabernacles—Succoth) . . ."

John 7:14, "Now about the midst of the feast (of tabernacles) Jesus went up into the temple, and taught."

Luke 2:41-43, "Now his parents went to Jerusalem every year at the feast of passover. And when he was twelve years old, they went up to Jerusalem after the custom of the feast. And when they had fulfilled the days . . ."

Matthew 26:17,19 (Mark 14:12,16) (Luke 22:7-9,13), "Now the first day of the feast of unleavened bread the disciples came to Jesus, saying unto him, Where wilt thou that we prepare for thee to eat the passover? And the disciples did as Jesus had appointed them; . . . and they made ready the passover."

Luke 22:15, "And he said unto them, With desire I have desired to eat this passover with you . . ."

Mark 14:20 (Matthew 26:23), ". . . It is one of the twelve, that dippeth with me in the (ceremonial) dish."

Mark 14:22 (Matthew 26:26) (Luke 22:19), "And as they did eat, Jesus took (unleavened—matzoh) bread, and blessed, and brake it, and gave it to them . . ."

Mark 14:23 (Matthew 26:27) (Luke 22:17), "And he took the (wine) cup, and when he had given thanks, he gave it to them . . ."

Mark 14:26 (Matthew 26:30), "And when they had sung (the Hallel) an hymn . . ."

COMMENT: Not only did Jesus observe Judaism's laws, but the much maligned Pharisees are shown in the New Testament to have been valued dispensers of the word of God in Jesus' own estimation. Furthermore, Jesus had friends among the Pharisees. Christianity should place the Pharisees in the proper regard and end disparagement of this name. Read here where we plainly see that the Pharisees even sought to save his life. In addition, many came to him to be healed.

Matthew 23:1-3, "Then spake Jesus to the multitude, and to his disciples, Saying, The scribes and the Pharisees sit in Moses' seat: All therefore whatsoever they bid you observe, that observe and do . . ."

Luke 13:31, "The same day there came certain of the Pharisees, saying unto him, Get thee out, and depart hence; for Herod will kill thee."

Luke 5:17, ". . . as he was teaching . . . Pharisees . . . were come out of every town of Galilee, and Judea, and Jerusalem: and the power of the Lord was present to heal them."

Luke 7:36 (Luke 11:37), "And one of the Pharisees desired him that he would eat with him. And he went into the Pharisee's house, and sat down to meat."

Luke 14:1, ". . . he went into the house of one of the chief Pharisees to eat bread on the sabbath day . . ."

As a final observation here, it is interesting to note that Jesus is depicted as wearing the Jewish man's religious tsitsit garment. The wearing of this garment is a command by God in *Numbers 15:38-39* reading, ". . . *that they make them fringes on the borders of their garments . . . (to) remember all the commandments . . ."* In *Matthew 14:36* we infer Jesus is wearing this tsitsit garment as we read, *"And (men) besought him that they might only touch the hem of his garment: . . ."*

6

Laws Are Good For Salvation

This chapter is a truly startling one. Read it and re-read it, for it demonstrates that in the New Testament Jesus was a Jew who believed in Judaism and taught others to be faithful to his religion's precepts and laws forever!

Certainly, if the verses quoted in this chapter remained in the New Testament they must be the word of God, for they are irreconcilably contradictory to the Christian message found in the New Testament. These passages have remained included in the New Testament through God's power it seems to us for a purpose. The purpose could well be to reassure Jews who are in doubt about their Judaism, and are thinking of leaving Judaism for Christianity, that Judaism has always been and will always be the road to God for the people of Jewish heritage. Those unsure Jews perhaps can have their belief in Judaism kindled and can be kept on God's pathway for Jews by the very same Christian Book through which they would desert their people and God! Indeed, Jews who already have left our burdened road will have their eyes opened. Prayerfully, many will return as baal teshuvah and through repentance turn to the God of Israel, who surely is waiting with fatherly understanding and forgiveness. Believe Jesus in this matter:— Eternal life is obtained through Judaism.

For devout Jews, the revelations in this chapter will be very comfortable corroboration of their firm faith in the holiness of Judaism. Christians and others who read these verses will bring to them their own heritage and will make of them what they will.

These pages of reverse proof-texts are intended to strengthen the course God set up for Jews and to fortify our faith and devotion to His plan for us and mankind. In effect, here you will discover confirmation of Judaism's everlasting truth and validity through the words of Jesus and others in the New Testament. Now, let's get into it.

Matthew 5:17-19, "Think not that I am come to destroy the law, or the prophets: I am not come to destroy, but to fulfil. For verily I say unto you, Till heaven and earth pass, one jot or one tittle shall in no wise pass from the law, till all be fulfilled. Whosoever therefore shall break one of these least commandments, and shall teach men so, he shall be called the least in the kingdom of heaven: but whosoever shall do and teach them, the same shall be called great in the kingdom of heaven."

COMMENT: You can read this over and over and never end your astonishment. Remember, these are Jesus' words saying he is here to follow the law of Moses, not end the law. Until the world ends, the law as written will be in effect. Jews who obey the law and teach it are greatly loved by God, while those who transgress the law and teach its transgression are not. NOTE that although the word "fulfil" could mean "to complete or end," in this case and context it clearly means "to obey and do." We know this because the following sentence continues the idea that the law will not change until the world ends, which still has not occurred two thousand years later.

Luke 16:16-17, "The law and the prophets were until John (the Baptist): since that time the kingdom of God is preached, and every man presseth into it. And it is easier for heaven and earth to pass, than one tittle of the law to fail."

COMMENT: Preaching the kingdom is emphasized since John the Baptist, Jesus said. But the laws of the Torah are still effective and good, to be fulfilled until the world ends. NOTE that in no way does "until John" signify the end of the law, because the very next sentence substantiates the law's validity forever.

Luke 16:19-20,22-24,27-31, "There was a certain rich man, . . . And there was a certain beggar named Lazarus, . . . the beggar died, and was carried by the angels into Abraham's bosom: the rich man also died, and was buried; And in hell he lift up his eyes, being in torments, . . . And he cried and said, Father Abraham, have mercy on me, . . . I pray thee . . . send him (Lazarus) to my father's house: . . . that he may testify unto them, lest they also come into this place of torment. Abraham saith unto him, They have Moses and the prophets; let them hear them. And he said, Nay, father Abraham: but if one went unto them from the dead, they will repent. And he said unto him, If they hear not Moses and the prophets, neither will they be persuaded, though one rose from the dead."

COMMENT: Jesus clearly relates in this story that the laws of Moses and the words of the prophets which teach repentance lead the faithful to Abraham's bosom, instead of hell. Moses and the prophets are the pathway to eternal life in heaven. Jesus taught this.

Matthew 19:16-19 (Mark 10:17,19) (Luke 18:18,20), ". . . Good Master, what good thing shall I do, that I may have eternal life? And he said unto him . . . if thou wilt enter into life, keep the commandments . . . Which? Jesus said, Thou shalt do no murder, Thou shalt not commit adultery, Thou shalt not steal, Thou shalt not bear false witness, Honor thy father and thy mother: and, thou shalt love thy neighbor as thyself."
COMMENT: There you have it. The way to eternal life, salvation in heaven, is being a good Jew and submitting to the laws of the commandments. These detailed instructions by Jesus are plainly presented. NOTE that in the following verses the man asks what more he need do. And Jesus replies, to be perfect he should sell everything he owns and give it to the poor and receive treasure in heaven: "and come and follow me." The man, on hearing this, leaves disturbed because he has great wealth and doesn't want to lose it. There is no indication that the "follow me" means anything else but to accompany Jesus pennyless. The message remains intact that observing Torah law gives eternal life. Perfection is another story.

Mark 12: 28-31 (Matthew 22:36-40), ". . . Which is the first (great commandment in the law) commandment of all? And Jesus answered him, The first of all the commandments is, Hear, O Israel: The Lord our God is one Lord: And thou shalt love the Lord thy God with all thy heart, and with all thy soul, and with all thy mind, and with all thy strength: this is the first commandment. And the second is like, namely this, Thou shalt love thy neighbor as thyself. There is none other commandment greater than these. (On these two commandments hang all the law and the prophets)."
COMMENT: So, Jesus selected *Deuteronomy 6:4-5* and *Leviticus 19:18* as the greatest two laws. This was very Jewish of him, as most rabbis would completely agree, especially Rabbi Hillel. He chose the Shema prayer, the Jew's affirmation of God's oneness and dedication to love of Him together with Judaism's great moral teaching of loving people with the love you have for yourself. What could be more indicative of the essence of Judaism?

Luke 10:25-28, ". . . Master, what shall I do to inherit eternal life? He said unto him, What is written in the law? how readest thou? And he answering said, Thou shalt love the Lord thy God with all thy

heart, and with all thy soul, and with all thy strength, and with all thy mind: and thy neighbor as thyself. And he said unto him. Thou hast answered right: this do, and thou shalt live."
COMMENT: This goes one step further than the just given, *Mark 12:28-31.* Here we have the indisputable link between the commandments and eternal life, which is the reward for obeying them. It is evident that Jesus said that the law of Moses, as epitomized in *Deuteronomy 6:5* and *Leviticus 19:18,* is the pathway to personal salvation and eternal life. Yes, Jesus said this as found in the New Testament.

Mark 12:32-34, "And the scribe said unto him, Well, Master, thou hast said the truth: for there is one God; and there is none other but he: And to love him with all the heart, and with all the understanding, and with all the soul, and with all the strength, and to love his neighbor as himself, is more than all burnt offerings and sacrifices. . . . Jesus . . . said unto him, Thou art not far from the kingdom of God . . ."
COMMENT: This is a straight follow-through of *Mark 12:28-31,* which connects the acknowledgement of the oneness of God, loving Him, and loving ones neighbor as written in the law, with the reward of God's kingdom. Burnt offerings and sacrifices are secondary to the commandments in Judaism and always have been. With no Temple, there is no doubt about this low degree of importance. This passage demonstrates Jesus' Judaism through and through. NOTE that the term "Master" means good teacher, not anything more. Also note that the question of "one God" will be thoroughly examined in the next chapters.

Matthew 7:12 (Luke 6:31), "Therefore all things whatsoever ye would that men should do to you, do ye even so to them: for this is the law and the prophets."
COMMENT: If you thought that "do unto others" is not Judaic or that it is different from "love your neighbor as yourself" you see here that it is totally of Jewish origin. Jesus declared that it is the law and the prophets. It is Judaic.

Luke 11:28, ". . . blessed are they that hear the word of God and keep it."
Matthew 7:21, "Not every one . . . shall enter into the kingdom of heaven; but he that doeth the will of my Father which is in heaven."
Matthew 3:15, ". . . it becometh us to fulfill all righteousness . . ."
COMMENT: These powerful statements are tucked in between verses which emphasize other ideas. But they can stand alone. And, standing alone they are Judaism's own. Jesus believed that the will of God is

revealed in the word of God, the Hebrew Bible. In the Hebrew Scriptures we learn the law of Moses (Torah) and the Prophets. Thereby, we can perform righteousness as God desires. This Jesus believed.

Luke 19:8-9, ". . . half of my goods I give to the poor; and if I have taken any thing from any man by false accusation, I restore him fourfold. And Jesus said unto him, This day is salvation come to this house forsomuch as he also is a son of Abraham."
COMMENT: It appears that Jesus believed that even a partial fulfillment of the commandments of the Torah is sufficient to be accepted by God. In fact, even by rectifying transgression of the Torah's laws and doing good deeds a person is deserving of salvation. As Jews trust, it is the trying to please God, it is the effort, not the success in total compliance with God's ordinances which is required of us to be righteous.

Luke 13:28, "There shall be weeping and gnashing of teeth, when ye shall see Abraham, and Isaac, and Jacob, and all the prophets, in the kingdom of God, and you yourselves thrust out."
COMMENT: Here Jesus said that the fathers of Judaism and the goodly Hebrew prophets are all accepted into the kingdom of God. Evidently, good Jews need nothing more than the Hebrew religion for life eternal in Jesus' own belief. NOTE that Jesus also said that many of his followers will not get into God's kingdom because of their sinfulness. There is no Christologic "belief" presented here curing wickedness.

John 4:22, "(to Samaritan) Ye worship ye know not what: we know what we worship: for salvation is of the Jews."
COMMENT: Jesus "worships" what Jews worship, namely God. Salvation is of whom?

I Corinthians 6:9-10, (Paul) "Know ye not that the unrighteous shall not inherit the kingdom of God? Be not deceived: neither fornicators, nor idolaters, nor adulterers, nor effeminate, nor abusers of themselves with mankind, Nor thieves, nor covetous, nor drunkards, nor revilers, nor extortioners, shall inherit the kingdom of God."
COMMENT: Although Paul adds some of his own, the listing of "thou shalt nots" is derived from the commandments. He stresses what he considers unrighteousness and says that transgression prevents people from earning reward of heaven. Paul, here, reveals his Judaic background. NOTE that the next verse says that those who "were" transgressors had been helped by the Christologic message. Of course, if you give up evil you are closer to God, Christianity's way, Judaism's way, or any other way.

Luke 1:46-47,50-55, "And Mary said, My soul doth magnify the Lord, And my spirit hath rejoiced in God, my Savior. And his mercy is on them that fear him from generation to generation. He hath showed strength with his arm; he hath scattered the proud in the imagination of their hearts. He hath put down the mighty from their seats, and exalted them of low degree. He hath filled the hungry with good things; and the rich he hath sent empty away. He hath holpen his servant Israel in remembrance of his mercy; As he spake to our fathers, to Abraham, and to his seed for ever."

COMMENT: Mary, Jesus' mother, called the God of Judaism her Savior. Hence, Jews have had salvation by God the Father and need no second or alternate source of salvation. She spoke of God's greatness and His help of His servant, Israel. She spoke of God's message to Abraham's children, that the Covenant is eternal. This was the understanding of Mary after she was allegedly informed that she would have a miraculous virgin birth and that the child would be the Messiah. As you surely can see, she spoke as a traditional, believing Jewish person, not the holy figure of Christianity.

Luke 1:6, (Luke) "And they (Zacharias and Elizabeth) were both righteous before God, walking in all the commandments and ordinances of the Lord blameless."

COMMENT: Jews can be free of sin, blameless, following the law of Moses, as exemplified by these two people. Therefore, we know, the law does give justification for eternal life.

Romans 4:3, (Paul) "For what saith the scripture? Abraham believed God, and it was counted unto him for righteousness."

COMMENT: Consequently, righteousness in God's eyes is believing God's instructions and doing as God commands. In Abraham's situation, it was offering his son Isaac as a sacrifice. In our situation, it is following God's commandments in His Torah.

I John 5:2-3, (John) ". . . we love the children of God, when we love God, and keep his commandments. For this is the love of God, that we keep his commandments: and his commandments are not grievous."

COMMENT: Loving God requires fidelity to His laws, which are not hard to bear or perform. So, we read here that the commandments of the Torah are to be kept and can be kept. They should be observed to demonstrate our love of God and our fellow man. It may be beyond human ability to perform all our duties to God, always and perfectly. But, God gave the commandments which are not hard to uphold, when you use all your good intentions with all your heart. The laws require your effort, not perfection.

Romans 7:12,14,16,22, (Paul) "Wherefore the law is holy, and the commandment holy, and just, and good. For we know that the law is spiritual: . . . I consent unto the law that it is good. For I delight in the law of God after the inward man:"

I Timothy 1:8, (Paul) "But we know that the law is good, if a man use it lawfully;"

II Timothy 3:16-17, (Paul) "All scripture is given by inspiration of God, and is profitable for doctrine, for reproof, for correction, for instruction in righteousness: That the man of God may be perfect, thoroughly furnished unto all good works."

I Peter 1:25, (Peter) "But the word of the Lord endureth for ever. . . ."

COMMENT: Amazingly, the verses presented above affirm the validity of the laws and the commandments of the Torah. They are described as sacred and beneficial, effective and everlasting. Stop here and ask yourself this:—If the Torah is all these things of God, shouldn't the laws be performed and Judaism be observed by all Jews?

Romans 10:5, (Paul) "For Moses describeth the righteousness which is of the law, That the man which doeth those things shall live by them."

COMMENT: The Hebrew Bible teaches that the Torah's laws lead to virtue, which is rewarded by everlasting life. Paul, in this passage, admits that this is the message of Moses in the Holy Scriptures, who communicated God's will to the Hebrew people.

James 5:16, (James) ". . . The effectual fervent prayer of a righteous man availeth much."

I John 3:22, (John) "And whatsoever we ask, we receive of him, because we keep his commandments, and do those things that are pleasing in his sight."

COMMENT: These two verses show that keeping commandments and being righteous are connected. Both lead to God's hearing us, being pleased, and helping us. NOTE that John's next verse changes commandments to singular and then designates it as belief in Jesus Christ. Never mind this twist into Christologics. The verse quoted is Judaic, and that's a fact.

James 2:8, (James) "If ye fulfill the royal law according to the scripture, Thou shalt love thy neighbor as thyself, ye do well:"

COMMENT: A person is good if he obeys the golden rule as given in the law of Moses.

James 1:27, (James) "Pure religion and undefiled before God and the Father is this, To visit the fatherless and widows in their affliction, and to keep himself unspotted from the world."

COMMENT: Here is the golden rule made specific and said to be the basis of religious requirements. Also, to be pure from worldly evils in general makes for a religious person. These are Jewish ideas, totally.

Galatians 3:21, (Paul) "Is the law then against the promise of God? God forbid: for if there had been a law given which could have given life, verily righteousness should have been by the law."

COMMENT: Strange as it may be to read, Paul is here ostensibly lending support to the validity of the law of Moses. For he says "if" the law could be effective Moses' law would suffice for salvation. Well, we have already seen that Jesus said that keeping the commandments is the path to salvation and the law is effective to this end. Therefore, Paul, if he "believes" Jesus, must conclude that righteousness is obtained by the Scriptural laws. NOTE that Paul actually contradicts Jesus on this essential matter and, in effect, created Christianity's separation from its roots in Judaism. Paul claims that sin is not overcome, but is created, by the law. It is Paul's teaching, not Jesus', which invalidated the law for the budding Church. Let's read what Jesus said about this kind of opposition. In *Matthew 10:24 (Luke 6:40) (John 13:16)* Jesus said, *"The disciple is not above his master, nor the servant above his lord."* So we ask, whose statements take precedence? Who is to be believed? We here present a twist from Christologics to Judaics, which fits very comfortably into our exposure of Jesus the Jew:—If you should "believe" on Jesus to be saved, believe his teachings about the eternal and effective holy law of God revealed by Moses. And you will be saved as a Jew.

Romans 14:14, (Paul) "I know . . . that there is nothing unclean of itself: but to him that esteemeth any thing to be unclean, to him it is unclean."

COMMENT: Certainly, this is true. Jews consider things unclean because God announced it in the Torah, not because they are unclean of themselves. The law of kashruth (kosher) is God's law, as detailed by those who seek Him. God's ordinances create uncleanliness, not the thing itself. And Jews who want to please God and get close to Him keep the kosher laws. This is what God desires of us.

Romans 3:1-2, (Paul) "What advantage then hath the Jew? or what profit is there of circumcision? Much every way: chiefly, because that unto them were committed the oracles of God."

Romans 9:4, Romans 10:2, (Paul) "Who are Israelites: to whom pertaineth the adoption, and the glory, and the covenants, and the giving of the law, and the service of God, and the promises: For I bear them record that they have a zeal of God . . ."

Romans 11:29, (Paul) "For the gifts and calling of God are without repentance."

Acts 2:5, (author) "And there were dwelling at Jerusalem Jews, devout men . . ."

COMMENT: Jews have a fervor for God and are devout, said Paul. In other words, Judaism promoted enthusiasm for God. Jews were given the Covenant, the law, the prophets, and the promises. Jews minister to God by being His Chosen People. There is benefit, much benefit, in being Jewish. Paul even bolsters the firm foundation of the Torah, God's gift, lasting for eternity, without God changing His mind, without repenting of His Torah. That is what Paul actually said. NOTE that Paul, however, believed that all these positive features of being Jewish are cancelled, and of no avail, due to the Jew's lack of belief in Jesus Christ. We will leave Paul's reasoning to others. Instead, we ask you to keep in mind his positive appreciation of Judaism. And also remember that Jesus said, in effect, that Judaism is of God. Jesus, himself, taught that "Jews for Judaism" is the way. We have shown abundant evidence of this in our present chapter. Who is the authority you choose, Jesus or Paul?

Ephesians 6:2-3, (Paul) "Honor thy father and mother; which is the first commandment with promise; That it may be well with thee, and thou mayest live long on the earth."

Matthew 15:4 (Mark 7:10), "For God commanded (Moses said), saying, Honor thy father and mother: and, He that curseth father or mother, let him die the death."

COMMENT: These verses are Paul's and Jesus' utterances, condemning anyone who doesn't bestow honor upon his parents, as taken from the Ten Commandments. This means dutifully regarding them and respecting them, and implicitly honoring your heritage as well. This commandment is considered important enough to be put forward separately. Therefore, shaming your parents and their teaching by turning from them and the God of their heritage is prohibited and deserving of worldly death as well as loss of life in the hereafter. This is what we read in the New Testament.

Luke 5:37-39, "And no man putteth new wine into old bottles; else the new wine will burst the bottles, and be spilled, and the bottles shall perish. But new wine must be put into new bottles; and both are preserved. No man also having drunk old wine straightway desireth new: for he saith, The old is better."

COMMENT: Jesus' saying appears to fit Judaism and its offspring, Christianity. To carry this analogy through, the new wine, Christianity, should not be placed into the old, Judaism. This, of course, is just what happened. In order for it to be good, the new should be nurtured separately. Both are then properly maintained, the old as it should be and the new as it should be. This did not occur. Sadly, the new has caused great harm to the old by claiming to succeed it, while mixing with it. And the new, by so doing, has harmed itself. Isn't that the proper conclusion to be drawn? Taken one step further, Jesus also said that those who know the old, Judaism, prefer it. Shouldn't you, as a Jew, prefer it too?

7

His God Is Judaism's God

Now that we have shown that the New Testament affirms that the Torah gives salvation, let's proceed to the very interesting study of finding the God of Jesus. Would it surprise you to learn that in the New Testament's pages Jesus' God is described in Judaic terms? The God of Israel, as Judaism understands God, is the Deity Jesus knew, professed, and worshiped! The verses presented in this chapter should prove this beyond any doubt, using unbiased reasoning. These quotes should clear the mind of those Jews who are questioning Judaism and may think that Christianity properly describes God. From these selected reverse proof-texts it can be seen that the light of Judaism is its pure, monotheistic God, the same God spoken of by Jesus. Jesus never propounded a triune Divinity at all. Christianity has done this, not Jesus.

In these reverse proof-texts Jesus tells us to worship the only God, our Father, who is his God and our God, perfect, all-powerful, and all-knowing. The words "God" and "Father" are used synonomously, while the name Jesus Christ is not. Our forgiving Father judges and rewards everyone according to his works. God is the only Savior. The Deity is not a multiple of persons, but a oneness. And He never is seen by man as He has no form.

In regard to who Jesus is in relation to God our Father, we read that Jesus himself asserted he does not have the knowledge or power of the Father, who is greater than he. Moreover, Jesus prayed to and asked help from God. He even expressed abandonment by God. Truly, he worshiped the Father as a good Jew would. We see Jesus Christ is not an element in an only true God, not at all part of an equally venerated triune Deity. Jesus, it is written, did claim to have been "sent" (perhaps inspired) to do what God wants done. Nevertheless, he did not claim divinity. He appeared to be a man with a mission, in an obvious subordinate relationship to God. At times, the New Testament says he can do things which God can do, while at other times it is stated that only God can do these things. But, this contradiction notwithstanding, from the beginning to the end of Christianity's Book, there is not one word proclaiming that Jesus and God are the same. Nowhere is it expressed that Jesus is the same essence as God. In fact, it is Christianity, not the New Testament, which has declared Jesus is God.

A question is raised here:—How could the basic beliefs about Judaism's God remain in the New Testament? The answer is that they were included, and not expunged, for the simple reason they are authentic early Christianity. They reveal the early creed of the Jesus movement. Read by an advocate of Judaism, these verses are powerful and conclusive verification of the eternal sacredness of Judaism and its teaching concerning God being a unity, alone, and indivisible. Christianity has much to do to make these passages fit alongside the concept of the Trinity. Read ahead and see.

WORSHIP OF THE LORD OUR GOD, OUR FATHER IN HEAVEN.

Matthew 4:10 (Luke 4:8), ". . . for it is written, Thou shalt worship the Lord thy God, and him only shalt thou serve."

Matthew 5:16, ". . . and glorify your Father which is in heaven."

Matthew 6:9-13 (Luke 11:2-4), ". . . pray ye: Our Father which art in heaven, Hallowed be thy name. Thy kingdom come. Thy will be done in earth, as it is in heaven. Give us this day our daily bread. And forgive us our debts, as we forgive our debtors. And lead us not into temptation, but deliver us from evil: For thine is the kingdom, and the power, and the glory, for ever. Amen."

Matthew 7:11, ". . . how much more shall your Father which is in heaven give good things to them that ask him?"

Romans 14:11, (Paul) "For it is written, as I live, saith the Lord, every knee shall bow to me, and every tongue shall confess to God."

I Timothy 1:17, (Paul) "Now unto the King eternal, immortal, invisible, and only wise God, be honor and glory for ever and ever. Amen."

I Peter 3:12, (Peter) "For the eyes of the Lord are over the righteous, and his ears are open unto their prayers . . ."

COMMENT: Worship our Father in heaven, and only He, said Jesus, for God listens and responds to prayer. Perfect Judaism is found in these words. NOTE that God hears prayers directly. There is no intercessor or mediator mentioned as being required. There is no "in Jesus' name" called for when we pray to God. The Lord's Prayer does not state such a thing.

MY GOD AND YOUR GOD, THE SAME PERFECT GOD.

Matthew 5:45, "That ye may be the children of your Father which is in heaven . . ."

Matthew 5:48, "Be ye therefore perfect, even as your Father which is in heaven is perfect."

John 20:17, ". . . my Father, and your Father; . . . my God, and your God."

II Corinthians 6:18, (Paul) "And (I) will be a Father unto you, and ye shall be my sons and daughters, saith the Lord Almighty."

COMMENT: God is his Father, Jesus said, the same as the Father of us all. We are the children of a perfect God. And, Jesus is talking about the God of Israel, as Jews know Him. NOTE that a perfect God could not present laws to His Chosen People which were not completely excellent and wise. A perfect God could not and would not change His plans, His faultless plans.

GOD IS ALL-KNOWING AND ALL-POWERFUL.

Matthew 6:32 (Luke 12:30), ". . . for your heavenly Father knoweth that ye have need of all these things."

Matthew 10:29 (Luke 12:6), ". . . and one of them (sparrows) shall not fall on the ground without your Father (God)."

Matthew 19:26 (Mark 10:27) (Luke 18:27) (Luke 1:37), "But Jesus . . . said unto them, With men this is impossible: but with God all things are possible (For with God nothing is impossible)."

Acts 17:24-27, (author) "God that made the world and all things therein, seeing that he is Lord of heaven and earth, . . . seeing he giveth to all life, and breath, and all things: And hath made of one blood all nations . . . and hath determined the times before appointed, and the bounds of their habitation: That they should seek the Lord, . . . and find him, though he be not far from every one of us:"

Romans 13:1, (Paul) "Let every soul be subject unto the higher powers. For there is no power but of God: the powers that be are ordained of God."

I Corinthians 10:26, (Paul—Psalm) "For the earth is the Lord's and fullness thereof."

Colossians 1:12,16, (Paul) "Giving thanks unto the Father... For by him were all things created, that are in heaven, and that are in earth, visible and invisible, whether they be thrones, or dominions, or principalities, or powers: all things were created by him, and for him:"

Hebrews 2:10, (Paul) "For it became him (God), for whom are all things, and by whom are all things, . . . (to make the captain of their salvation (Jesus) perfect through sufferings)."

COMMENT: In Hebrews above, we included the Christologics so there can be no doubt whatsoever that it is God our Father, not Jesus, "for whom and by whom are all things." God of creation is all-knowing and all-powerful, and no other power is like His. The earth and the heavens and everything therein are by Him and for Him. God determines all. Judaism teaches exactly this. NOTE that even if we were to imagine that Jesus possessed any power it would necessarily be power made by God our Father and distributed to Jesus. God's supremacy and uniqueness cannot be incorporated into an alleged Trinity, using these verses as our reference.

GOD IS MERCIFUL AND THE FORGIVER OF SINS.

Matthew 6:14-15 (Mark 11:25-26), "For if ye forgive men their trespasses, your heavenly Father will also forgive you: But if ye forgive not men their trespasses, neither will your Father forgive your trespasses."

Matthew 18:35, "So likewise shall my heavenly Father do also unto you, if ye from your hearts forgive not every one his brother their trespasses."

Luke 6:36, "Be ye therefore merciful, as your Father also is merciful."

Luke 23:34, ". . . Father, forgive them . . ."

II Corinthians 1:3, (Paul) "Blessed be God . . . the Father of mercies, and the God of all comfort:"

COMMENT: It is the merciful Father who has the power of forgiveness. NOTE that Jesus asks his Father, God, to forgive. Consequently, we know that Jesus does not have the authority to forgive or take sin away. Jesus' own words indicate this. Apparently, as recorded here in the New Testament, Jesus is not able to confer forgiveness, either together with or apart from God our Father.

GOD JUDGES AND REWARDS ACCORDING TO WORKS.

Matthew 6:1,4,18, ". . . otherwise ye have no reward of your Father which is in heaven. . . . and thy Father which seeth in secret himself shall reward thee openly."

I Peter 1:16-17, (Peter) "Because it is written. Be ye holy; for I am holy. And if ye call on the Father, who without respect of persons judgeth according to every man's work . . ."

Romans 14:12, (Paul) ". . . every one of us shall give account of himself to God."

COMMENT: All people are judged by God our Father and are rewarded according to our actions. This is Judaic, thoroughly and completely. NOTE that God's reward is in no way linked to Christologic belief.

GOD OUR FATHER IS OUR ONLY SAVIOR.

Luke 1:46-47, "And Mary said, My soul doth magnify the Lord,

And my spirit hath rejoiced in God my Savior."

Luke 20: 37-38 (Matthew 22: 31-32) (Mark 12: 26-27), "Now that the dead are raised, even Moses showed at the bush, when he calleth the Lord the God of Abraham, and the God of Isaac, and the God of Jacob. For he is not a God of the dead, but of the living: for all live unto him."

I Timothy 1:1, (Paul) ". . . by the commandment of God our Savior, (and Lord Jesus Christ, which is our hope);"

I Timothy 2:3, (Paul) "For this is good and acceptable in the sight of God our Savior;"

Titus 3:4, (Paul) ". . . the kindness and love of God our Savior . . ."

James 4:12, (James) "There is one lawgiver (God), who is able to save and to destroy . . ."

Jude (1):25, (Jude) "To the only wise God our Savior, be glory and majesty, dominion and power, both now and ever. Amen."

I Timothy 4:10, (Paul) ". . . because we trust in the living God, who is the Savior of all men, specially of those that believe."

COMMENT: Take a good look again at the above verses. It is written that the only Savior is God, our lawgiver. He alone bestows salvation and accomplishes resurrection of the dead. Jews believe this, and here is confirmation in the New Testament of our belief. NOTE that "specially those that believe" actually reinforces the proof that God is our only Savior. It signifies that all children of the living God are capable of receiving God's love. Pointedly, it means that those who "believe" (perhaps the message of Christianity) are not uniquely saved. Others are saved as well. The Christologics in Timothy 1:1 is presented so that you can clearly see that God our Father is the Savior, not Jesus Christ, who is designated otherwise.

THE LORD GOD IS A UNITY, HE IS ONE.

Mark 12:29, "And Jesus answered him, The first of all the commandments is, Hear, O Israel; The Lord our God is one Lord:"

COMMENT: That's right. Jesus said that the Shema prayer, the prayer Jews say daily and at impending death, is the most important. This prayer, which every religious Jew hopes to utter as his last words, has significance as Judaism's affirmation of the oneness of God, the singleness of His essence, His aloneness, and His uniqueness.

Mark 12:32, ". . . Well, Master, thou hast said the truth: for there is one God; and there is none other but he:"

James 2:19, (James) "Thou believest that there is one God; thou doest well . . ."

Matthew 23:9, "And call no man your father upon the earth: for one is your Father, which is in heaven."

Ephesians 4:6, (Paul) "(There is) One God and Father of all, who is above all, and through all, and in you all."

I Corinthians 8:4-6, (Paul) ". . . there is none other God but one. For though there be that are called gods, whether in heaven or in earth, . . . But to us there is but one God, the Father, of whom are all things . . ."

COMMENT: All the foregoing passages announce what Jews know, that God is one God, and He is the Father. That is what is written. Right here, we have New Testament acknowledgement that God is the Father, and no other is God. In other words, if the essence is not the Father and nothing other, it is not entitled to be called God. NOTE that Christianity does not claim that Jesus is the Father. The claim is that the Father, Jesus, and the Holy Ghost are one essence in the Godhead, but separate "persons." This is the so-called mystery of the Christian "monotheistic" triune God. However, without challenging this concept here and now, we can with assurance maintain that Jesus, who is "God the Son," is not "God the Father" also. Consequently, he is not God as is proclaimed in Christianity. And this conclusion is drawn from plain verses.

GOD IS INVISIBLE, HAVING NO FORM SEEN.

John 1:18, "No man hath seen God at any time; the only begotten Son, which is in the bosom of the Father, he hath declared him."

John 5:37, "And the Father . . . Ye have neither heard his voice at any time, nor seen his shape."

I John 4:12,20, (John) "No man hath seen God at any time. If we love one another, God dwelleth in us, and his love is perfected in us. . . . for he that loveth not his brother whom he hath seen, how can he love God whom he hath not seen?"

COMMENT: The invisible and incorporeal God of Judaism is confirmed, whether called the Father or called God. See *Exodus 33:20, "And he said, Thou canst not see my face: for there shall no man see me, and live."* In addition, we are told that when we do God's will and love one another, we bring God closer to ourselves. NOTE that John's words were after Jesus lived, and that he believed the message of Jesus. The verses are a sharp blow to the concept of a triune God. Obviously, Jesus was visible and seen, if you read the New Testament. Yet, we are made aware of the truth that God is never seen. Therefore, John did not believe that Jesus was God in any shape, incarnation, or mystical presence. Whatever else he may have been to John, Jesus was not God. And we know from *Numbers 23:19, "God is not a man, . . ."*

THE "GOOD GOD" IS NOT JESUS.

Matthew 19:16-17 (Mark 10:17-18) (Luke 18:18-19), ". . . And, behold, one came and said unto him, Good Master, what good thing

shall I do, that I may have eternal life? And he said unto him, Why
callest thou me good? there is none good but one, that is, God: . . .
(none is good, save one, that is, God)."
COMMENT: This passage is probably one of the most amazing presented in this chapter. Simply told, Jesus denied being God. If you
don't believe it, read the passage again. He declared he should not be
called good, because only God is good. Thus, Jesus clearly contradicts
Christianity's formulation of the Trinity. This is irrefutable evidence of
Jesus the Jew believing in the God of Judaism. And this God has nothing to do with himself together in one entity.

JESUS DOES NOT HAVE CO-EQUAL KNOWLEDGE WITH GOD.
Mark 13:32 (Matthew 24:36), "But of that day and that hour
knoweth no man, no, not the angels which are in heaven, neither the
Son, but the Father."
Acts 1:7, ". . . It is not for you to know the times or the seasons,
which the Father hath put in his own power."
COMMENT: The Father, only, has knowledge of when events are to
occur. Jesus does not have this information. NOTE that if there were a
formulation called a triune God, Jesus in these verses denies that he is
part of it. For, with a unity of the Godhead, there must be equal
knowledge by the unified substance of God. Jesus says he doesn't have
co-equal knowledge with the Father. Can one part of God be ignorant
of what another part of God knows? No. So, evidently, Jesus is not
part of a Trinity.

JESUS DOES NOT HAVE GOD'S POWER.
Matthew 20:23 (Mark 10:40), "And he saith unto them . . . but to
sit on my right hand, and on my left, is not mine to give, but it shall be
given to them for whom it is prepared of my Father."
COMMENT: It is in the Father's power to grant favors and rewards.
Jesus openly asserted he does not have the power of the Father. NOTE
that if Jesus were part of a triune Godhead, he would have co-equality
of power. He does not. Therefore, this verse gives proof that God the
Father and Jesus have no oneness in a Godhead.

JESUS' PRAYER IS DIRECTED TO THE FATHER.
Matthew 11:25-26 (Luke 10:21), ". . . Jesus . . . said, I thank
thee, O Father, Lord of heaven and earth, . . . Even so, Father: for it
seemed good in thy sight."
Luke 23:46 (Psalm 31:5), ". . . Father, into thy hands I commend
my spirit . . ."
John 14:16, "And I will pray the Father . . ."
COMMENT: The Father hears all prayers, including the prayers of
Jesus. NOTE that Christianity's triune God would be praying to itself,

if you can imagine this preposterous situation.

GOD IS GREATER THAN ALL, INCLUDING JESUS.

John 10:29, "My Father, . . . is greater than all . . ."

John 13:16, ". . . The servant is not greater than his lord; neither he that is sent (Jesus) greater than he that sent him (God)."

John 14:28, ". . . for my Father is greater than I."

COMMENT: Jesus' Father, who is God the Father of us all, is called by Jesus greater than himself. NOTE that this is further verification that Jesus is not part of a Trinity having co-equality of power and importance. Whoever Jesus may have thought he was, he did not envisage himself a part of a triune Divinity.

THE FATHER'S WILL IS GREATER THAN ALL, INCLUDING JESUS'

Matthew 26:39,42 (Mark 14:35-36) (Luke 22:42), "And he went a little farther, and fell on his face, and prayed, saying, O my Father, if it be possible, let this cup pass from me: nevertheless not as I will, but as thou wilt . . . O my Father, if this cup may not pass away from me, except I drink it, thy will be done. (Abba, Father, all things are possible unto thee . . .)."

COMMENT: This certainly is clear enough, isn't it? The Father, not Jesus, has the power. The Father's will is differentiated from his and can be contrary to what Jesus' desire is. NOTE that this is additional indication, of a substantial nature, that Jesus is not part of a Godhead unity. For if he were, he could not plead with himself. Think about it. It is senseless.

HE INCREASED IN WISDOM.

Luke 2:52, (Luke) "And Jesus increased in wisdom and stature, and in favor with God and man."

COMMENT: Here is what one would say about any human being who was growing up as a good person. NOTE that if Jesus were God, he could never be described as increasing in wisdom, because he would be all-wisdom. Moreover, Jesus is said to obtain greater approval from God as he matured. Could he, in the Godhead, consider himself more favorably as he grew up as Jesus the person? This question exposes the illogic of Jesus being considered God. This is not Christianity's mystery. It is simply a verse in the New Testament which, among others, makes Christianity's Trinity inconceivable, using God-given reasoning.

HE WAS MADE LOWER THAN THE ANGELS.

Hebrews 2:9, (Paul) "But we see Jesus, who was made a little lower than the angels . . . that he by the grace of God . . ."

COMMENT: In *Psalm 8:5,* man is said to be made *"a little lower than the angels."* Therefore, Paul is saying that Jesus was a man of stature lower than the angels which attend God in heaven. As such he received

God's favor. NOTE that not only is Jesus described as lower than the angels, and consequently obviously not God, but that God offered him grace. God could not dispense grace to himself in any logical manner. This verse makes the concept of Jesus in the Trinity an impossibility.

HE WAS FORSAKEN BY GOD.

Mark 15:34 (Matthew 27:46), "And at the ninth hour Jesus cried with a loud voice saying, Eloi, Eloi, lama sabachthani? which is, being interpreted, My God, my God, why hast thou forsaken me?"
COMMENT: This is one of the clearest verses refuting Jesus' alleged divinity. How could this utterance come from the Jesus Christ of Christianity? It really could not. But, from Jesus the Jew, it is simply a despairing cry to God, one of far too many in the long and tragic history of Jews being tortured and put to death. NOTE that the question must be asked, "Can God abandon himself?" But, the question is not for Judaism to answer, as it is Christianity's concept to ponder. Outside of Christianity the absurdity is profound. Also, notice that in this verse Jesus called on the name "God," while in others he used the name "Father." So, we can be certain that for Jesus the two names are for one and the same Deity. The terms for the Divinity are interchangeable, just as they are in Judaism. Jesus' God is our own God, the God of the Jewish people as we know Him! This is the only proper conclusion to be made from the reading of the verses given in this chapter.

8

His God Is Not a Trinity

The previous chapter used reverse proof-texts to show Jesus' God was Judaism's God. In this chapter, we shall quote Christologic passages from the New Testament as further reinforcement of the confidence Jews should have in the Judaic understanding of God. These verses belong to Christianity and are its bedrock, as Christians interpret them. The Christologic layers of the New Testament are of no relevance to Jews, who are secure in the revealed God of the Hebrew Scriptures. Understand that we are not challenging Christian theology here. Our subject is God, as Jesus knew Him, as written in the New Testament. It is incredible, but true:—Even within the Christologic passages there is confirmation of the monotheistic God of Judaism as known by Jews.

In no place did Jesus say he is God, or God incarnate, or part of a Trinity, or in any unique way the substance of God! He never said he was of one essence with God in any special union. Nevertheless, Christianity does believe this. Don't you think Jesus would have said so, and said so plainly, if it were truly his belief?

How, then, did the concept of the Trinity become a basic dogma of Christianity? It wasn't clearly comprehended from the pages of Christianity's Book, so it was mandated as a belief three hundred years after Jesus' death by Christianity's Council of Nicaea in 325 C.E. Hence, for three centuries, Jesus did not have the designation as God the Son of the Trinity. A council said this is the truth, not Jesus.

Also, ask yourself this:—If God is all-powerful, why wouldn't He, and only He, be the one who "saves" eternally? Why would He need another entity to do part of His work, when He can do everything? Power to do all things certainly includes saving souls. In other words,

49

why would God need to be a Trinity when He is an all-capable Unity! Use your God-given logic to think and answer. Your reasoning will surely make you put God in His place as the one-in-one God. This should be another interesting chapter, so let's start our investigation of these passages.

ONLY BEGOTTEN SON OF GOD.

I John 4:9, (John) ". . . God sent his only begotten Son . . ."
COMMENT: Jesus is not God's only begotten Son. For proof we present verses from the Hebrew Scriptures. Read these:—*Exodus 4:22, ". . . Thus saith the Lord, Israel is my son, even my firstborn:" Deuteronomy 14:1, "Ye are the children of the Lord your God . . ." Hosea 1:10, ". . . Ye (children of Israel) are the sons of the living God." Psalm 2:7, ". . . The Lord hath said unto me, Thou art my Son; this day have I begotten thee."*

JESUS AND THE FATHER ARE ONE.

John 10:30, "I and my Father are one."
COMMENT: It was so taken for granted that he didn't mean he was God in substance when he said this that he doesn't even bother refuting blasphemy on this account. Instead, he denies that he blasphemed when he said he was the Son of God. Jesus then quoted from *Psalm 82:6, "I have said, Ye are gods; and all of you are children of the most High."* Jesus says he means he is the Son of God in a similar manner and is not a blasphemer. In this verse, Jesus was announcing that he had a special harmony with God in doing His will. This can be confirmed by the verse *Mark 12:29, ". . . Hear, O Israel! The Lord our God is one Lord,"* where Jesus quoted *Deuteronomy 6:4.* In this affirmation of the oneness of God, the Shema, no doubt can exist that Jesus was referring to a one-in-one God, not a three-in-one God which includes himself. As he denies blasphemy when he calls himself the Son of God and shows its innocuous intent, he surely would not call himself "one" with the Father in Christianity's sense either.

FATHER IS IN JESUS—JESUS IS IN THE FATHER.

John 10:38. ". . . believe, that the Father is in me, and I in him."
COMMENT: This does not signify that God and Jesus are together in a triune Godhead. Here is proof. Read *John 17:23, "I in them (followers) and thou in me, that they may be made perfect in one . . ." John 14:20, ". . . I am in my Father, and ye (followers) in me, and I in you." John 17:21, "That they all may be one; as thou, Father, art in me, and I in thee, that they also may be one in us . . ." I John 4:12, ". . . If we love one another, God dwelleth in us and his love is perfected in us."* These verses are evidence that no idea of a three-in-one God is propounded. A multitudinous assemblage of persons in the

Godhead would be the result of taking the verse literally, with all the followers in the Godhead also.

Matthew 10:40, "He that receiveth you (disciples) receiveth me, and he that receiveth me receiveth him that sent me."

COMMENT: Here "in me" is replaced by "receiveth me." Similarly, God would be a fifteen-in-one God, if this were to be taken literally. By the way, have you noticed that the "Holy Spirit" is ignored in all of this? Why should this be, if all three parts of the Trinity are equally important? The Holy Spirit is omitted in all these verses because these verses simply have nothing to do with a triune Deity.

I Corinthians 3:23, (Paul) "And ye are Christ's; and Christ is God's."

COMMENT: If something belongs to something, it isn't the essence of it. It simply belongs to it and is its possession. A relationship exists, nothing more.

JESUS IS SUBJECT TO GOD.

I Corinthians 15:28, (Paul) "And when all things shall be subdued unto him, then shall the Son also himself be subject unto him that put all things under him, that God may be all in all."

COMMENT: We will not disturb this concept of the end of time, for it is Christianity's to consider. However, in this verse, we have further refutation of Jesus being God. For, if Jesus is to be subject to God, he could not be part of a Trinity which is equally powerful and equally eternal. Is it possible, or even conceivable, that God could be made subject to himself? Christian theologists might say that with God all things are possible. Judaism's advocate would reply that all things are possible except God becoming not God. Refutation of Judaism's concept of God in this area of thought is difficult for Christianity, for it is their concept as well. Let us take one step further and offer that the Trinity, similarly, could not dissolve itself and make itself a non-Trinity, if the Trinity really were the essence of God.

POWER IS GIVEN TO JESUS BY THE FATHER.

Matthew 28:18, Matthew 11:27 (Luke 10:22), ". . . All power is given unto me in heaven and in earth. All things are delivered unto me of my Father . . ."

COMMENT: We will bypass the Christologic concept of power distribution. Remember that we have already shown Jesus saying he does not have God's power. However, it must be agreed that God is all-powerful. Consequently, he could not receive power or capability. Jesus, therefore, if he had power given to him, could not be claiming to be God who already is the Almighty.

THE SON REVEALS THE FATHER.

Matthew 11:27 (Luke 10:22), ". . . no man knoweth the Son, but the Father; neither knoweth any man the Father, save the Son, and he to whomsoever the Son will reveal him."

COMMENT: Let us pursue our fundamental search to find that the God of Jesus is not a triune God. Set Christologics aside. Here he describes his Father-to-Son relationship. These words in no way signify that Jesus is actually God. He made no such assertion. He has taken a position that his knowledge of God is supreme and unique. At most, we could say that these words are very odd, and even destructive of Christianity, if taken literally. We would have to conclude that all Hebrew Scripture contact with God by Abraham, Moses, and the Prophets was of naught. If this were so, it would cut Christianity's foundation, as the Hebrew Scriptures would not be the word of God. Certainly, *Isaiah 59:21* contradicts this when we read, *". . . My spirit that is upon thee, and my words which I have put in thy mouth, shall not depart out of thy mouth . . ."* Isaiah said that God's spirit and words are upon the people of Israel. The Father has revealed Himself to His Chosen People through His Scriptures. Jesus elsewhere contradicts his words here. For example in *Matthew 6:6,9 (Luke 11:2)* he declares that we should pray directly to God, *". . . when thou prayest, enter into thy closet, . . . pray to thy Father . . . pray ye: Our Father which art in heaven . . ."* There is our direct contact. In addition, notice that Jesus says that only the Father knows him. Apparently, he is not an intermediary between God and man either, if we take this verse literally. Christianity can make of these words what they will, but no Trinity is to be found.

John 14:6-7,9 (John 8:19) (John 12:45), ". . . no man cometh unto the Father, but by me. If ye had known me, ye should have known my Father also: and from henceforth ye know him, and have seen him. . . . he that hath seen me hath seen the Father . . ."

COMMENT: Needless to say, this passage is contradicted and refuted by much of what was presented in the previous chapter. It is a Christologic layer in the New Testament. Let's select a few verses which show the conflict of layers. See these:—*John 5:37, "And the Father . . . Ye have neither heard his voice at any time, nor seen his shape."* I Timothy 1:17, *(Paul) "Now unto the King eternal, immortal, invisible . . ."* I John 4:12, *(John) "No man hath seen God at any time. . . ."* Acts 17:27, *(author) "They that should seek the Lord, . . . though he be not far from every one of us:"* I Peter 1:17, *(Peter) "And if ye call on the Father . . ."* And don't forget The Lord's Prayer. A verse from the Hebrew Scriptures would also be of instruction here, namely *Numbers 23:19, "God is not a man, that he should lie . . ."* The conflict is

clear. However, let's concentrate on our search for indications of the
Trinity. Notice, again, that Jesus did not say he is the Father. If he did,
it would be contrary to the Christian concept of the Trinity, where the
Father and Jesus are separate persons in the Godhead. What Jesus reasonably could have meant is that he is able to convey God's will to
man. Jesus, it seems, is being described by John as an intercessor
between God and man, the hellenistic Logos. The passage must be
taken as figurative, not literal, for it to fit properly. But, in any way of
looking at it, we do not see that Jesus said he is the substance of the
Father. At most, we can interpret Jesus claiming that he is so attuned
to God that he mirrors and reflects Him.

   *John 1:18, (John) "No man hath seen God at any time; the only
begotten Son, which is in the bosom of the Father, he hath declared
him."*
   *John 6:46, "Not that any man hath seen the Father, save he which
is of God, he hath seen the Father."*
COMMENT: First observe that "God" and the "Father" are interchangeable appellations here. Then notice that Jesus confirms the fact
that he is not the Father, not God, because obviously Jesus has been
seen. Next think about the words "he who is of God hath seen the
Father." Again, this means Jesus is not God, because God has no need
to see himself. God is God, and one part of the Godhead is the same
substance as the other parts. Therefore, the parts need not contact one
another, if they belong to a Trinity. But, it is for Christianity to express
the functioning of their triune concept of God, and we leave the explanations to them and for them. One more comment is due. We are not
disputing that Jesus was an inspired religious person who had seen the
Father in ways all the Hebrew prophets and holy ones of God had seen
Him and declared Him. All goodly religious teachers make God
known. And all devout men hope to attain the bosom of the Father in
heaven as an eternal reward. The first subject in this chapter discusses
"Only Begotten Son," showing that Jesus was not this.

JESUS CHRIST IS MEDIATOR.
   *I Timothy 2:5, (Paul) "For there is one God, and one mediator
between God and men, the man Jesus Christ;"*
COMMENT: This presents complete destruction of the idea that Jesus
is actually the one God, in any manner at all. Jesus is termed a "mediator," the only intermediary between God and man. Whether this is or
is not true is not of concern here. It is Christianity's topic. What is of
importance in this quote is that, because God cannot mediate between
Himself and man, Jesus is clearly shown to be other than God. The
language is straightforward. As a final blow, Timothy calls Jesus

Christ "the man." Although Christianity's dogma is that he is man as well as God, Timothy intimates no such thing. He says "man" only.

HOLY GHOST IS GREATER THAN JESUS.

Luke 12:10 (Matthew 12:32) (Mark 3:28-29), "And whosoever shall speak a word against the Son of man (Jesus), it shall be forgiven him: but unto him that blasphemeth against the Holy Ghost it shall not be forgiven."

COMMENT: Here is plain indication that Jesus is not joined together with the Holy Spirit in a Trinity. He stated that the Holy Ghost should never be blasphemed, for to do so is unforgivable. We leave this concept to Christianity, as the Holy Ghost is their dogma. However, we are interested in the fact that Jesus is not in the category of the Holy Ghost. So, we see that the equality of the three-in-one God is undone. The basics of the Trinity belief is undercut. And now take good note that it is forgivable to talk against Jesus. He said so himself.

THEY BE WHERE I AM.

John 17:24, "Father, I will that they . . . be with me where I am . . ."

COMMENT: Jesus asked the Father to allow his followers to be with him in heaven to behold his glory. Doesn't this signify a differentiation between the Father, and His place, and Jesus, and his place in the time to come? It surely signals that God and Jesus are not of one substance, together in heaven.

JESUS TEMPTED BY THE DEVIL—HOLY GHOST ENTERS JESUS.

Luke 4:1-2 (Matthew 4:1-2) (Mark 1:12-13), "And Jesus being full of the Holy Ghost returned from Jordan and was led by the Spirit into the wilderness. Being forty days tempted of the devil. . . ."

COMMENT: Can God the Son of the Trinity be tempted by the devil by any stretch of the imagination? Surely, the devil cannot affect God who rules the world. End of comment. Another point here is that if the Holy Ghost can enter Jesus it cannot be presented as a separate entity apart from Jesus, making up the Trinity with the Father. Try to capture the picture. It's impossible. The Trinity is impossible from this.

BEFORE ABRAHAM WAS JESUS.

John 8:58, ". . . I say unto you, Before Abraham was, I am."

COMMENT: A pre-existence of some kind seems to be declared. Many philosophical ideas could be put forward to fit. Notice that a co-existence with God from eternity, in the same essence, is not presented at all. Other beings, such as angels, are said to be in co-existence with God from eternity. But, the angels are not God. Whatever else it does mean, "before Abraham" does not qualify as a statement of eternal existence of Jesus in a co-eternal Godhead.

BEFORE THE WORLD'S FOUNDATION.
John 17:24, ". . . for thou lovest me before the foundation of the world."
COMMENT: Jesus said the Father loved him before creation. He did not assert co-substantiation with the Father. Could Jesus call himself "thou," and could he say he loved himself? That is what this passage would mean if Jesus were in a triune Godhead. Don't you think that it would be beyond credibility? We leave this verse for Christianity to explain, for it is theirs to use as believed. It, however, does not figure in an explanation of the Trinity.

JESUS IS THE FIRST AND LAST.
Revelation 1:17-18, ". . . I am the first and the last: I am he that liveth and was dead; and, behold, I am alive for evermore . . ."
COMMENT: This is not Jesus saying he is *"the first, and . . . the last"* God of *Isaiah 44:6.* He is not saying he is God. Observe that Jesus is discussing his supposed resurrection, his being the first and the last brought into everlasting life by God in this manner. The Christian concept of Jesus' resurrection is not our subject. And the Trinity is not the subject of this verse from Revelation.

THREE BEAR RECORD IN HEAVEN.
I John 5:7, (John) "For there are three that bear record in heaven, the Father, the Word and the Holy Ghost: and these three are one."
COMMENT: You're right. This verse seems to give confirmation of the existence of a triune God. Actually it does not, because it is recognized by authorities that it was not part of the original New Testament versions. It probably was inserted by copyists who wanted to legitimize this belief. So that ends that.

FATHER, SON, AND HOLY GHOST.
Matthew 28:19 (Mark 16:15) (Luke 24:47), "Go ye therefore, and teach all nations, baptizing them in the name of the Father, and of the Son, and of the Holy Ghost:"
COMMENT: We have three names mentioned as needed for baptism of Christians. Notice that there is no link to a triune God. It doesn't read, "of God the Father, God the Son, and God the Holy Ghost." Christianity has made that unity of connection. Furthermore, the words themselves can be labeled as spurious. For Mark's version, which is the earliest, reads, "preach the gospel," with no "in the name of" given. Luke's version, which is later than Matthew's, reads, "preached in his (Jesus') name." Matthew is alone in his unique listing of the alleged participants in the Trinity. Baptism, as offered in this verse, has no parallel in the New Testament. By examination of the text, it can be deduced that this verse's verbage is the product of an

overzealous copyist devoted to the Trinity at a later time. But, in any case, no unity of linkage of the three is made, except by Christianity's post-interpretation.

THE LORD'S SUPPER.

Matthew 26:26-29 (Mark 14:22-25) (Luke 22:17-20), ". . . Jesus took bread, and blessed it, and brake it, and gave it to the disciples, and said. Take, eat; this is my body. And he took the cup, and gave thanks, and gave it to them, saying, Drink ye all of it; For this is my blood of the new testament, which is shed for many for the remission of sins. But I say unto you, I will not drink henceforth of this fruit of the vine, until the day when I drink it new with you in my Father's kingdom."

COMMENT: Let's go straight to our search for Jesus' God. In spite of the Christian concept of the remission of sins as spoken of here, you will observe that in no place in this passage did Jesus say he is God. There is no claim for the transubstantiation of God at all. It is Jesus' body and blood, not God's, which is spoken of here. And Jesus made no connection between God and himself, while presenting his message of vicarious atonement. Christianity takes it from there. But, notice that Jesus blessed God over the bread and wine as Jews do and gave thanks to God as Jews do during the Passover ceremony. It is a ritual of thanks and remembrance in Judaism, having nothing to do with the pagan rituals of substance transformation. Therefore, Jesus thanked God in a traditional manner, never uttering one word about God being in the bread and wine. His words about his own body and blood could perhaps be his special way of asking his disciples to remember him until they all meet in the kingdom of God. The alleged vicarious remission of sins is a separate issue entirely and need not be discussed at this point.

GOD EXALTED JESUS.

Philippians 2:9, (Paul) "Wherefore God also hath highly exalted him, and given him a name which is above every name:"

COMMENT: Jesus, if he were God or a part of God, would not have to be raised in status or dignity by God or another part of God. Do you get the point here?

FROM GOD TO GOD.

John 13:3, (John) ". . . he was come from God, and went to God;"

COMMENT: Jesus cannot come from God and go back to God in any rational manner, if he himself were part of God. Right? Christian theologians would answer this question by referring to it as a mystery, God's own mystery. The mystery is beyond human comprehension,

they might say, but not beyond our knowing of it. Well, we must admit
that it is very difficult to challenge anything which is called a mystery.
They have all irrationality covered with the designation of "mystery."
Therefore, the mysterious unsubstantiated theology of the Trinity is
left for Christianity to unravel, as it is of, by, and for themselves. By
the way, concerning this verse, don't we all come from and return to
God as His devoted children? Looking at it this way, there is no irrational mystery at all. In this simple explanation, Jesus is one of God's
own, nothing more.

JESUS IS NOT GOD, BUT CHRIST.
   *John 17:3, ". . . that they might know thee the only true God, and
Jesus Christ, whom thou hast sent."*
   *I Corinthians 8:6, (Paul) ". . . one God, the Father, . . . and one
Lord Jesus Christ . . ."*
   *James 1:1, (James) ". . . a servant of God and of the Lord Jesus
Christ . . ."*
   *II Peter 1:2, (Peter) ". . . the knowledge of God, and of Jesus our
Lord."*
   *I Peter 1:3, (Peter) "Blessed be the God and Father of our Lord
Jesus Christ . . ."*
   I Peter 2:5, (Peter) ". . . acceptable to God by Jesus Christ."
   *Ephesians 1:3,17, (Paul) "Blessed be the God and Father of our
Lord Jesus Christ, . . . the God of our Lord Jesus Christ . . ."*
   *Revelation 11:15, (John) ". . . are become the kingdoms of our
Lord, and of his Christ . . ."*
COMMENT: In all the above verses, God and Jesus are identified as
different. Jesus is called "Christ," while God is called "Father." The
term "Lord" is a term of authority, not a synonym for God. It is evi-
dent that Jesus is considered Christ, the Messiah, not God the Father.
And the language is sharp and clear, with no mistaking the separateness "and" indicates. See the following chapters "The Hebrew Messiah" and "Jesus Is Not the Hebrew Messiah" for our refutation.

GOD'S WILL, NOT JESUS' WILL.
   John 4:34, ". . . to do the will of him that sent me . . ."
   *John 5:30, ". . . I seek not mine own will, but the will of the
Father which hath sent me."*
   *John 6:38, "For I came down from heaven, not to do mine own
will, but the will of him that sent me."*
   John 6:39, ". . . the Father's will which hath sent me . . ."
COMMENT: Jesus is on earth to do what his Father wants done.
Jesus' will and the Father's are not the very same, not identical, and
they could differ. This is dramatically demonstrated in *Matthew 26:39*
where Jesus says, ". . . *O my Father, if it be possible, let this cup pass*

from me: nevertheless not as I will, but as thou wilt . . ." Other passages we have shown prove that the names "God" and "Father" are interchangeable appellations. Jesus might have said that God's will and his will are one will, but he did not. Obviously, with any detachment of viewpoint, God and Jesus here are not one in a unity, as shown by their separation of wills described by Jesus himself.

OF GOD OR OF JESUS.

John 7:17, ". . . whether it be of God, or whether I speak of myself."

COMMENT: These plain words indicate God and Jesus are distinctly separate, as ". . . God or . . . myself" denotes. Trinitarian belief has a separateness of persons together with a unity of three in the Godhead. But, Jesus did not express any substantiation of this concept. As the New Testament is about Jesus, shouldn't he have declared that he is part of a triune Deity, often and clearly, if this were true? If you look at the pages of the Hebrew Scriptures, you will find God identifying Himself as "the Lord your God" over and over again. Yet, Jesus did not once identify himself as "God the Son" of a Trinity. He never so identified himself, nor did others so call him. Remember that the "Son of God" is not equivalent to the meaning of "God the Son" of the Trinity. The two phrases are worlds apart in significance. The Trinity is the Church's mystery, not Jesus' mystery.

THE FATHER SENT AND TAUGHT JESUS.

John 12:49, "For I have not spoken of myself; but the Father which sent me, he gave me a commandment, what I should say, and what I should speak."

John 7:16, ". . . My doctrine is not mine, but his that sent me."

John 8:26, ". . . he that sent me . . . I speak . . . those things which I have heard of him."

John 8:28, ". . . I do nothing of myself; but as my Father hath taught me . . ."

John 8;40, ". . . me, a man that hath told . . . which I have heard of God . . ."

John 14:31, ". . . as the Father gave me commandment, even so I do. . . ."

John 15:15, ". . . for all things that I have heard of my Father I have made known unto you."

Hebrews 5:8, (Paul) "Though he were a Son, yet learned he obedience . . ."

COMMENT: Jesus said God sent him and gave him knowledge of what he should say and do. He obeys the orders he received to do God's will. This Christian fundamental is theirs to explore. We will examine the concept of the Trinity in relation to these verses. It is astonishing to find passages such as these, which are implicit contradictions of the doctrine of Jesus being part of a triune God. These verses are irreconcilable, in any rational manner, with the trinitarian doctrine. In this doctrine, God is supposed to be three persons of equal power in a united Godhead. Consequently, will power, knowledge, and authority must be equally shared by the Father, Son, and Holy Ghost. Take special notice that *John 8:40* demonstrates that "God" is the equivalent to "Father" used elsewhere. Now, observe that Jesus said he has not spoken of himself or done anything of himself, but has spoken and done what God taught him. Christianity can claim that the New Testament shows that Jesus had a special mission from God as imparted by these words. That certainly is so, if you believe the New Testament. However, Christianity lacks confirmation of the doctrine of the Trinity in the pages of the New Testament! These verses, plus so many others, are contradictions of this Christian belief. He never was included in the substance of God, by himself or by others in the Christian Scriptures.

Just look at the absurdity created were we to say Jesus is included in a triune Divinity:—

1—God sends God away from himself.

2—God teaches himself what he already knows.

3—God's doctrine belongs to only part of himself.

4—God gives himself his own commandment to do.

Some final observations are in order. Note that the Holy Ghost is strangely neglected, even though it is equally of importance in the concept of the three-on-one God. Note also that in *John 8:40* Jesus explicitly says he is "a man." And this, of course, eliminates the possibility of Jesus being God as we know from *Numbers 23:19, "God is not a man . . ."* It is asserted elsewhere, and Jesus here confirms, that he is a human. So, if Jesus said he is a man and never called himself God, shouldn't you believe him? In sum:—The Trinity is seen as not the religious teaching of Jesus, but the religious teaching about Jesus by Christianity.

9

Personal Salvation Through Judaism

In this important chapter, we present proof of the soul's salvation through Judaism from the pages of the Hebrew Bible. These words, of course, are holy to Christians as well as Jews. The Hebrew Scriptures will substantiate what has already been shown from the pages of the New Testament, that personal salvation is obtained by Jews! Know that damnation through the concept of original sin is absent in the Hebrew Bible. The entire Holy Scriptures are permeated with a feeling of the closeness to God which does not end with death. Regard the word "soul," which is found throughout. Through the Torah, we are given knowledge of God's presence, desires, and requirements for us to obtain eternal life. We are told to keep the commandments with deep commitment. Thereby, we are bonded to our Creator forever. Perfection is not required. What is required of us is performing God's will with all our heart.

Remember, what Jesus said is exactly that. Read these:—*Matthew 5:19, ". . . but whosoever shall do an teach them (commandments) the same shall be called great in the kingdom of heaven." Matthew 19:17, ". . . if thou wilt enter into life, keep the commandments." Mark 12:33-34, "And to love him (God) with all the heart, . . . understanding, . . . soul, . . . strength, and to love his neighbor as himself, . . . Jesus . . . said unto him, Thou art not far from the kingdom of God . . ." Luke 10:25-28, ". . . Master, what shall I do to inherit eternal life? He said unto him, What is written in the law? how readest thou? And he answering said, Thou shalt love the Lord thy God with all thy heart . . . and thy neighbor as thyself. And he said unto him. Thou hast answered right: do this and thou shalt live."*

Without doubt, this chapter is an essential presentation for the Jew who doubts Judaism's spiritual nature. This chapter is the ultimate counterattack to the Christian missionary wanting to convert the Jew. Fundamentally, the attraction of Christianity is its news of personal salvation. Jews, who might be mislead to believe its message, would convert to Christianity for this hope. We all long for the reward of eternal life. It makes life meaningful, offers solace, and helps ease the dread of death. Christianity has a deep satisfaction to offer. Its message is simple:—Just believe and be saved. Common sense is a poor match to this appeal.

For the unenlightened, there exists a mistaken idea that Judaism does not offer eternal life. The prospect of God's heavenly reward through Judaism is somehow lost to Jews who look elsewhere for personal salvation. But, the never changing truth is that God bestowed the means for man's eternal reward through Judaism, before Christianity's Christ, and therefore Jews need no other plan, no matter what its authenticity! Our road is sure, effective, and forever valid. The Holy Bible says so.

Whether the supposed sacrifice of Jesus is revealed unnecessary, in the light of God's pre-existing salvation path, is for Christianity to think about. In *Galatians 2:21* Paul said, *". . . for if righteousness come by the law, then Christ is dead in vain."* However, by establishing the truth of our share of eternity through the Hebrew Scriptures, we do not intend to disprove Christianity's claim. We could not do so. We are, nevertheless, stating our rightful claim.

We would appreciate reciprocity of tolerance and understanding, even respect, from Christians, after two thousand years of harmful attack on our house of God. Read Jesus' words in *Mark 11:17 (Matthew 21:13) (Luke 19:46)*, which quote *Isaiah 56:7*, *". . . My house shall be called of all nations the house of prayer . . ."* Even though anti-Judaism originates in hate-filled passages of the New Testament, and in spite of need to vindicate its arrival on the scene, Christianity must halt its terrible attack on Judaism and evil attitude towards Jews. For, it should be realized, when Christians who have abetted the degredation and destruction of Jews finally meet their Creator they will be asked "lama (why)?" Why have they sinned thus and so harmed God's Chosen People?

Now, let's get to the revelation of Judaism's salvation. The word "salvation" is often connected with the promised Messianic times or with the hope of God's deliverance from troubles on earth. And, certainly, Jews do anxiously await the Messiah who will bring peace, justice, and happiness to the world. However, Jews also have great expectation of everlasting bliss co-existing with Messianic hope in the Scriptures. Through the Torah, Jews grasp life eternal. The verses presented here should convince anyone who has an open mind and uses his God-given power of thinking.

Ask this:—Wouldn't it be senseless for God, who has extended personal salvation through Judaism, to offer Jews another way, a second way? If we already have an eternally effective route to save our souls from sin, as planned by God, a Jew who leaves his heritage's faith and looks to Christianity would be guilty of abandoning his pathway, his God-given pathway. When he finally meets his Creator he will be asked "lama (why)?" Why has he sinned thus and so harmed God's Chosen People? Read the Hebrew Scriptures and believe God's holy word. Personal salvation through Judaism is assured and is the only certainty Jews have concerning eternal life.

LET'S START WITH OUR KNOWLEDGE OF GOD BEING A SINGLE UNITY, WITH NONE BESIDE HIM, ALONE, OUR ONLY SAVIOR, AND NOT A MAN.

Deuteronomy 6:4, ". . . The Lord our God is one Lord:"

Deuteronomy 4:35, "Unto thee it was shown, that thou mightest know that the Lord he is God; there is none else beside him."

Deuteronomy 4:39, "Know therefore this day, and consider it in thine heart, that the Lord he is God in heaven above, and upon the earth beneath: there is none else."

Deuteronomy 32:39, "See now that I, even I, am he, and there is no god with me: . . . neither is there any that can deliver out of my hand."

I Chronicles 17:20, "O Lord, there is none like thee, neither is there any God beside thee . . ."

Nehemiah 9:6, "Thou, even thou, art Lord alone . . ."

Psalm 86:10, "For thou art great, . . . thou art God alone."

Isaiah 43:3, "For I am the Lord thy God, the Holy One of Israel, thy Savior . . ."

Isaiah 43:10-11, ". . . before me there was no God formed, neither shall there be after me. I, even I, am the Lord; and beside me there is no savior."

Isaiah 44:24, "Thus saith the Lord, thy redeemer, and he that formed thee from the womb, I am the Lord that maketh all things; that stretcheth forth the heavens alone; that spreadeth abroad the earth by myself;"

Isaiah 45:5-6, "I am the Lord, and there is none else, there is no God beside me: . . . That they may know . . . that there is none beside me. I am the Lord, and there is none else."

Isaiah 45:21-22, ". . . and there is no God else beside me; a just God and a Savior; there is none beside me. Look unto me, and be ye saved, all the ends of the earth: for I am God, and there is none else."

Isaiah 48:11-12, ". . . and I will not give my glory unto another. . . . I am he: I am the first, I also am the last."

Hosea 13:4, "Yet I am the Lord thy God from the land of Egypt, and thou shalt know no god but me: for there is no savior beside me."

Numbers 23:19, "God is not a man, that he should lie; neither (is he) the son of man . . ."

NOW LET'S QUOTE VERSES WHICH SHOW THAT WE ARE REWARDED BY GOD IN DIFFERENT WAYS. AS A PEOPLE WE ARE PROMISED MESSIANIC SALVATION AND PROMISED POSSESSION OF THE LAND OF ISRAEL.

Jeremiah 30:10, "Therefore fear thou not, O my servant Jacob, saith the Lord; neither be dismayed, O Israel: for, lo, I will save thee from afar, and thy seed from the land of their captivity; and Jacob shall return, and shall be in rest, and be quiet, and none shall make him afraid."

Deuteronomy 6:18, "And thou shalt do that which is right and good in the sight of the Lord: that it may be well with thee, and that thou mayest go in and possess the good land which the Lord sware unto thy fathers."

A THIRD MANNER OF REWARD IS ALSO GIVEN AS A REWARD IN THE HEREAFTER. IT IS THIS MEANING WHICH WE ARE PURSUING.

Certainly, many verses in the Hebrew Scriptures suggest that the reward of the just is obtained in an afterlife with God. The implications of much of the Biblical language lead to this conclusion by those who study the verses. Many verses need interpretation, however, to reveal their meaning of life eternal. Other quotations are plain and evident assertions of personal salvation in Judaism, which need no learned explanation. Let's go on.

MEN ARE TAKEN DIRECTLY TO HEAVEN.

Genesis 5:24, "And Enoch walked with God: and he was not; for God took him."

II Kings 2:11, ". . . there appeared a chariot of fire, and horses of fire, and parted them both asunder; and Elijah went up by a whirlwind into heaven."

THE SOUL AT DEATH IS EITHER GATHERED TO ITS FOREFATHERS, WHERE IS FOUND THE PRESENCE OF GOD, OR IS CUT OFF FROM THIS DESIRED DESTINATION FOR ETERNITY.

Genesis 25:8, "Then Abraham gave up the ghost, and died in a good old age, . . . and was gathered to his people."

Genesis 25:17, ". . . Ishmael . . . gave up the ghost and died; and was gathered unto his people."

Leviticus 7:27, "And whosoever soul it be that eateth any manner of blood, even that soul shall be cut off from his people."

Leviticus 22:3, "Say unto them, Whosoever he be . . . that goeth unto the holy things, . . . having his uncleanness upon him, that soul shall be cut off from my presence: I am the Lord."

Leviticus 23:28-29, "And ye shall do no work in that same day: for it is a day of atonement, to make an atonement for you before the Lord your God. For whatsoever soul it be that shall not be afflicted in that same day, he shall be cut off from among his people."

Numbers 15:31, "Because he hath despised the word of the Lord, and hath broken his commandment, that soul shall utterly be cut off; his iniquity shall be upon him."

Deuteronomy 31:16, "And the Lord said to Moses, Behold, thou shalt sleep with thy fathers . . ."

Deuteronomy 32:48-50, "And the Lord spake unto Moses . . . Get thee up into this mountain . . . and behold the land of Canaan, which I give unto the children of Israel for a possession: And die in the mount whither thou goest up, and be gathered unto thy people; as Aaron thy brother died . . . and was gathered unto his people:"

Psalm 49:19, "He shall go to the generation of his fathers . . ."

RIGHTEOUSNESS RESULTS IN THE REWARD OF RISING AFTER DEATH WITH THE NEARNESS OF GOD.

Psalm 17:15, "As for me, I will behold thy face in righteousness: I shall be satisfied, when I awake, with thy likeness."

THE LAW IS FAULTLESS, AND EFFECTIVE, AND REWARDING. THE GREAT REWARD IS NONE OTHER THAN LIFE ETERNAL FROM GOD OUR REDEEMER.

Psalm 19:7,11,14, "The law of the Lord is perfect, converting the soul; . . . Moreover by them is thy servant warned: and in keeping of them there is great reward. . . . Let the words of my mouth, and the meditation of my heart, be acceptable in thy sight, O Lord, my strength, and my redeemer."

Leviticus 18:5, "Ye shall therefore keep my statutes, and my judgments: which if a man do, he shall live in them: I am the Lord."

THE GOODNESS IN STORE IS EVERLASTING LIFE.

Psalm 31:19, "Oh how great is thy goodness, which thou hast laid up for them that fear thee . . ."

WE HAVE IMMORTAL EXISTENCE WITH GOD.

Psalm 116:8-9, "For thou hast delivered my soul from death, mine eyes from tears, and my feet from falling. I will walk before the Lord in the land of the living."

HAPPY IN THIS WORLD—WELL WITH THEE IN THE WORLD TO COME.

Psalm 128:2, ". . . happy shalt thou be, and it shall be well with thee."

THE PEOPLE OF ISRAEL ARE TO HAVE EVERLASTING SALVATION.
Isaiah 45:17,25, "But Israel shall be saved in the Lord with an everlasting salvation: ye shall not be ashamed nor confounded world without end. In the Lord shall all the seed of Israel be justified, and shall glory."

DO GOD'S WILL AND RECEIVE A PLACE AMONG THE ANGELS.
Zechariah 3:7, "Thus saith the Lord of hosts; If thou wilt walk in my ways . . . I will give thee places to walk among those that stand by."

THE LAW IS FOR YOUR DAYS ON EARTH AS WELL AS YOUR LIFE ETERNAL.
Deuteronomy 32:46-47, ". . . to do, all the words of this law. For it is not a vain thing for you; because it is your life; and through this thing ye shall prolong your days in the land . . ."
Deuteronomy 30:6, ". . . to love the Lord thy God with all thine heart, and with all thy soul, that thou mayest live."

GOD HAS THE POWER OF RAISING THE DEAD. HE MAKES ALIVE AND MAKES DIE.
Deuteronomy 32:39, "See now that I, even I, am he, and there is no god with me: I kill, and I make alive; I wound, and I heal . . ."
I Samuel 2:6, "The Lord killeth, and maketh alive: he bringeth down to the grave, and bringeth up."

LIVE ETERNALLY AND NOT DIE FOREVER.
Deuteronomy 33:6, "Let Reuben live, and not die . . ."

THE RIGHTEOUS HAVE AN ENVIOUS END, WHILE THE UNRIGHTEOUS DO NOT.
Numbers 23:10, ". . . Let me die the death of the righteous, and let my last end be like his!"

GOD AND THE SOUL ARE BOUND TOGETHER.
I Samuel 25:29, "Yet a man is risen to pursue thee, and to seek thy soul: but the soul of my lord shall be bound in the bundle of life with the Lord thy God; and the souls of thine enemies, them shall he sling out . . ."

SAMUEL IS BROUGHT UP FROM THE EARTH ALIVE.
I Samuel 28:13-16, ". . . I saw gods ascending out of the earth. . . . What form is he of? And she said, An old man cometh up; and he is covered with a mantle. And Saul perceived that it was Samuel, and he stooped with his face to the ground, and bowed himself. And Samuel said to Saul, Why hast thou disquieted me, to bring me up? . . ."

DELIVERY TO LIFE IN THE HEREAFTER IS BY CONFESSION AND REPENTANCE.

Job 33:27-28, "He looked upon men, and if any say, I have sinned, and perverted that which was right, and it profited me not; He will deliver his soul from going into the pit, and his life shall see the light."

EVIL MEN AND NATIONS GO TO HELL, WHILE THOSE IN NEED HAVE EXPECTATION OF HEAVEN.

Psalm 9:17-18, "The wicked shall be turned into hell, and all the nations that forget God. For the needy shall not alway be forgotten: the expectation of the poor shall not perish for ever."

GOD SEND SOULS TO HELL AND DECAY OR ETERNAL LIFE.

Psalm 16:10-11, "For thou wilt not leave my soul in hell; neither wilt thou suffer thine Holy One to see corruption. Thou wilt show me the path of life: in thy presence is fullness of joy; at thy right hand there are pleasures for evermore."

SOULS EXIST IN PEACE IN HEAVEN, WHILE DESCENDANTS HAVE HAPPINESS ON EARTH.

Psalm 25:13, "His soul shall dwell at ease; and his seed shall inherit the earth."

SOULS OF SINNERS AND THE RIGHTEOUS ARE TAKEN BY GOD SEPARATELY.

Psalm 26:9, "Gather not my soul with sinners, nor my life with bloody men;"

GOD IS OUR ETERNAL LIFE-GIVER.

Psalm 36:9, "For with thee is the fountain of life: in thy light shall we see light."

OUR SOULS GO TO GOD, OUR REDEEMER, INSTEAD OF BEING LOST IN THE GRAVE FOREVER IN DEATH.

Psalm 49:15, "But God will redeem my soul from the power of the grave: for he shall receive me. Selah."

THE WICKED ARE BLOTTED OUT, WHILE THE RIGHTEOUS ARE WRITTEN IN THE BOOK OF THE LIVING FOR ETERNAL LIFE.

Psalm 69:28, "Let them (the iniquitous) be blotted out of the book of the living, and not be written with the righteous."

GOD RECEIVES SOULS IN HEAVEN.

Psalm 73:24-25, "Thou shalt guide me with thy counsel, and afterward receive me to glory. Whom have I in heaven but thee? and there is none upon earth that I desire beside thee."

WE GO TO HEAVEN OR HELL WHERE GOD IS FOUND.

Psalm 139:8, "If I ascend up into heaven, thou art there: if I make my bed in hell, behold, thou art there."

GOD SAVES THE GODLY ETERNALLY, BUT DESTROYS THE UNGODLY.

Psalm 145:20, "The Lord preserveth all them that love him: but all the wicked will he destroy."

A MAN COULD CHOOSE A PATHWAY WHICH SEEMS GOOD, BUT LOSE LIFE EVERLASTING THEREBY, (WHILE THE LAW'S WAY IS SURE).

Proverbs 14:12 (Proverbs 16:25), "There is a way which seemeth right unto a man, but the end thereof are the ways of death."

AT DEATH THE GOOD MAN'S HOPE OF ETERNAL SALVATION IS FULFILLED, WHILE THE EVIL MAN'S HOPE IS EXTINGUISHED.

The following verses give unmistakable evidence of the expectation of eternal life by doing God's will and being righteous. No learned explanation is necessary. All is clear.

Proverbs 10:28, "The hope of the righteous shall be gladness: but the expectation of the wicked shall perish."

Proverbs 11:7, "When a wicked man dieth, his expectation shall perish: and the hope of unjust men perisheth."

Proverbs 11:19, "As righteousness tendeth to life; so he that pursueth evil pursueth it to his own death."

Proverbs 14:32, "The wicked is driven away in his wickedness: but the righteous hath hope in his death."

Proverbs 23:17-18, "Let not thine heart envy sinners: but be thou in the fear of the Lord all the day long. For surely there is an end; and thine expectation shall not be cut off."

Proverbs 24:14, "So shall the knowledge of wisdom be unto thy soul: when thou hast found it, then there shall be a reward, and thy expectation shall not be cut off."

Proverbs 24:20, "For there shall be no reward to the evil man; the candle of the wicked shall be put out."

DUST RETURNS TO DUST, BUT THE SPIRIT RETURNS TO GOD.

Here are the great words of comfort and hope! It is with clarity and simplicity that we learn of the soul's return to God at death. This is Judaism's understanding of God's reward of everlasting life for the faithful.

Ecclesiastes 3:20-22, "All go unto one place; all are of the dust, and all turn to dust again. Who knoweth the spirit of man that goeth upward, and the spirit of the beast that goeth downward to the earth? . . . for who shall bring him to see what shall be after him?"

Ecclesiastes 12:7, "Then shall the dust return to the earth as it was: and the spirit shall return unto God who gave it."

THE PEOPLE OF ISRAEL ARE TOLD TO CHANGE THEIR WAYS AND COME TO GOD WITH ALL OF THEIR SPIRITUAL MIGHT, SO THAT THEIR SOULS ARE HEALED AND THEY ARE REWARDED.

Isaiah 6:10, ". . . lest they see with their eyes, and hear with their ears, and understand with their heart, and convert, and be healed."

GOD'S PROMISE OF EARTHLY REWARD IS COUPLED HERE WITH THE REWARD OF EVERLASTING LIFE, TO "SWALLOW UP DEATH IN VICTORY."

Isaiah 25:8, "He will swallow up death in victory; and the Lord God will wipe away tears from off all faces; and the rebuke of his people shall he take away from off all the earth: for the Lord hath spoken it."

OUR RESURRECTION IS ASSURED IN THESE WORDS.

Isaiah 26:19, "Thy dead men shall live, together with my dead body shall they arise. Awake and sing, ye that dwell in dust: for thy dew is as the dew of herbs, and the earth shall cast out the dead."

THE PEOPLE OF ISRAEL SHALL HAVE EVERLASTING SALVATION IN THIS WORLD AND THE WORLD WITHOUT END.

Isaiah 45:17, "But Israel shall be saved in the Lord with an everlasting salvation: ye shall not be ashamed nor confounded world without end."

LISTENING TO GOD AND DOING HIS WILL BINDS US TO GOD ETERNALLY, ON THIS EARTH AND IN HEAVEN.

Isaiah 55:3, "Incline your ear, and come unto me: hear, and your soul shall live; and I will make an everlasting covenant with you, even the sure mercies of David."

GOOD MEN WILL SPEND ETERNITY IN THE PRESENCE OF GOD.

Isaiah 58:8, "Then shall thy light break forth as the morning, and thine health shall spring forth speedily: and thy righteousness shall go before thee; the glory of the Lord shall be thy reward."

GOD REWARDS THE RIGHTEOUS WITH EVERLASTING LIFE AND PUNISHES THE SINNER WITH DEATH.

Assuredly, all souls belong to God. The following verses by Ezekiel are confirming evidence of Judaism's expectation. We know that God punishes the sinner so that he does not have eternal life. Just as surely we know that God rewards the good person with life eternal in heaven. Each person is responsible for his own soul's life or death. Repentance changes the heart and creates a new spirit which finds God and thereby life eternal.

Ezekiel 18:13, "(a son) . . . shall he then live? he shall not live; he hath done all these abominations; he shall surely die; his blood shall be upon him."

Ezekiel 18:4, "Behold, all souls are mine; as the soul of the father, so also the soul of the son is mine; the soul that sinneth, it shall die."

Ezekiel 18:18, "As for his father, because he cruelly oppressed, spoiled his brother by violence, and did that which is not good among his people, lo, even he shall die in his iniquity."

Ezekiel 18:20, "The soul that sinneth, it shall die. The son shall not bear the iniquity of the father, neither shall the father bear the iniquity of the son: the righteousness of the righteous shall be upon him, and the wickedness of the wicked shall be upon him."

Ezekiel 18:24 (Ezekiel 18:26), "But when the righteous turneth away from his righteousness, and committeth iniquity, and doeth according to all the abominations that the wicked man doeth, shall he live? All his righteousness that he hath done shall not be mentioned: in his trespass that he hath trespassed, and in his sin that he hath sinned, in them shall he die."

Ezekiel 18:30, "Therefore I will judge you, O house of Israel, every one according to his ways, saith the Lord God. Repent, and turn yourselves from all your transgressions; so iniquity shall not be your ruin."

Ezekiel 18:31, "Cast away . . . all your transgressions, whereby ye have transgressed; and make you a new heart and a new spirit: for why will ye die, O house of Israel?"

GOD'S REQUIREMENTS FOR OUR OBTAINING LIFE ETERNAL ARE THAT WE KEEP HIS COMMANDMENTS, DO WORKS OF RIGHTEOUSNESS, AND REPENT OUR TRANSGRESSIONS.

The following passages from Ezekiel give God's sure and undeniable promise of life eternal for the observant Jew. The pious Jew, who follows the Torah, lives forever and does not die. The sinner, who turns to God and repents, can receive life everlasting. Moreover, we are told in direct language that each individual is responsible for himself, for his own soul's salvation. This reveals the error of vicarious atonement for the Jew.

Ezekiel 18:9, "(he that) Hath walked in my statutes, and hath kept my judgments, to deal truly; he is just, he shall surely live, saith the Lord God."

Ezekiel 18:17, "(a son) That hath taken off his hand from the poor, that hath not received usury nor increase, hath executed my judgments, hath walked in my statutes; he shall not die for the iniquity of his father, he shall surely live."

Ezekiel 18:19, "Yet say ye, Why? doth not the son bear the iniquity of the father? When the son hath done that which is lawful and right, and hath kept all my statutes, and hath done them, he shall surely live."

Ezekiel 18:21 (Ezekiel 18:27) (Ezekiel 18:28), "But if the wicked

will turn from all his sins that he hath committed, and keep all my stat-
utes, and do that which is lawful and right, he shall surely live, he
shall not die (he shall save his soul alive)."

Ezekiel 18:22, "All his transgressions that he hath committed, they
shall not be mentioned unto him: in his righteousness that he hath done
he shall live."

Ezekiel 18:23 (Ezekiel 18:32), "Have I any pleasure at all that the
wicked should die? saith the Lord God: and not that he should return
from his ways, and live?"

Ezekiel 20:11 (Ezekiel 20:13), "And I gave them my statutes, and
showed them my judgments, which if a man do, he shall even live in
them."

HERE WE HAVE EZEKIEL'S "VALLEY OF THE DRY BONES" PROPHESY OF THE RESURRECTION OF THE NATION OF ISRAEL, PERSON BY PERSON.

Ezekiel 37:5-7,10-14, "Thus saith the Lord God unto these bones:
Behold, I will cause breath to enter into you, and ye shall live: And I
will lay sinews upon you, and will bring up flesh upon you, and cover
you with skin, and put breath in you, and ye shall live; and ye shall
know that I am the Lord. . . . and the bones came together, bone to
his bone, . . . and they lived, and stood up upon their feet, an exceed-
ing great army . . . these bones are the whole house of Israel: . . .
Thus saith the Lord God; Behold, O my people, I will open your
graves, and cause you to come up out of your graves, and bring you
into the land of Israel. . . . And ye shall know that I am the Lord,
when I have opened your graves, O my people, and brought you up out
of your graves, And shall put my spirit in you, and ye shall live . . ."

THE "END OF DAYS" VERSES IN DANIEL PROMISE US RESURRECTION AND ETERNAL LIFE OR ETERNAL REJECTION.

Daniel 12:13, "But go thou thy way till the end be: for thou shalt
rest, and stand in thy lot at the end of days."

Daniel 12:1-2, ". . . and at that time thy people shall be deliv-
ered, every one that shall be found written in the book. And many of
them that sleep in the dust of the earth shall awake, some to everlast-
ing life, and some to shame and everlasting contempt."

As a final illumination in this chapter, let's go again to the pages
of the New Testament. Let's present confirmation of the Jew's heavenly salvation in Jesus' own words. They were spoken before his supposed mission was completed and are proof of Jesus' affirmation of
the pre-existing salvation of Judaism. This book's chapter "Laws Are
Good for Salvation" shows that Jesus' belief is Judaism's.

Luke 13:28, "There shall be weeping and gnashing of teeth, when ye shall see Abraham, and Isaac, and Jacob, and all the prophets, in the kingdom of God, and you yourselves thrust out."

Luke 16:22-23, "And it came to pass, that the beggar died and was carried by the angels into Abraham's bosom: the rich man also died, and was buried; And in hell he lift up his eyes, being in torments, and seeth Abraham afar off, and Lazarus in his bosom."

Luke 20:37-38, "Now that the dead are raised, even Moses showed at the bush, when he calleth the Lord the God of Abraham, and the God of Isaac, and the God of Jacob. For he is not a God of the dead, but of the living: for all live unto him."

Now read the words of Paul, which deny salvation through Judaism.

Romans 5:14, "Nevertheless death reigned from Adam to Moses, even over them that had not sinned after the similitude of Adam's transgression . . ."

COMMENT: Why didn't Paul say "from Adam to Jesus" instead? He did not, and hence Paul's words here acknowledge that God meant the law of Moses to be effective for salvation. Another observation is that Paul said death came to all before Moses. This conflicts with the verses by Jesus that we just quoted from Luke. Well, who is the authority, Jesus or Paul? Again we read in *Matthew 10:24, "The disciple is not above his master . . ."* Therefore, you should not believe Paul. It is clear from Jesus that salvation, not death, was in place before Moses and after.

Romans 3:20, "Therefore by the deeds of the law there shall no flesh be justified in his sight . . ."

COMMENT: We see that Paul said that eternal life was apparently made possible by the law of Moses, as indicated by the words *"death reigned from Adam to Moses"* in *Romans 5:14.* Or did God make a mistake? Is your concept of God that He can blunder in this matter or any other matter? Did He make laws which are not effective and do not accomplish what they were meant to do? Paul believed so. He believed that the laws give death, rather than life. Therefore, to complete the analysis, if you agree with Paul that the laws bring death, then you are saying that God is not Almighty God. You are saying that God is imperfect. Think this over.

There is another approach to this subject. If you know God is all-perfect and therefore created laws as he wished them to be, then perhaps you believe He meant to give laws to condemn His Chosen People. Instead of giving laws to make Jews righteous and worthy of eternal life, perhaps the laws were given to create sin and death. Is this your concept of God, that He can be cruel or unreasonable? If you believe this then you are saying that God is not all-good and is lacking in loving purpose for the world. Can you not understand, that whatever way you look at it, if you believe Paul when he said the laws do not offer salvation you are, in effect, denying God is the Supreme Being?

Let's direct our final words to the Jew who has converted or is thinking of converting to Christianity. You have been shown in this chapter Hebrew Scriptures expressing the reality of personal salvation through Judaism. Also, verses from the New Testament have been gathered to confirm this fact. What more on earth need be done to convince you of the truth of salvation through Judaism? If you expect a bolt from the blue, you won't get it. Six million Jews went to their eternity with no heavenly bolt. So will you. And at your death your regrets will be too late. Your desertion of Judaism will be on the record of the book of your soul. When you meet God you will be asked "lama (why)?" Why did you believe Paul and so harm God's Chosen People. Why did you leave your heritage's pathway?

But, it is not too late. As you are reading these words, there still is time for your return. You can become a baal teshuvah and turn to the God of your people. Your return to the people of Israel, God's suffering servant, is always welcomed and is your only sure salvation as a born Jew. Believe it. God said it. We have proved it.

Perhaps you know in your innermost parts that Judaism is of God, but you're afraid to return. You're afraid of losing the "sweet salvation of Christ." You're afraid of damnation falling upon you. You're afraid of being wrong and afraid of the unknown awaiting you. Actually the profound fears in you have you in tow, while the one fear you should have is lost in the outer region of your being. The one fear you should have is of the consequences of forsaking the God of your fathers, Judaism's Almighty God, and abandoning His pathway for you! You should fear forsaking God for—who knows what? Your abandonment will lie heavy on your soul when you die, if you die a willing apostate from Judaism. Read this carefully:—See what God said in *Deuteronomy 30:17-18 (Deuteronomy 8:19-20)* concerning apostates, *"But if thine heart turn away (from God), . . . and worship other gods, and serve them; I denounce unto you this day, that ye shall surely perish . . ."* In other words, apostates will not have eternal life. These are God's words. Think of all of this when you are alone.

10

God and His Chosen People

Now that you have read the Biblical evidence of the truth that God offers personal salvation to His Chosen People, we'll outline here Judaism's basic understanding of God and His relationship to the people of Israel. Our comprehension rests solidly on the word of God as revealed abundantly in the Hebrew Bible. It is fundamental Scripture teaching. God's relationship to the Jewish people is described as holy, unique, awesome, and eternal! His laws and commandments were given to His Chosen People so that Jews would be a light to the nations to impart spirituality and righteousness to the whole world. Through faith in God and acceptance of the yoke of the Torah, Jews have become the suffering servants of the God of Israel, the one God of all the earth.

Jews are uplifted in extraordinary spiritual contact with God in all we do throughout our life. Our prayers and trust are forever sure. The Lord God, our Father in heaven, and we, His children, are in blessed linkage. With the Torah as our guide, we find the pathway to God on earth, which leads to our home with Him in heaven. In this chapter, we'll quote selected Biblical verses which illustrate the concepts expressing basic Judaism.

THE GOD OF ISRAEL IS THE ONLY GOD OF THE WHOLE WORLD ETERNALLY.

Deuteronomy 6:4, "Hear, O Israel: the Lord our God is one Lord:"

Exodus 15:18, "The Lord shall reign for ever and ever."

Isaiah 45:23, ". . . unto me every knee shall bow, every tongue shall swear."

Isaiah 48:12, "Harken unto me, O Jacob and Israel, my called; I am he; I am the first, I also am the last."

Isaiah 54:5, ". . . and thy Redeemer the Holy One of Israel; the God of the whole earth shall be called."

GOD REWARDS THE RIGHTEOUS AND PUNISHES THE SINNER.

Psalm 18:20, "The Lord rewarded me according to my righteousness; according to the cleanness of my hands hath he recompensed me."

Isaiah 1:28, "And the destruction of the transgressors and of the sinners shall be together, and they that forsake the Lord shall be consumed."

Isaiah 3:10, "Say ye to the righteous, that it shall be well with him: for they shall eat the fruit of their doings."

Isaiah 13:11, "And I will punish the world for their evil, and the wicked for their iniquity . . ."

Malachi 3:18, "Then shall ye return, and discern between the righteous and the wicked, between him that serveth God and him that serveth not."

GOD FORGIVES SINNERS WHO REPENT AND BECOME WORTHY.

Leviticus 26:40-42, "If they shall confess their iniquity, . . . and that also they have walked contrary unto me; . . . if then their uncircumcised hearts be humbled, and they then accept of the punishment of their iniquity: Then will I remember my covenant with Jacob, (Isaac), and (Abraham) . . . and I will remember the land."

Isaiah 1:18-19, "Come now, and let us reason together, saith the Lord: though your sins be as scarlet, they shall be as white as snow; . . . If ye be willing and obedient, ye shall eat the good of the land:"

Jeremiah 31:34, ". . . for they shall all know me, . . . saith the Lord: for I will forgive their iniquity, and I will remember their sin no more."

Jeremiah 33:8, "And I will cleanse them from all their iniquity, . . . and I will pardon all their iniquities, whereby they have sinned, and whereby they have transgressed against me."

Micah 7:18-19, "Who is a God like unto thee, that pardoneth iniquity, and passeth by the transgression of the remnant of his heritage? he retaineth not his anger for ever, because he delighteth in mercy. He will turn again, he will have compassion upon us; he will subdue our iniquities; and thou wilt cast all their sins into the depths of the sea."

A HOLY RELATIONSHIP BETWEEN GOD AND HIS CHOSEN PEOPLE.

Genesis 12:3, "And I will bless them that bless thee, and curse him that curseth thee: and in thee shall all families of the earth be blessed."

Exodus 19:6, "And ye shall be unto me a kingdom of priests, and an holy nation . . ."

Deuteronomy 7:6, "For thou art an holy people unto the Lord thy God: the Lord thy God hath chosen thee to be a special people unto himself, above all people that are upon the face of the earth."

Psalm 135:4, "For the Lord hath chosen Jacob unto himself, and Israel for his peculiar treasure."

Jeremiah 30:22, "And ye shall be my people, and I will be your God."

RELATIONSHIP BONDED BY COVENANT AND COMMANDMENTS FOREVER.

Exodus 19:5, ". . . if ye will obey my voice indeed, and keep my covenant, then ye shall be a peculiar treasure unto me above all people: . . ."

Exodus 24:3, "And Moses came and told the people all the words of the Lord, and all the judgments: and all the people answered with one voice, and said, All the words which the Lord hath said will we do."

Deuteronomy 11:1, Therefore thou shalt love the Lord thy God, and keep his charge, and his statutes, and his judgments, and his commandments, alway."

Deuteronomy 12:28, "Observe and hear all these words which I command thee, that it may go well with thee, and with thy children after thee for ever . . ."

Isaiah 59:21, ". . . this is my covenant with them, saith the Lord: My spirit that is upon thee, and my words which I have put in thy mouth, shall not depart out of thy mouth, nor out of the mouth of thy seed, . . . from henceforth and for ever."

THE COVENANT IS AN ETERNAL COVENANT.

Genesis 17:7,13, "And I will establish my covenant between me and thee and thy seed after thee in their generations for an everlasting covenant, to be a God unto thee and to thy seed after thee. . . . and my covenant shall be in your flesh for an everlasting covenant."

Leviticus 26:44, ". . . I will not cast them away, neither . . . break my covenant with them: for I am the Lord their God."

Deuteronomy 7:9, "Know therefore that the Lord thy God, he is God, the faithful God, which keepeth covenant and mercy with them that love him and keep his commandments to a thousand generations;"

Judges 2:1, ". . . and I (God) said, I will never break my covenant with you."

I Chronicles 16:15-17, "Be ye mindful always of his covenant; the word which he commanded to a thousand generations; Even of the covenant which he made with Abraham, . . . and to Israel for an everlasting covenant."

SPECIAL COMMANDMENTS OF GOD—NEVER ABROGATED

Exodus 12:17, "And ye shall observe the feast of unleavened bread; . . . therefore shall ye observe this day . . . for ever."

Exodus 31:16, "Wherefore the children of Israel shall keep the sabbath, to observe the sabbath throughout their generations, for a perpetual covenant."

Leviticus 23:31, "(Day of Atonement) . . . it shall be a statute for ever throughout your generations . . ."

Numbers 15:38-39, "Speak unto the children of Israel, and bid them that they make them fringes on the borders of their garments throughout their generations, . . . that ye may look upon it, and remember all the commandments . . ."

Deuteronomy 28:1, ". . . harken diligently unto the voice of the Lord thy God, to observe and to do all his commandments which I command thee this day . . ."

LAW OF MOSES (TORAH) OFFERS ETERNAL LIFE.

Leviticus 18:5, "Ye shall therefore keep my statutes, and my judgments: which if a man do, he shall live in them . . ."

Deuteronomy 30:6,10, "And the Lord thy God will circumcise thine heart, . . . that thou mayest live. If thou shalt harken unto the voice of the Lord thy God, to keep his commandments and his statutes which are written in this book of the law, and if thou turn unto the Lord thy God with all thine heart, and with all thy soul."

Ezekiel 18:9, "(he that) Hath walked in my statutes, and hath kept my judgments, to deal truly; he is just, he shall surely live, saith the Lord God."

Ezekiel 18:21,27, "But if the wicked will turn from all his sins that he hath committed, and keep all my statutes, and do that which is lawful and right, he shall surely live, he shall not die. . . . he shall save his soul alive."

Ezekiel 33:19, "But if the wicked turn from his wickedness, and do that which is lawful and right, he shall live thereby."

CHOSEN PEOPLE (ISRAEL) BELOVED BY GOD ETERNALLY.

Isaiah 45:25, "In the Lord shall all the seed of Israel be justified, and shall glory."

Isaiah 65:24, "And it shall come to pass, that before they call, I will answer; and while they are yet speaking, I will hear."

Ezekiel 37:27-28, ". . . yea, I will be their God, and they shall be my people. And the heathen shall know that I the Lord do sanctify Israel . . ."

Hosea 2:19, "And I will betroth thee unto me for ever; yea, I will betroth thee unto me in righteousness, and in judgment, and in lovingkindness, and in mercies."

Hosea 2:23, ". . . I will say to them . . . Thou art my people; and they shall say, Thou art my God."

GOD ACCOMPLISHES FOR HIS OWN NAME'S SAKE.

Isaiah 43:25, "I, even I, am he that blotteth out thy transgressions for mine own sake, and will not remember thy sins."

Isaiah 48:9,11, "For my name's sake will I defer mine anger, and for my praise will I refrain for thee, that I cut thee not off. For mine own sake, even for mine own sake, will I do it: for how should my name be polluted? and I will not give my glory unto another."

Jeremiah 14:7, "O Lord, though our iniquities testify against us, do it for thy name's sake: for our backslidings are many; we have sinned against thee."

Ezekiel 20:44, "And ye shall know that I am the Lord, when I have wrought with you for my name's sake, not according to your wicked ways . . . O ye house of Israel, saith the Lord God."

Daniel 9:18-19, "O my God, incline thine ear, . . . for we do not present our supplications before thee for our righteousnesses, but for thy great mercies. O Lord, hear; (forgive); (harken); and do; defer not, for thine own sake . . ."

GOD'S WORK IS PERFECT.

Deuteronomy 4:2, "Ye shall not add unto the word which I command you, neither shall ye diminish ought from it, that ye may keep the commandments of the Lord your God which I command you."

Deuteronomy 32:4, "He is the Rock, his word is perfect . . ."

Psalm 19:7, "The law of the Lord is perfect, converting the soul . . ."

Psalm 111:7, "The works of his hands are verity and judgment; all his commandments are sure."

Isaiah 40:8, "The grass withereth, the flower fadeth: but the word of our God shall stand for ever."

GOD'S PROMISES ARE UNBREAKABLE.

Numbers 23:19, "God is not a man, that he should lie; neither the son of man, that he should repent: hath he said, and shall he not do it? or hath he spoken, and shall he not make it good?"

Isaiah 34:16, "Seek ye out of the book of the Lord, and read: no one of these shall fail . . ."

Isaiah 51:6, ". . . the heavens shall vanish away like smoke, and the earth shall wax old like a garment, and they that dwell therein shall die in like manner: but my salvation shall be for ever, and my righteousness shall not be abolished."

Isaiah 54:10, "For the mountains shall depart, and the hills be removed; but my kindness shall not depart from thee, neither shall the covenant of my peace be removed, saith the Lord that hath mercy on thee."

Isaiah 55:11, ". . . my word . . . that goeth forth out of my mouth: it shall not return unto me void, but it shall accomplish that which I please, and it shall prosper in the thing whereto I sent it."

If all this is true, and it is because it is quoted from the Scriptures holy to both Jews and Christians, then it must be that Christianity is in Biblical error when it maintains that Judaism is no longer of God. It is claimed by Christian missionaries that Christianity is heir to the promises God made to the Chosen People of Israel. Is there any possibility that Christianity has the right to claim to be the "New Israel" when God never said there would be another people to take His Chosen People's place? Do you see anything in these verses in this chapter which state that Israel will be supplanted by another body of people? Is there anything which could even remotely be interpreted to allow for such a broken pledge from the Lord God of Israel? God says he doesn't speak falsely, that His word is sure and true. Nowhere is anything said in the Hebrew Scriptures about others being successors or the Covenant being transferred. In fact, quite the opposite is found. God's Chosen are to be His beloved forever. God said it very clearly.

Well then, what about Christianity's claim? Does it fail as a religion if it is not the "New Israel?" We think not. There never has been a need for Christianity to dispute and deny Judaism's role in the world. Surely, Christianity's spirituality has been deeply marred by its attack on Judaism and the ensuing tragic effect on the Jewish people throughout the Christian Era.

By propounding Judaism's truth, we are not attacking Christianity's holiness. Similarly, Christianity need not attack Judaism's sacredness. Judaism's advocates are only interested in asserting and verifying our rightful relationship to God. Christianity has its own relationship, which they believe is true and which need not concern Jews. What does deeply concern us, however, is that Jews who have considered conversion to Christianity be aware of the never-ending attachment of God to the Jewish people. Due to this bond, Jews are obligated to travel Judaism's pathway to the God of our fathers. It is what God expects of Jews and what He requires of us, as revealed in the Holy Scriptures. A person of Jewish heritage is not able to justify conversion to Christianity, to himself or to his Creator, in light of the Biblical passages presented in this chapter!

11

The Hebrew Messiah

Christian missionaries to the Jews don't want to shock the Jew by handing out leaflets which proclaim Jesus is God. This belief is kept in the background, waiting for the potential convert to become interested by the declaration of Jesus being our own Hebrew Messiah. After all, if Jews are waiting for the Messiah (the Moshiach), maybe Jesus is he. But, Jews are not waiting for God. Consequently, the missionaries merely declare Jeshua ben Joseph is the Moshiach. His being God the Son of the Christian Trinity is advanced to the potential convert later. The full-page ads of the so-called "Jews for Jesus" organizations don't say a word about the Trinity, not a single word. Well, Jews need not contemplate this non-Jewish concept of a triune God. The Scriptural evidence presented in this book is sufficient proof that Jesus did not claim to be God incarnate and that he believed in the God of unity of the Hebrew Scriptures. The concept of the Trinity does not affect Jews, because it has no basis in the Hebrew Bible.

However, Jews are deeply concerned about the Hebrew Messiah. Our Scriptures are filled with words of Messianic expectation. Our Jewish souls wait for him daily. The question which is of interest to us is whether Christianity's Christ is the Hebrew Messiah. Have Jews neglected to recognize that Jesus is their Messiah, because Christianity has claimed him as God the Son? After all, it might be that if we separate the Christologic Christ from the Jewish Jesus, we would find we are looking straight at the Moshiach of the Hebrews. In other words, let's put aside the claims of Christianity and discover if Jesus fits the role of the Hebrew Messiah, as Judaism understands him from our own Scriptures. Let's first look at the attributes of the Messiah and the Messianic Era expectations as presented in the Hebrew Bible. Then we can ascertain if Jesus fulfilled the Messianic requirements and if he, indeed, is the Moshiach of the Jewish people.

Clearly, if his role was not that of the Messiah, as expressed in the written word of God, the Hebrew Scriptures, what Christianity has made of the Messiah is not Judaism's concern. However, it certainly would be of very great concern and importance to us if his performance were that of the expected Messiah. Has the Hebrew Messiah already come? We must use traditional interpretation of Biblical Messianic passages to find our answer. What do you think we will discover?

Have our Jewish ancestors been in error through the centuries? When they refused to succumb to conversion, and instead suffered martyrdom for Kiddush Ha-Shem (sanctification of God's name), were they wrong? When persecution, torture, and death could be avoided, were our learned and pious forefathers mistaken to remain with their Judaism? How easy it would have been to accept conversion to Christianity. They could have prospered socially, and economically, and obtained peace in a diaspora of disdain and degradation for Jews. Actually, it is surprising that so few were lost to Judaism due to conversion. It seems surely a "sign" that Judaism's remnant in dispersion remained steadfast, even when offered the choice of the Christian cross or the Christian curse!

We shall find in these pages that Jews have rejected Jesus as the Hebrew Messiah because of our intimate and profound knowledge of the Holy Scriptures, together with our devotion to the God of Israel! Scriptural passages are the basis of Judaism's understanding of the Messiah and Messianic expectations. Much must be fulfilled. Much must be established. The Messiah's tasks are still to be accomplished.

Christianity has tried to avoid the unfulfilled Messianic hopes by either minimizing them or changing them to fit their Christology. When this could not be done, they advanced the time of fulfillment to a "second coming." Well, it must be understood that the Biblical foundation of Messianic hope cannot be disregarded or changed to suit Christianity's circumstances. It must be understood that their belief that Jesus is the Messiah has to measure up to verses as written in the Hebrew Scriptures. Expectations must be satisfied as written. After all, this is where the hope of the Messiah originated. If we find Messianic expectations unfulfilled in traditional terms, other terms will not do! What God says will occur is exactly what will occur. God said it clearly and repeatedly in His Holy Book.

Moreover, what is to occur is to occur when expected, which is at the arrival of the Messiah. The Messiah's achievements cannot legitimately be placed forward to a future time, a "second coming," unless this is explicitly described in these holy verses. By now, it should be of no surprise to you to learn that no such double arrival, in order to accomplish the Messianic Era, is written. The Scriptures do not describe a Messiah coming—dying—not achieving—leaving—returning—and then making the Messianic times a reality. Nowhere is it said that the Messiah is to return after having once failed in doing what the Messiah is to do. A "second coming" as well as Christologics, both, have absolutely no foundation in Judaism's Bible! Such a "second coming" is anticipated only in the New Testament, and we shall examine this error later in this book.

Consequently, if the Scriptural expectations for the Messiah are unfulfilled and no "second coming" is propounded, it would appear that the Christian Messiah (Christ) and Hebrew Messiah (Moshiach) are two different entities! Now, let's read carefully the Hebrew Bible passages about the Messiah and see if Jesus fits these Messianic expectations.

Daniel 7:13-14, ". . . one like the Son of man came with the clouds of heaven, and came to the Ancient of days, . . . And there was given him dominion, and glory, and a kingdom, that all people, nations, and languages, should serve him: his dominion is an everlasting dominion, which shall not pass away, and his kingdom that which shall not be destroyed."

Zechariah 9:9-10, ". . . thy King cometh unto thee: he is just, and having salvation; lowly, and riding upon an ass, . . . and he shall speak peace unto the heathen; and his dominion shall be from sea even to sea, and from the river even to the ends of the earth."

COMMENT: It seems, curiously, two very different appearances of the Messiah are depicted in the Bible, as interpreted by Christianity. But actually, Daniel describes the Messiah's arrival before God in heaven, not on earth. Read it again and see. The arrival can be described fancifully, as in Zechariah, because it lacks relevance to the Messianic expectations. What is completely relevant is what he achieves. And both Daniel and Zechariah agree that the Messiah is to have an earthly kingdom, whose dominion shall be throughout the world. It shall be a non-ending kingdom, teaching peace. The Messiah will have great honor and service from all people, and he will save the people of Israel from earthly troubles. These are the descriptions of the Messiah and his rule. NOTE that Jesus does not fit these descriptions because he did not rule a kingdom on earth. Also, note that nothing is said about coming one way (on an ass), leaving (dying), and returning another way. Further, understand, Christianity's interpretation notwithstanding, there is no Christologic other-worldly kingdom spoken of here in either verse. The Messianic kingdom is depicted as earthly and interpreted as such in Judaism. It is so interpreted because that is precisely what is written.

Daniel 2:44, ". . . *the God of heaven (shall) set up a kingdom, which shall never be destroyed: . . . and it shall stand for ever."*

Daniel 7:18, "But the saints of the most High shall take the kingdom, and possess the kingdom for ever, even for ever and ever."

Psalm 89:3-4, "I have made a covenant with my chosen, I have sworn unto David my servant, Thy seed will I establish for ever, and build up thy throne to all generations. Selah."

II Samuel 7:8,12-13,16 (I Chronicles 17:7,11-12,14), ". . . say unto my servant David, . . . I took thee . . . to be ruler over my people, over Israel: . . . I will set up thy seed after thee, . . . and I will establish his kingdom. He shall build an house for my name, and I will stablish the throne of his kingdom for ever. And thine house and thy kingdom shall be established for ever before thee: thy throne shall be established for ever."

COMMENT: God will create a kingdom which will last for all time. In it the Messiah and those after him will rule His Chosen People, Israel. The Messiah is to build a Temple for God which will be everlasting, as the kingdom will be everlasting. NOTE that there is no such kingdom created. There is no such Temple built. Jesus did not make this happen. Also, note that the Messiah himself is not to exist forever. It is his kingdom which will last forever, not he. And it is given that the saints of the most High, which are the Israel People, will eventually self-rule. That is what these passages impart.

Numbers 24:17, 19, ". . . there shall come a Star out of Jacob, and a Sceptre shall rise out of Israel, . . . Out of Jacob shall come he that shall have dominion . . ."

Psalm 72:8, 11, "He shall have dominion also from sea to sea, and from the river unto the ends of the earth. Yea, all kings shall fall down before him: all nations shall serve him."

Isaiah 11:10, "And in that day there shall be a root of Jesse, which shall stand for an ensign of the people; to it shall the Gentiles seek: and his rest shall be glorious."

Daniel 7:27, "And the kingdom and dominion, and the greatness of the kingdom under the whole heaven, shall be given to the people of the saints of the most High, whose kingdom is an everlasting kingdom, and all dominions shall serve and obey him."

COMMENT: All countries and people will look to the Messiah of the Hebrew people and serve him. NOTE that besides Jesus' lack of rule over an earthly kingdom, he never had dominions under him, serving and obeying him. Moslems, Hindus, and Buddhists, etc., certainly are not under his rule, in this world or any other. In fact, not only was he not served by nations, but the Romans put him to death. Not only was he not obeyed and glorious, but Jesus' death was apparently against his own desires and certainly inglorious, hanging between two thieves.

Isaiah 11:1-2,4-5, "And there shall come forth a rod out of the stem of Jesse, and a Branch shall grow out of his roots: And the spirit of the Lord shall rest upon him, the spirit of wisdom and understanding, the spirit of counsel and might, the spirit of knowledge and of the fear of the Lord; . . . with righteousness shall he judge the poor, and reprove with equity for the meek of the earth: and he shall smite the earth: with the rod of his mouth, and with the breath of his lips shall he slay the wicked. And righteousness shall be the girdle of his loins, and faithfulness the girdle of his reins."

Jeremiah 33:15, "In those days, and at that time, will I cause the Branch of righteousness to grow up unto David; and he shall execute judgment and righteousness in the land."

COMMENT: The Hebrew Messiah will properly administer God's desires for human beings' goodness and virtue. He will, with excellence, judge, rebuke, and punish the evil-doers in this world. He will perform justice and righteousness for the poor and meek. NOTE that the designation of his rule is "the earth" and "in the land." This eliminates Christianity's interpretation of heavenly judgment. And plainly, Jesus was not then, and is not now, in the land righteously judging in the Messianic kingdom on earth as described. In addition, can it be said in any rational manner that God the Son of the Trinity possesses "the fear of the Lord," when he is supposed to be the salfsame in a unity?

Psalm 72:7, "In his days shall the righteous flourish; and abundance of peace so long as the moon endureth."

Isaiah 52:7, "How beautiful upon the mountains are the feet of him that bringeth good tidings, that publisheth peace; that bringeth good tidings of good, that publisheth salvation; that saith unto Zion, Thy God reigneth!"

Isaiah 9:6-7, "For unto us a child is born, unto us a son is given: and the government shall be upon his shoulder: . . . Of the increase of his government and peace there shall be no end, upon the throne of David, and upon his kingdom, to order it, and to establish it with judgment and with justice from henceforth even for ever . . ."

COMMENT: In the thriving kingdom of the Messiah, there will be endless peace and justice. He will have a government ruling over righteous people who flourish and know the God of Israel, who is their rescuer. NOTE that Jesus did not establish peace on earth or rule over a kingdom of righteous people. Note also, the "child" is not Christianity's Christ child at all, who had no government.

Psalm 28:8, "The Lord is their strength, and he is the saving strength of his anointed."

Jeremiah 30:9, "But they shall serve the Lord their God, and David their king, whom I will raise up unto them."

COMMENT: These verses are presented to show that there is a clear differentiation between the Lord God and the Messiah. NOTE that Christianity has joined the two and made their Messiah God himself.

Psalm 89:3, ". . . I have sworn unto David my servant."

II Samuel 7:8 (I Chronicles 17:7), ". . . say unto my servant David, Thus saith the Lord of hosts, I took thee . . ."

Ezekiel 34:23-24, "And I will set up one shepherd over them, and he shall feed them, even my servant David; . . . And I the Lord will be their God, and my servant David a prince among them . . ."

COMMENT: The Messiah is to function as the servant of God. He will be God's shepherd. NOTE that God and His servant are separate entities, with God bringing the Messiah into his position. Nothing is said here, or elsewhere in the Hebrew Scriptures, about the Messiah being the substance of the Lord God, which Christianity believes. In a previous chapter, "His God Is Not a Trinity," we have shown that the New Testament similarly makes a clear differentiation between God and Jesus Christ. Nevertheless, Christianity has blended the two.

Isaiah 19:20, ". . . for they shall cry unto the Lord because of the oppressors, and he shall send them a savior, and a great one, and he shall deliver them."

Isaiah 55:3-4, ". . . I will make an everlasting covenant with you, even the sure mercies of David. Behold, I have given him for a witness to the people, a leader and commander to the people."

Psalm 18:50, "Great deliverance giveth he to his king; and showeth mercy to his anointed, to David, and to his seed for evermore."

COMMENT: The Messiah of the Hebrew people is sent by God to rescue God's Chosen People. Jews will have deliverance through the Messiah. NOTE that it is unfortunate, but true, that Christianity's Messiah has been made the cause of great troubles for the people of Israel, rather than the opposite. God promised deliverance, not further oppression.

Ezekiel 37:24-25, "And David my servant shall be king over them; . . . they shall also walk in my judgments, and observe my statutes, and do them. And they shall dwell in the land that I have given unto Jacob my servant, wherein your fathers have dwelt; and they shall

dwell therein, even they, and their children, and their children's chil-
dren for ever; and my servant David shall be prince for ever."
COMMENT: With the Messiah as king, the Jewish people are to
inherit the Promised Land forever. The Davidic dynasty of the Messiah
is established as God's royalty for all time. And the people will follow
the laws of God and do them in this Messianic kingdom. NOTE that
for two thousand years after Jesus there has not been any Jewish kingdom in the Promised Land with the Messiah and those following
ruling.

Psalm 132:9-12,15,17, "Let thy priests be clothed with righteous-
ness; and let thy saints shout for joy. For thy servant David's sake turn
not away the face of thine anointed. The Lord hath sworn in truth unto
David; . . . If thy children will keep my covenant . . . their children
shall also sit upon thy throne for evermore. I will abundantly bless her
provision . . . There will I make the horn of David to bud . . ."

Jeremiah 23:4-6, "And I will set up shepherds over them which
shall feed them: and they shall fear no more, nor be dismayed, neither
shall they be lacking, saith the Lord. . . . I will raise unto David a
righteous Branch, and a King shall reign and prosper, and shall exe-
cute judgment and justice in the earth. In his days Judah shall be
saved, and Israel shall dwell safely . . ."

Jeremiah 33:14, 16, "Behold, the days come, saith the Lord, that I
will perform that good thing which I have promised unto the house of
Israel and the house of Judah. In those days shall Judah be saved, and
Jerusalem shall dwell safely . . ."
COMMENT: In the time to come, the Messiah and his Davidic
descendants will rule forever over the people of Israel who will have
kept God's Covenant. The Messiah will supervise and dispense justice
and judgment in the earth. It says, "in the earth." People will have
plenty and live in abundance, with no fear. They will be rescued and
live in safety. NOTE these questions:—Does Jesus fit this picture?
Either then or now, have the Jewish people dwelt in safety and plenty?
The quotes state that in the time of the Messiah the people of Israel
"shall dwell safely." As this is the description of the Messianic age for
the Hebrew people, it is obvious that it has not arrived! As Jesus does
not fit this outline of Messianic achievement, it is similarly obvious
that he is not the Hebrew Messiah! The Holy Bible is our source.
Whatever else he may be in Christianity, Jesus is not the Messiah of
the Hebrew Scriptures awaited in Judaism.

In summary, from the Biblical passages about the Messiah, it is
evident that Jews reject Jesus as the Messiah because they know he did
not perform the role or accomplish the tasks of the Messiah, as writ-

ten. We are not in the Messianic Era. We do not have the Messianic expectations fulfilled. Neither Jews nor the earth has peace, abundance, safety, and happiness. In this book's next chapter, the Messianic Era is fully explored and revealed.

The real question is not why Jews do not believe Jesus was the Hebrew Messiah but why Christians do, when the Messianic times did not unfold as prophesied in the Book of God! There is really no answer they can offer which can satisfy this simple question. It is clear that the Christian Christ has a supposed function which differs from the one given in the Hebrew Bible for the Messiah. Christ's mission, as explained in Christianity, is to offer personal salvation through vicarious atonement. The Messiah's mission of earthly redemption is changed by Christianity into heavenly salvation. But, their belief does not concern us here. We just want to make it understood that Judaism's Messiah and Christianity's Messiah are not the same in essence or function.

The Hebrew Scriptures' Messiah is Judaic. The early followers of Jesus did hope he was this Messiah. His Jewish followers fully understood the need for the Messiah to accomplish his mission of being the ruler in God's earthly Messianic kingdom. This was their hope. When he died without the Messianic hopes being achieved, they must have been very disappointed. But, instead of complete discouragement at his execution by the Romans, they were somehow prompted to expect his imminent return. In this return, he would fulfill the expectations. Needless to say, Jesus did not return in their lifetime as they had expected and the New Testament reported was to occur.

The early Church had to minimize Messianic expectations and orientation and postulate that Jesus would return at some future unknown time. They still await his second coming. The trouble with this is that, although Christians can await his return to earth, they have absolutely no basis for this happening in any of the Hebrew Bible's prophesies! Nothing at all is written about a second coming to complete what a first coming left undone. Their await is Christologic, not Messianic.

With great hope and reason, Jews also await. But, we await what God has promised in the Hebrew Scriptures. The Messiah is to come to fulfill all the marvelous expectations as written. Judaism is permeated with the faith of his coming, and though he tarry, he shall surely appear.

12

Scriptural Messianic Expectations

In this chapter, we shall present Biblical verses which illustrate the heart of the Messianic times. The selected passages are representative of the very many which are in the Bible. Of course, the Messiah has the function of presiding over the Messianic world, and his role as ruler is alone the reason for his being God's anointed! Therefore, the Messiah cannot be contemplated apart from the Messianic Era and its expectations.

First, let's explain the word "Messiah." The Hebrew word "moshiach" is simply a word meaning "anointed one." Messiah or Moshiach is a title of honor which was given to ancient Hebrew kings. The Hebrew Messiah is to be a divinely appointed human being, with an earthly mission from God for the Chosen People and, through them, all mankind.

It is of interest to learn that the Bible does not always tell of a personality being the Messiah. Sometimes only Messianic occurrences are described, with God being the redeemer who brings about His people's rescue. At other times, the collective house of David, the whole people of Israel, is meant when expressing Messianic powers. It should be grasped that the Messiah is not described as the redeemer, but as the head of the redeemed people. God is the Redeemer of His people. The Lord's spirit and strength will be upon His anointed, yet, there is no merging of identity indicated.

When the Messiah is mentioned as a person, however, he is certainly of lofty spiritual stature. He has wisdom, discernment and righteousness. He obeys God. He administers justice and judgment successfully as a perfect leader in the kingdom of God on earth, a kingdom which will exist eternally. We have presented verses which describe the

Messiah in our previous chapter, "The Hebrew Messiah."

Here will be shown what the Messianic kingdom will be like. The Chosen People will reside in God's kingdom in Zion forever. Israel's enemies will be destroyed. The Hebrew people will have material abundance and spiritual excellence! There will be full joy, fruitfulness, tranquility, safety, and well-being. The Torah will be perfectly followed in a new, profound way. God's laws will be written on the hearts of the people so they cannot be broken or neglected. The people will be spiritually perfect, free from transgression, and sin will be overcome. God's spirit will be in the midst of the people and the Temple will be rebuilt permanently.

Moreover, all nations will look to Israel's spirituality, praise it, submit to it, and through Israel's light be guided to God and religious excellence! Idol worship will end. Peace will cover the earth, with oppression, suffering, and war at an end. What a glorious vision of earthly bliss and spiritual perfection for the Hebrews and Gentiles in Judaism's Messianics! It would be too mild to call it the supreme golden age of mankind, but that is, in essence, the vision.

It is plain that the promises of the Messianic times did not flower when a portion of the Hebrew people returned from exile in Babylon to Jerusalem. The Second Temple was not the Messianic Temple. No Messiah had built it. It was missing the Ark of the Covenant and essential holiness. Moreover, it was destroyed, which cannot be the fate of the Messianic Temple. Nothing which occurred during the time of the Second Temple approximates the Messianic expectations. Indeed, the consequences of captivity continued even in the return from Babylon. God promised all tribes would be returned and gathered, but they were not. And so, the Messiah is awaited and still awaited.

The people of Israel have been brought into great misery, almost total destruction, due to sinfulness through disobedience to God's Torah. But, God wants to bring His people back to righteousness, not to punish them only. Therefore, although harshly treated by God, the remnant will repent and return to God, be given His help, and receive great blessing in the latter days. This blessing is the redemption. At the time of the redemption the Jewish people will all be gathered from exile throughout the earth into the Promised Land. With Israel's enemies destroyed, the Chosen People will build the land to which they have returned and prosper there for eternity. As a light to the Gentiles, Israel will bring all the world to worship God and have spiritual perfection, all this while material abundance is our happy lot.

FIRST, WE PRESENT GENERAL PASSAGES WHICH DESCRIBE THE SORROW AND THE PROMISE.

Leviticus 26:15-17,31,38,44, "And if ye shall despise my statutes,

*or if your soul abhor my judgments, so that ye will not do all my com-
mandments, but that ye break my covenant: . . . I will . . . appoint
over you terror . . . and cause sorrow of heart: and ye shall sow your
seed in vain, for your enemies shall eat it. And I will set my face
against you, and ye shall be slain before your enemies: they that hate
you shall reign over you: and ye shall flee when none pursueth you.
And I will make your cities waste, and bring your sanctuaries unto
desolation, . . . And ye shall perish among the heathen, and the land
of your enemies shall eat you up. And they that are left of you shall
pine away in their iniquity in your enemies' lands; . . . (If they confess) . . . I will not cast them away, neither will I abhor them, to
destroy them utterly, and to break my covenant with them: for I am the
Lord their God."*

Isaiah 64:7,10-11, Isaiah 65:8-9, 19, *". . . for thou hast hid thy
face from us, and hast consumed us, because of our iniquities. Thy
holy cities are a wilderness, Zion is a wilderness, Jerusalem a desolation. Our holy and our beautiful house, where our fathers praised thee,
is burned up with fire: and all our pleasant things are laid waste. . . .
for my servants' sakes . . . I may not destroy them all. And I will
bring forth a seed out of Jacob, and out of Judah an inheritor of my
mountains: and mine elect shall inherit it, and my servants shall dwell
there. And I will rejoice in Jerusalem, and joy in my people: and the
voice of weeping shall be no more heard in her . . ."*

Jeremiah 30:7-11,17, *"Alas! for that day is great, so that none is
like it: it is even the time of Jacob's trouble; but he shall be saved out
of it. For it shall come to pass in that day, saith the Lord of hosts, that
I will . . . burst thy bonds, and strangers shall no more serve themselves of him: But they shall serve the Lord their God, and David their
king, whom I will raise up unto them. Therefore fear thou not, O my
servant Jacob, saith the Lord; neither be dismayed, O Israel: for, lo, I
will save thee from afar, and thy seed from the land of their captivity;
and Jacob shall return, . . . and none shall make him afraid . . .
though I make a full end of all nations whither I have scattered thee,
yet will I not make a full end of thee: . . . For I will restore health unto
thee, and I will heal thee of thy wounds, saith the Lord . . ."*

Jeremiah 32:42, *"For thus saith the Lord; Like as I have brought
all this great evil upon this people, so will I bring upon them all the
good that I have promised them."*

Hosea 3:4-5, *"For the children of Israel shall abide many days
without a king . . . and without a sacrifice . . . Afterward shall the
children of Israel return, and seek the Lord their God, and David their
king; and shall fear the Lord and his goodness in the latter days."*

Amos 8:10, Amos 9:8,14-15, *"And I will turn your feasts into
mourning and all your songs into lamentation; . . . and I will make it*

as the mourning of an only son, and the end thereof as a bitter day. Behold, the eyes of the Lord God are upon the sinful kingdom, and I will destroy it from off the face of the earth; saving that I will not utterly destroy the house of Jacob, saith the Lord. And I will bring again the captivity (gathering) of my people of Israel (to Zion), and they shall build the waste cities, and inhabit them; and they shall plant vineyards, and drink the wine thereof; they shall also make gardens, and eat the fruit of them. And I will plant them upon their land, and they shall no more be pulled up out of their land which I have given them, saith the Lord thy God."

Nahum 1:12, *"Thus saith the Lord; . . . Though I have afflicted thee, I will afflict thee no more."*

Zephaniah 3:19, *"Behold, at that time I will undo all that afflict thee: and I will save her that halteth . . ."*

VERSES THAT TELL GOD WILL COMPASSIONATELY GATHER HIS CHOSEN PEOPLE FROM ALL THE WORLD INTO THE PROMISED LAND.

Deuteronomy 30:3, 5, *". . . the Lord thy God will turn thy captivity, and have compassion upon thee, and will return and gather thee from all the nations, whither the Lord thy God hath scattered thee. And . . . bring thee into the land which thy fathers possessed, and thou shalt possess it . . ."*

Isaiah 11:12, *"And he shall . . . assemble the outcasts of Israel, and gather together the dispersed of Judah from the four corners of the earth."*

Jeremiah 12:15, *". . . after that I have plucked them out I will return, and have compassion on them, and will bring them again, every man to his heritage, and every man to his land."*

Ezekiel 34:13, *"And I will bring them out from the people, and gather them from the countries, and will bring them to their own land, and feed them upon the mountains of Israel by the rivers, and in all the inhabited places of the country."*

Zechariah 8:7-8, *". . . I will save my people from the east country, and from the west country; And I will bring them, and they shall dwell in the midst of Jerusalem: . . ."*

VERSES THAT TELL ISRAEL WILL BE FRUITFUL AND PROSPEROUS.

Deuteronomy 28:11, *"And the Lord shall make thee plenteous in goods, in the fruit of thy body, (cattle), (ground), in the land which the Lord sware unto thy fathers to give thee."*

Isaiah 65:21, *"And they shall build houses, and inhabit them; and they shall plant vineyards, and eat the fruit of them."*

Jeremiah 23:3, *"And I will gather the remnant of my flock out of the countries whither I have driven them, and will bring them again to their folds; and they shall be fruitful and increase."*

Joel 2:24, 26, "And the floors shall be full of wheat, and the vats shall overflow with wine and oil. And ye shall eat in plenty, and be satisfied . . ."

Zechariah 8:12, "For the seed shall be prosperous; the vine shall give her fruit, and the ground shall give her increase, and the heavens shall give their dew; and I will cause the remnant of this people to possess all these things."

VERSES THAT TELL THERE WILL BE EVERLASTING HAPPINESS FOR THE HEBREW PEOPLE.

Isaiah 25:8, ". . . and the Lord God will wipe away tears from off all faces; and the rebuke of his people shall he take away . . ."

Isaiah 35:10, "And the ransomed of the Lord shall return, and come to Zion with songs and everlasting joy upon their heads: they shall obtain joy and gladness, and sorrow and sighing shall flee away."

Isaiah 55:12, "For ye shall go out with joy, and be led forth with peace . . ."

Isaiah 61:3, "To appoint unto them that mourn in Zion, to give unto them beauty for ashes, the oil of joy for mourning, the garment of praise for the spirit of heaviness . . ."

Jeremiah 31:4,13, ". . . (Thou) shalt go forth in the dances of them that make merry. . . . Then shall the virgin rejoice in the dance, both young men and old together: for I will turn their mourning into joy, and will comfort them, and make them rejoice from their sorrow."

VERSES THAT TELL ILLNESSES WILL CEASE AND LONG LIFE BE GIVEN TO THE ISRAEL PEOPLE.

Deuteronomy 7:15, "And the Lord will take from thee all sickness, and will put none of the evil diseases of Egypt, which thou knowest, upon thee . . ."

Job 5:26, "Thou shalt come to thy grave in a full age, like a shock of corn cometh in his season."

Isaiah 29:18, Isaiah 33:24, "And in that day shall the deaf hear the words of the book, and the eyes of the blind shall see out of obscurity, and out of darkness. And the inhabitant shall not say, I am sick . . ."

Isaiah 65:20, "There shall be no more thence an infant of days, nor an old man that hath not filled his days: for the child shall die an hundred years old . . ."

Zechariah 8:4, ". . . There shall yet old men and old women dwell in the streets of Jerusalem, and every man with his staff in his hand for very age."

VERSES THAT TELL THERE WILL BE SAFETY AND NO FEAR IN THE PROMISED LAND FOR THE CHOSEN PEOPLE.

Isaiah 54:13-14,17, ". . . great shall be the peace of thy children. . . . thou shalt be far from oppression; for thou shalt not fear: and from terror; for it shall not come near thee. No weapon that is formed against thee shall prosper . . ."

Jeremiah 46:27, "But fear not thou, O my servant Jacob, and be not dismayed, O Israel: . . . Jacob shall return, and be in rest and at ease, and none shall make him afraid."

Ezekiel 38:8,11, ". . . and they shall dwell safely all of them. And thou shalt say, I will go up to the land of unwalled villages; I will go to them that are at rest that dwell safely, all of them dwelling without walls, and having neither bars nor gates,"

Zephaniah 3:13,15, ". . . for they shall feed and lie down, and none shall make them afraid. . . . thou shalt not see evil any more."

Zechariah 14:11, "And men shall dwell in it, . . . Jerusalem shall be safely inhabited."

VERSES THAT TELL OF WORLDWIDE PEACE.

Psalm 72:7, "In his days shall the righteous fluorish; and abundance of peace so long as the moon endureth."

Isaiah 32:18, "And my people shall dwell in a peaceable habitation, and in sure dwellings, and in quiet resting places;"

Ezekiel 39:9, "And they that dwell in the cities of Israel shall go forth, and shall set on fire and burn the weapons, both the shields and the bucklers, the bows and the arrows, and the handstaves, and the spears . . ."

Hosea 2:18, ". . . and I will break the bow and the sword and the battle out of the earth, and will make them to lie down safely,"

Micah 4:3-4 (Isaiah 2:4), ". . . and they shall beat their swords into plowshares, and their spears into pruninghooks: nation shall not lift up a sword against nation, neither shall they learn war any more. But they shall sit every man under his vine and under his fig tree; and none shall make them afraid . . ."

VERSES THAT TELL OF WILD ANIMALS CAUSING NO HARM.

Isaiah 11:6,9, "The wolf also shall dwell with the lamb, and the leopard shall lie down with the kid; and the calf and the young lion and the fatling together; . . . They shall not hurt nor destroy in all my holy mountain . . ."

Isaiah 65:25, "The wolf and the lamb shall feed together, and the lion shall eat straw like the bullock: and dust shall be the serpent's meat. They shall not hurt nor destroy in all my holy mountain, saith the Lord."

Ezekiel 34:25, "And I will . . . cause the evil beasts to cease out of the land: and they shall dwell safely in the wilderness, and sleep in the woods."

Hosea 2:18, *"And in that day will I make a covenant for them with the beasts of the field, and with the fowls of heaven, and with the creeping things of the ground: . . . and will make them to lie down safely."*

VERSES THAT TELL THE ENEMIES OF GOD'S CHOSEN WILL BE DESTROYED.

Isaiah 14:2, Isaiah 41:11, *". . . and the house of Israel . . . shall take them captives, whose captives they were; and they shall rule over their oppressors. Behold, all they that were incensed against thee shall be ashamed and confounded: they shall be as nothing; and they that strive with thee shall perish."*

Jeremiah 30:16, *"Therefore all they that devour thee shall be devoured; and all thine adversaries, every one of them, shall go into captivity; and they that spoil thee shall be a spoil, and all that prey upon thee will I give for a prey."*

Daniel 2:44, *"And in the days of these kings shall the God of heaven set up a kingdom, which shall never be destroyed: and the kingdom shall not be left to other people, but it shall break in pieces and consume all these kingdoms . . ."*

Joel 3:19-20, *"Egypt shall be a desolation, and Edom shall be a desolate wilderness, for the violence against the children of Judah, because they have shed innocent blood in their land. But Judah shall dwell for ever . . ."*

Micah 5:9, *"Thine hand shall be lifted up upon thine adversaries, and all thine enemies shall be cut off."*

VERSES THAT TELL ISRAEL WILL RECEIVE HER FORMER ENEMIES' WEALTH AND SERVICE.

Psalm 2:8, *"Ask of me, and I shall give thee the heathen for thine inheritance, and the uttermost parts of the earth for thy possession."*

Isaiah 60:5-6,10,12,14, *". . . the Gentiles shall come unto thee. . . . they shall bring gold and incense; . . . And the sons of strangers shall build up thy walls, and their kings shall minister unto thee: . . . For the nation and kingdom that will not serve thee shall perish; . . . The sons also of them that afflicted thee shall come bending unto thee; and all they that despised thee shall bow themselves down at the soles of thy feet; and they shall call thee, The city of the Lord, The Zion of the Holy One of Israel."*

Isaiah 61:5-6, *"And strangers shall stand and feed your flocks, and the sons of the alien shall be your plowmen and your vinedressers. . . . ye shall eat the riches of the Gentiles, and in their glory shall ye boast yourselves."*

Zephaniah 2:9, ". . . the residue of my people shall spoil them, and the remnant of my people shall possess them."

Zechariah 14:14, "And Judah also shall fight at Jerusalem; and the wealth of all the heathen round about shall be gathered together, gold, and silver, and apparel, in great abundance."

WE HAVE JUST BEEN DESCRIBING THE MATERIAL EXCELLENCE. NOW WE WILL START DESCRIBING THE SPIRITUAL EXCELLENCE.

FIRST, WE PRESENT PASSAGES THAT TELL ISRAEL'S REDEEMER IS THE LORD GOD OF ISRAEL.

Job 19:25, "For I know that my redeemer liveth, and that he shall stand at the latter day upon the earth;"

Psalm 19:14, "Let the words of my mouth, and the meditation of my heart, be acceptable in thy sight, O Lord, my strength, and my redeemer."

Isaiah 48:20, ". . . The Lord hath redeemed his servant Jacob."

Isaiah 49:7, "Thus saith the Lord, the Redeemer of Israel . . ."

Isaiah 49:26, ". . . and all flesh shall know that I the Lord am thy Savior and thy Redeemer, the mighty One of Jacob."

VERSES THAT TELL THE CHOSEN PEOPLE WILL BE PRAISED AND CALLED GREAT BY THE NATIONS BECAUSE OF ISRAEL'S SPIRITUAL EXCELLENCE, WHICH IN TURN WILL BLESS THE WORLD.

Genesis 12:2-3, "And I will make of thee a great nation, and I will bless thee, and make thy name great; and thou shalt be a blessing: . . . in thee shall all families of the earth be blessed."

Genesis 18:18, "Seeing that Abraham shall surely become a great and mighty nation, and all the nations of the earth shall be blessed in him . . ."

Isaiah 61:6,9, Isaiah 62:12, "But ye shall be named the Priests of the Lord: men shall call you the Ministers of our God: . . . And their seed shall be known among the Gentiles, . . . all that see them shall acknowledge them, that they are the seed which the Lord hath blessed. And they shall call them, The holy people, The redeemed of the Lord: and thou shalt be called Sought out, A city not forsaken."

Malachi 3:12, "And all nations shall call you blessed: for ye shall be a delightsome land, saith the Lord of hosts."

Zephaniah 3:19-20, ". . . I will get them praise and fame in every land where they have been put to shame . . . for I will make you a name and a praise among all people of the earth . . ."

VERSES THAT TELL ISRAEL WILL BE FREE OF SIN.

Isaiah 60:21, "Thy people also shall be all righteous: they shall inherit the land for ever, . . . that I may be glorified."

Jeremiah 3:17, Jeremiah 50:20, ". . . neither shall they walk any more after the imagination of their evil heart. In those days, and in that time, saith the Lord, the iniquity of Israel shall be sought for, and there shall be none; and the sins of Judah, and they shall not be found: for I will pardon them whom I reserve."

Ezekiel 37:23, "Neither shall they defile themselves anymore . . . with their detestable things, nor with any of their transgressions: but I will save them out of all their dwelling places, wherein they have sinned, and will cleanse them: so shall they be my people, and I will be their God."

Zephaniah 3:13, "The remnant of Israel shall not do iniquity, nor speak lies; neither shall a deceitful tongue be found in their mouth . . ."

Zechariah 8:16-17, "These are the things that ye shall do; Speak ye every man the truth to his neighbor; execute the judgment of truth and peace in your gates: And let none of you imagine evil in your hearts against his neighbor; and love no false oath . . ."

VERSES THAT TELL IDOL WORSHIP WILL CEASE.

Isaiah 2:18, "And the idols he shall utterly abolish."

Isaiah 2:20, "In that day a man shall cast his idols of silver, and his idols of gold, which they made each one for himself to worship, to the moles and to the bats;"

Ezekiel 36:25, "Then will I sprinkle clean water upon you, and ye shall be clean: from all your filthiness, and from all your idols, will I cleanse you."

Micah 5:13, "Thy graven images also will I cut off, and thy standing images out of the midst of thee; and thou shalt no more worship the work of thine hands."

Zechariah 13:2, ". . . in that day, saith the Lord of hosts, . . . I will cut off the names of the idols out of the land, and they shall no more be remembered . . ."

VERSES THAT TELL A NEW MANNER OF KNOWING THE COVENANT WILL REPLACE THE OLD MANNER, WHEN THE LAWS WILL BE INGRAINED ON THE HEART.

Deuteronomy 30:6, "And the Lord thy God will circumcise thine heart, and the heart of thy seed, to love the Lord thy God with all thine heart, and with all thy soul, that thou mayest live."

Jeremiah 31:31,33-34, "Behold, the days come, saith the Lord, that I will make a new covenant with the house of Israel and with the house of Judah: But this shall be the covenant . . . I will put my law in their inward parts, and write it in their hearts; . . . they shall teach no more every man his neighbor (brother), saying, Know the Lord: for they shall all know me . . ."

Jeremiah 32:40, "And I will make an everlasting covenant with them, that I will not turn away from them, to do them good; but I will put my fear in their hearts, that they shall not depart from me."

Ezekiel 36:26, "And a new heart also will I give you, and a new spirit will I put within you; and I will take away the stony heart out of your flesh, and I will give you an heart of flesh."

Zephaniah 3:9, "For then will I turn to the people a pure language, that they may all call upon the name of the Lord, to serve him with one consent."

VERSES THAT TELL THE TORAH'S LAWS WILL BE OBSERVED ETERNALLY.

Deuteronomy 4:6, "Keep therefore and do them; for this is your wisdom and your understanding in the sight of the nations, which shall hear all these statutes, and say, Surely this great nation is a wise and understanding people."

Deuteronomy 29:29, ". . . those things which are revealed belong unto us and to our children for ever, that we may do all the words of this law."

Isaiah 2:3 (Micah 4:2), Isaiah 52:1, "And many people shall. . . go up to the mountain of the Lord, . . . and he will teach us of his ways, and we will walk in his paths: for out of Zion shall go forth the law, and the word of the Lord from Jerusalem. . . . O Jerusalem, the holy city: for henceforth there shall no more come unto thee the uncircumcised and the unclean."

Isaiah 59:21, ". . . My spirit that is upon thee, and my words which I have put in thy mouth, shall not depart out of thy mouth, nor out of the mouth of thy seed . . . from henceforth and for ever."

Ezekiel 36:27, "And I will put my spirit within you, and cause you to walk in my statutes, and ye shall keep my judgments, and do them."

VERSES THAT TELL ISRAEL WILL BE A LIGHT TO THE NATIONS, WHEREBY THE KNOWLEDGE OF GOD WILL FILL THE EARTH.

Isaiah 42:1,6, "Behold my servant, whom I uphold; mine elect, in whom my soul delighteth; I have put my spirit upon him: he shall bring forth judgment to the Gentiles. I the Lord have called thee in righteousness, . . . and will keep thee, and give thee for a covenant of the people, for a light of the Gentiles;"

Isaiah 49:3,6, "And (He) said to me, Thou art my servant, O Israel, in whom I will be glorified. . . . I will also give thee for a light to the Gentiles, that thou mayest be my salvation unto the end of the earth."

Isaiah 55:5, ". . . nations that knew not thee shall run unto thee because of the Lord thy God, and for the Holy One of Israel; for He hath glorified thee."

*Isaiah 60:3-4, "And the Gentiles shall come to thy light, and kings
to the brightness of thy rising. . . . thy sons shall come from far, and
thy daughters shall be nursed at thy side."*

*Habakkuk 2:14, "For the earth shall be filled with the knowledge
of the glory of the Lord, as the waters cover the sea."*

**VERSES THAT TELL JUDAISM WILL BE THE ONE WORLDWIDE RELI-
GION, JERUSALEM WILL BE THE CENTRAL HOLY PLACE FOR ALL
PEOPLE, AND GENTILES WILL CONVERT TO THE LORD GOD OF
ISRAEL AND SERVE HIM.**

*Psalm 22:27, "All the ends of the world shall remember and turn
unto the Lord: and all the kindreds of the nations shall worship before
thee."*

*Psalm 102:15,22, "So the heathen shall fear the name of the Lord,
and all the kings of the earth thy glory. When the people are gathered
together, and the kingdoms, to serve the Lord."*

*Isaiah 2:2, ". . . the mountain of the Lord's house shall be estab-
lished . . . and all nations shall flow unto it."*

*Isaiah 14:1, ". . . and the strangers shall be joined with them,
and they shall cleave to the house of Jacob."*

*Isaiah 19:21, ". . . and the Egyptians . . . shall do sacrifice and
oblation; yea, they shall vow a vow unto the Lord, and perform it."*

*Isaiah 45:23, ". . . unto me every knee shall bow, every tongue
shall swear (to God)."*

*Isaiah 54:5, "For thy Maker is thine husband; the Lord of hosts is
his name; and thy Redeemer the Holy One of Israel; The God of the
whole earth shall he be called."*

*Isaiah 56:6-7, "Also the sons of the stranger, that join themselves
to the Lord, to serve him, and to love the name of the Lord, to be his
servants, every one that keepeth the sabbath from polluting it, and
taketh hold of my covenant; Even them will I bring to my holy mountain, and make them joyful in my house of prayer: their burnt offerings
and their sacrifices shall be accepted upon mine altar; for mine house
shall be called an house of prayer for all people."*

*Isaiah 66:18,20,23, ". . . it shall come, that I will gather all
nations and tongues; and they shall come, and see my glory. And they
shall bring all your brethren for an offering unto the Lord out of all
nations . . . to my holy mountain Jerusalem, . . . from one new moon
to another, and from one sabbath to another, shall all flesh come to
worship before me, saith the Lord."*

*Jeremiah 3:17, "At that time they shall call Jerusalem the throne
of the Lord; and all the nations shall be gathered unto it, to the name
of the Lord, to Jerusalem . . ."*

Jeremiah 16:19, "O Lord . . . the Gentiles shall come unto thee from the ends of the earth, and shall say, Surely our fathers have inherited lies, vanity, and things wherein there is no profit."

Zephaniah 2:11, *"The Lord . . . will famish all the gods of the earth; and men shall worship him, every one from his place, even all the isles of the heathen."*

Zechariah 2:11, *"And many nations shall be joined to the Lord in that day, and shall be my people . . ."*

Zechariah 8:22, *"Yea, many people and strong nations shall come to seek the Lord of hosts in Jerusalem, and to pray before the Lord."*

Zechariah 8:23, *"Thus saith the Lord of hosts; In those days it shall come to pass, that ten men shall take hold out of all languages of the nations, even shall take hold of the skirt of him that is a Jew, saying, We will go with you: for we have heard that God is with you."*

Zechariah 14:9, *"And the Lord shall be king over all the earth: in that day shall there be one Lord, and his name one."*

Zechariah 14:16, *"And it shall come to pass, that every one that is left of all the nations which came against Jerusalem shall even go up from year to year to worship the King, the Lord of hosts, and to keep the feast of tabernacles."*

VERSES THAT TELL ISRAEL EXALTS, GLORIFIES, AND SANCTIFIES GOD.

Isaiah 2:11, *"The lofty looks of man shall be humbled, . . . and the Lord alone shall be exalted in that day."*

Isaiah 17:7, *"At that day shall a man look to his Maker, and his eyes shall have respect to the Holy One of Israel."*

Isaiah 40:5, *"And the glory of the Lord shall be revealed, and all flesh shall see it together: for the mouth of the Lord hath spoken it."*

Isaiah 49:3, *"And (the Lord) said unto me, Thou art my servant, O Israel, in whom I will be glorified."*

Ezekiel 28:25, *"Thus saith the Lord God; When I shall have gathered the house of Israel from the people among whom they are scattered, and shall be sanctified in them in the sight of the heathen, then shall they dwell in their land that I have given to my servant Jacob."*

VERSES THAT TELL THE REDEMPTION OF GOD'S CHOSEN WILL BE FOREVER.

Isaiah 45:17, *"But Israel shall be saved in the Lord with an everlasting salvation: ye shall not be ashamed nor confounded world without end."*

Ezekiel 37:26, *"Moreover I will make a covenant of peace with them; it shall be an everlasting covenant with them: and I will place them and multiply them, and will set my sanctuary in the midst of them for evermore."*

Ezekiel 43:7, *". . . the place of my throne . . . where I will dwell in the midst of the children of Israel for ever . . ."*

Joel 3:20-21, "But Judah shall dwell for ever, and Jerusalem from generation to generation. For I will cleanse their blood that I have not cleansed: for the Lord dwelleth in Zion."

Micah 4:7, ". . . and the Lord shall reign over them in mount Zion from henceforth, even for ever."

VERSES THAT TELL GOD'S SPIRIT, THE SHEKINAH OF GOD, WILL DWELL IN THE MIDST OF THE PEOPLE OF ISRAEL.

Isaiah 44:3, ". . . I will pour my spirit upon thy seed, and my blessing upon thine offspring:"

Ezekiel 39:29, "Neither will I hide my face any more from them: for I have poured out my spirit upon the house of Israel, saith the Lord God."

Joel 2:27-28, "And ye shall know that I am in the midst of Israel, . . . I will pour out my spirit upon all flesh; and your sons and your daughters shall prophesy, your old men shall dream dreams, your young men shall see visions:"

Zephaniah 3:15,17, ". . . the king of Israel, even the Lord, is in the midst of thee: thou shalt not see evil any more. The Lord thy God in the midst of thee is mighty; he will save, he will rejoice over thee with joy . . ."

Zechariah 2:10-11, "Sing and rejoice, O daughter of Zion: for, lo, I come, and I will dwell in the midst of thee, saith the Lord. And many nations shall be joined to the Lord in that day, and shall be my people: and I will dwell in the midst of thee . . ."

VERSES THAT TELL THE TEMPLE OF JERUSALEM WILL BE REBUILT AND WILL LAST FOREVER.

Ezekiel 37:26-28, ". . . and (I) will set my sanctuary in the midst of them for evermore. My tabernacle also shall be with them . . . And the heathen shall know that I the Lord do sanctify Israel, when my sanctuary shall be in the midst of them for evermore."

Hosea 3:4-5, "For the children of Israel shall abide many days . . . without a sacrifice, and without an image, and without an ephod, and without terephim: Afterward shall the children of Israel return . . ."

Amos 9:11, "In that day will I raise up the tabernacle of David that is fallen, and close up the breaches thereof; and I will raise up his ruins, and I will build it as in the days of old:"

Zechariah 1:16, "Therefore thus saith the Lord; I am returned to Jerusalem with mercies: my house shall be built in it . . ."

Zechariah 6:12, "Behold the man whose name is The Branch; and he shall grow up out of his place, and he shall build the temple of the Lord:"

**VERSES THAT TELL THROUGH REPENTANCE WE EXPRESS SORROW
FOR WRONG-DOING AND RETURN TO GOD WHO FORGIVES OUR SINS
AND GIVES US REDEMPTION.**

*Deuteronomy 30:9-10, ". . . for the Lord will again rejoice over
thee for good, . . . If thou shalt harken unto the voice of the Lord thy
God, to keep his commandments and his statutes . . . and if thou turn
unto the Lord thy God with all thine heart, and with all thy soul."*

*Isaiah 55:7, "Let the wicked forsake his way, and the unrighteous
man his thoughts: and let him return unto the Lord, and he will have
mercy upon him; and to our God, for he will abundantly pardon."*

*Jeremiah 3:12, Jeremiah 36:3, ". . . Return, thou backsliding
Israel, saith the Lord; . . . for I am merciful, saith the Lord, and I will
not keep anger for ever. . . . that they may return every man from his
evil way; that I may forgive their iniquity and their sin."*

*Ezekiel 33:11,19, ". . . I have no pleasure in the death of the
wicked; but that the wicked turn from his way and live: . . . But if the
wicked turn from his wickedness, and do that which is lawful and
right, he shall live thereby."*

*Hosea 14:1-2,4, "O Israel, return unto the Lord thy God; for thou
hast fallen by thine iniquity. Take with you words, and turn to the
Lord: say unto him, Take away all iniquity, and receive us graciously:
. . . I will heal their backsliding, I will love them freely; for mine
anger is turned away from him."*

**NOW LET US CONCLUDE BY REVEALING SOME OTHER LATTER DAY
EXPECTATIONS OF HAPPENINGS.**

**FIRST, WE PRESENT THE VERSE WHICH TELLS THAT BEFORE JUDG-
MENT DAY ELIJAH THE PROPHET WILL APPEAR TO CALL PEOPLE TO
REPENT, SO THAT MORE ARE WORTHY AND RIGHTEOUS BEFORE
GOD.**

*Malachi 4:5-6, "Behold, I will send you Elijah the prophet before
the coming of the great and dreadful day of the Lord: And he shall turn
the heart of the fathers to the children, and the heart of the children to
their fathers . . ."*

VERSES THAT TELL OF STRANGE HAPPENINGS.

*Isaiah 11:15, "And the Lord shall utterly destroy the tongue of the
Egyptian sea; . . . and shall smite it in the seven streams, and make
men go over dryshod."*

*Ezekiel 47:12, "And by the river upon the bank thereof, . . . shall
grow all trees for meat, whose leaf shall not fade, neither shall the
fruit thereof be consumed: it shall bring forth new fruit according to
his months . . ."*

*Joel 3:18, "And it shall come to pass in that day, that the moun-
tains shall drop down new wine, and the hills shall flow with milk,*

. . . and a fountain shall come forth of the house of the Lord . . ."

Zechariah 14:4, " . . . and the mount of Olives shall cleave in the midst thereof toward the east and toward the west, and there shall be a very great valley; and half of the mountain shall remove toward the north, and half of it toward the south."

Zechariah 14:8, "And it shall be in that day, that living waters shall go out from Jerusalem; half of them toward the former sea, and half of them toward the hinder sea . . .

VERSES THAT TELL OF A DAY OF JUDGMENT, THE DAY OF THE LORD, WHICH IS TO COME. IT WILL BE TERRIBLE ON THAT DAY WHEN GOD WILL DESTROY SINNERS AND SAVE THE RIGHTEOUS. A NEW HEAVEN AND EARTH WILL BE CREATED WHERE ISRAEL WILL BE WITH THE LORD.

Joel 2:1,10,32, "Blow ye the trumpet in Zion, and sound an alarm in my holy mountain: let all the inhabitants of the land tremble: for the day of the Lord cometh, . . . The earth shall quake before them; the heavens shall tremble: the sun and the moon shall be dark, and the stars shall withdraw their shining: And it shall come to pass, that whosoever shall call on the name of the Lord shall be delivered: for in mount Zion and in Jerusalem shall be deliverance, as the Lord hath said, and in the remnant whom the Lord shall call."

Joel 3:14,16, " . . . for the day of the Lord is near in the valley of decision. The Lord also shall roar out of Zion . . . and the heavens and the earth shall shake: but the Lord will be the hope of his people, and the strength of the children of Israel."

Isaiah 13:9, Isaiah 65:17, Isaiah 66:22, "Behold, the day of the Lord cometh, . . . to lay the land desolate: and he shall destroy the sinners thereof out of it. For, behold, I create new heavens and a new earth: and the former shall not be remembered, nor come into mind. For as the new heavens and the new earth, which I will make, shall remain before me, saith the Lord, so shall your seed and your name remain."

Zechariah 14:1-3, "Behold, the day of the Lord cometh, and thy spoil shall be divided in the midst of thee. For I will gather all nations against Jerusalem to battle; and the city shall be taken, and the houses rifled, and the women ravished; and half of the city shall go forth into captivity, and the residue of the people shall not be cut off from the city. Then shall the Lord go forth, and fight against those nations, as when he fought in the day of battle."

VERSES THAT TELL OF THE WAR AGAINST ISRAEL BY GOG AND MAGOG, WHEN GOD WILL INTERVENE TO SAVE ISRAEL.

Ezekiel 38:18-23, "And it shall come to pass at the same time when Gog shall come against the land of Israel, saith the Lord God, that my fury shall come up in my face. . . . Surely in that day there shall be a great shaking in the land of Israel: . . . and the mountains shall be thrown down . . . And I will call for a sword against him throughout my mountains, . . . And I will plead against him with pestilence and with blood; . . . Thus will I magnify myself, and sanctify myself; and I will be known in the eyes of many nations, and they shall know that I am the Lord."

Ezekiel 39:4,6,11,13, "Thou shalt fall upon the mountains of Israel, thou, and all thy bands . . . And I will send a fire on Magog, and among them that dwell carelessly in the isles: . . . And . . . I will give unto Gog a place there of graves in Israel, . . . and it shall be to them a renown the day that I shall be glorified, saith the Lord God."

VERSES THAT TELL THE MESSIANIC EXPECTATIONS ARE TO OCCUR IN THE "LATTER DAYS."

Deuteronomy 4:30, ". . . even in the latter days, if thou turn to the Lord thy God . . ."

Isaiah 2:2, "And it shall come to pass in the last days, that the mountain of the Lord's house shall be established in the top of the mountains, and shall be exalted above the hills; and all nations shall flow into it."

Ezekiel 38:8, "After many days thou shalt be visited: in the latter years thou shalt come into the land . . ."

Daniel 2:28, "But there is a God in heaven that revealeth secrets, and maketh known to the king . . . what shall be in the latter days . . ."

Hosea 3:5, "Afterward shall the children of Israel return, and seek the Lord their God, and David their king; and shall fear the Lord and his goodness in the latter days."

IN THIS CHAPTER WE HAVE PRESENTED PASSAGES OF MESSIANIC EXPECTATIONS WHICH ARE CLEARLY UNFULFILLED. THEREFORE, WITH COMPLETE CERTAINTY, JUDAISM KNOWS THE MESSIAH HAS NOT YET COME.

Let's list in review all the Messianic expectations, as presented in this chapter, which are Biblically prophesied and are awaited in Judaism. These expected happenings must arise at the time of the Messiah. The Scriptures tell us this.

In those days, the Messiah is to preside over the land which has the Messianic expectations happening or fulfilled. We have the material prosperity expectations:—the Promised Land—fruitfulness—happiness—well-being—safety and no fear—peace—animals harmless—enemies destroyed—enemies wealth and service. In addition, we have the spiritual expectations:—We know Israel's Redeemer is the Lord God of Israel—His Chosen People will be made great—Israel will be free from sin—Idol worship will end—A new heart will perfect human righteousness in Jews—The Torah will be everlastingly observed—Israel's righteous conduct will be a spiritual light to the nations—Judaism will be the one worldwide religion—God will be exalted, glorified, and sanctified by His Chosen People—The redemption will be forever—God's spirit will be in the midst of Israel—The Temple will be permanently and perfectly rebuilt—Repentance is the means of returning to God for His forgiveness—Finally, we are to have Elijah the prophet, some strange happenings, the Day of Judgment, the war of Gog and Magog, and the designation of "latter days."

To bring your thoughts back to the theme of this book:—You don't find Jesus Christ in any of this!

13

Jesus Was Not the Messiah— Who Was He?

We have shown, in the previous chapters, that Jesus did not preside in the Messianic kingdom and did not achieve what the Messiah is to do on this earth. Consequently, he was not the Hebrew Messiah described in the Bible. Christianity has assigned him a function, but it is not that of Messiah as awaited in Judaism. What Jesus is in Christianity is not of concern to Judaism. For those who interpret Scripture within the traditional meanings, Jesus Christ and the Moshiach are obviously different figures.

Here, we shall inquire into the New Testament's association of Jesus and the Messianic hopes. Jesus the Jew and Messianic glimmerings will be separated from the Messiah-Christ of Christianity! We do this because it is of interest and it is a reasonable question to ask:— Who was Jesus?

First, let's get a little background into Jesus' world. Jesus grew up in the beautiful Galilee, which unfortunately was under an unhappy political situation. There was oppressive Roman occupation. The Jewish people longed to rid their land of the unjust foreign rulers. There was great unhappiness over burdonsome taxes, poverty, and disease. Devoutly religious people fervently prayed for the appearance of the Messiah to take away their worldly tribulations and bring to them the glorious Messianic promises. Pseudo-Messiahs were known to have appeared. The world of Jesus was psychologically prepared for the day of the Messiah's coming, the day of political, material and spiritual redemption. The words, "Repent, for the kingdom of God is at hand," were easily listened to and believed.

Now, we submit a short summary of what Jesus' association with the Messianic expectations may have been. This story is possible from the Jewish viewpoint. True, it cannot be proved. However, it is just as true that it cannot be disproved. It cannot be disproved because it is built on the verses of the New Testament itself.

As we have said, Jesus' world was religiously emotional, waiting for the Messiah to appear. He was caught up in this Messianic passion. Mentally he was able, in some way, to accept himself as God's messenger. In some mystical way, he saw himself as part of the vision of hope. He was a leader and a charismatic preacher and personality. The Jews who followed him throughout the Holy Land were gripped by his zeal and the aura surrounding him. Jesus preached repentance in order to enter into the Messianic kingdom of God. He performed miracles in order to attract multitudes to his Judaic message. He said he was sent by God to do God's will. He said his message was for the Jewish people only. Others would convert to Judaism, and join his people.

He performed miracles and had a successful ministry. God was glorified by the miracles he performed, not Jesus. People who had faith God could cure them were cured by Jesus. But, miracles were not a sign Jesus had any God-like or Messiah-like power, for evil people, Jesus' disciples, and even natural processes could perform miracles also. Of course, the Hebrew Bible abounds with God's miracles performed through human beings. In fact, both Jesus and his disciples did not believe miracles were a sign of his being special. If anything, Jesus tried to hide the fact he performed cures, cast out devils, raised the dead, etc., by asking those he helped not to tell about it to others.

Jesus preached about the necessity for repentance. He advised the multitudes that the kingdom was coming soon, so they should get back to doing what God has asked them to do through the Scriptures. Never did he preach to the multitudes a message that belief in his future death and resurrection would make vicarious atonement for their sins! Read that again. He never preached about his supposed vicarious atonement. His message of repentance was the traditional one of Judaism.

Some may have thought he was a prophet, and he said so himself. The people who followed him were confused about the mysteries of the kingdom as well as about who Jesus was. Very strangely, his own disciples were not made aware of his Messianic claim, until a certain time. Then, when Jesus did say he believed he was the Messiah, he asked for secrecy. Adding to this amazing situation, even after he openly laid claim to being the Messiah his disciples "doubted" him. Even after his disciples supposedly heard God call him His Son, they still doubted him. Indeed, some even doubted after viewing him supposedly risen from the dead. Jesus' disciples lacked faith in him and his power, lacked understanding of his religious teaching, and, most surprisingly, lacked even the slightest comprehension of his alleged role as vicarious atonement savior.

When he was killed by the Romans as a political danger, a presumed king of the Jews, those who believed he was the Messiah must have been aghast. In desperation, with no Biblical basis, but with a clinging to hope, they stretched his activities into a "second coming." Jesus' followers deemed necessary his return to fulfill the function of Messiah, as Biblically indicated. The generation around Jesus waited for his return during their lifetime, as stated in the New Testament. Those after his generation, disappointed that the expectation of his second coming came to naught, advanced his return to an unknown future time. And so, the non-Jewish environment in which Christianity thrived, after the parting from its Judaic roots, accepted the Messiah in terms of an indefinite and far in the future (two thousand years now) return. There is no Hebrew Scriptural foundation for this belief of Christianity.

Jesus' Jewish followers, who believed in repentance and the kingdom of God on earth, and who were attracted to his message by the miracles he performed, left him for good reason. They left him because his mission as Messiah was seen false at his execution. But, they also departed from his following during his lifetime because of their religious commitment to Judaism. First, Jesus taught that the laws of God as given by Moses in the Torah could be circumvented, and this on Jesus' own authority. This was not a denial of the truth and efficacy of the laws, which Paul did. Indeed, we have shown that Jesus believed in the holiness of God's laws. But, Jesus' interpretation of the laws went beyond acceptable Judaism. And Jews left his following because of this. Second, Jesus appeared to blaspheme God. He seemed to take away the glory belonging to God and give himself that glory. As we have shown, he did not call himself God, but his expression of the power of God as related to himself went beyond acceptability. And Jews left his following because of this. For these reasons, and for others Christianity has created, Jews did not then, and cannot now, follow Jesus. Yet, it is history that Christianity has flourished among the Gentiles on Christologic terms.

Let's continue now with the Scriptural verification of the Judaic understanding of the life of Jesus as well as questions as to who he was and what his mission was as presented in the pages of the New Testament.

JESUS WAS SENT TO DO GOD'S WILL.

John 5:30, ". . . I seek not mine own will, but the will of the Father, which hath sent me."

John 7:16-17, ". . . My doctrine is not mine, but his that sent me. If any man do his will, he shall know of the doctrine, whether it be of God, or . . . of myself."

John 8:26-29, ". . . I speak to the world those things which I have heard of him. . . . I do nothing of myself; but as my Father hath taught me, . . . And he that sent me is with me: the Father hath not left me alone; for I do always those things that please him."

John 12:49, "For I have not spoken of myself; but the Father which sent me, he gave me a commandment, what I should say, and what I should speak."

COMMENT: Jesus believed he had a special mission from God and a special relationship with God. He believed he knew God's will in a unique way. His mission was to do God's will, which is expressed in God's doctrine written in the Scriptures and known to Jews. His actions were derived from his feelings about God's desires, not his own. In reading these verses, we readily see, using unbiased judgment, that Jesus' mystical feelings about his special relationship with God did not impinge on God's sovereignty.

JESUS CAME TO JEWS ONLY.

Matthew 15:24, "But he answered and said, I am not sent but unto the lost sheep of the house of Israel."

Mark 1:38, "And he said unto them, Let us go into the next towns, that I may preach there also; for therefore came I forth."

Matthew 10:5-7, "These twelve Jesus sent forth, and commanded them, saying, Go not into the way of the Gentiles, and into any city of the Samaritans enter ye not: But go rather to the lost sheep of the house of Israel. And as ye go, preach, saying, The kingdom of heaven is at hand."

Matthew 7:6, Mark 7:27, "Give not that which is holy unto the dogs, neither cast ye your pearls before swine, . . . Let the children first be filled: for it is not meet to take the children's bread, and to cast it unto the dogs."

COMMENT: Jesus said his mission was for Jews only and told his disciples also to preach only to the people of Israel, Jews alone. His mission was to teach in the towns of Israel. His message was the message of Judaism concerning the coming of the kingdom of God, the Messianic earthly kingdom of God. He preached repentance so that those separated from God would be accepted by God into the Messianic kingdom.

OTHERS WOULD CONVERT TO JUDAISM—BUT NOT AS PAUL BELIEVED TO CHRISTIANITY.

Romans 9:24-26, (Paul) "Even us, . . . not of the Jews only, but also of the Gentiles . . . As he saith, . . . I will call them my people, which were not my people; . . . And it shall come to pass, that in the place where it was said unto them, Ye are not my people; there shall they be called the children of the living God."

COMMENT: Paul took this from *Hosea 1:10*, in which it is quite clear that the people of Israel are meant, not Gentiles. Jews will be returned to God through repentance and become beloved.

John 10:16, "And other sheep I have, which are not of this fold: them also I must bring, and they shall hear my voice; and there shall be one fold, and one shepherd."
COMMENT: Read *Isaiah 56:6,8, "Also the sons of the stranger, that join themselves to the Lord . . . every one that keepeth the sabbath from polluting it, and taketh hold of my covenant; The Lord God which gathered the outcasts of Israel saith, Yet will I gather others to him, beside those that are gathered unto him."* Also read *Ezekiel 34:23-24, "And I will set up one shepherd over them, . . . even my servant David; . . . And I the Lord will be their God . . . "* These two passages are the background. In reading them we see that they depict the gathering of the Gentiles to Judaism through the light of Israel in the time of the Messiah. The Hebrew Bible does not describe the Messiah getting a "second people," but that the Gentiles convert to Judaism. Furthermore, it is God's voice which will be heard and obeyed. The Davidic Messiah will be the leader of the people of Israel, not their God.

At this point, it would be interesting to discover what meaning the performance of miracles had in the ministry of Jesus. In spite of all the anti-Judaism sentiment in the New Testament, it is said repeatedly that the Jewish masses followed Jesus in his preaching activities throughout the Holy Land. How did he attract people? Let's look into the enormous excitement he created when he did miraculous things. Apparently, Jesus performed miracles, in large part, in order to attract the multitudes to his message. The miracles were not a sign of his having God's power, but of functioning for God. It was God's miracles. We know this because it was God who was praised, and God whom the people glorified, and God in whom they had faith. Furthermore, we see in the Bible that miracles are not of themselves a sign of holy power, but can be performed by the ungodly also. We should know, too, that miracles can be accomplished by nature's process itself. Jesus' followers were supposedly capable of performing miracles also. Therefore, this further strengthens the argument against miracles being a sign Jesus had the power of God in a unique manner, as his followers were assuredly not special like Jesus is claimed to be in Christianity. Now, we'll quote Scripture for all of the above.

JESUS WAS FOLLOWED BY THE MULTITUDES BECAUSE OF THE MIRACLES OF HEALING THE SICK, CASTING OUT DEVILS, RAISING THE DEAD, ETC.
Matthew 12:15, Matthew 14:14,36, ". . . and great multitudes fol-

lowed him, and he healed them all; . . . And Jesus went forth, and saw a great multitude, and was moved with compassion toward them, and he healed their sick. And besought him that they might only touch the hem of his garment: and as many as touched were made perfectly whole."

Mark 3:7-8 (Matthew 4:24-25) (Luke 6:17), ". . . and a great multitude from Galilee followed him, and from Judea, And from Jerusalem, . . . when they had heard what great things he did, came unto him."

Luke 5:15, Luke 6:18-19, Luke 7:21, "But so much the more went there a fame abroad of him: and great multitudes came together to hear, and to be healed by him of their infirmaties. And they that were vexed with unclean spirits: and they were healed. And the whole multitude sought to touch him: for there went a virtue out of him, and healed them all. . . . he cured many of their infirmaties and plagues, and of evil spirits; and unto many that were blind he gave sight."

John 6:2, John 12:9,11, "And a great multitude followed him, because they saw his miracles which he did on them that were diseased. Much people of the Jews . . . came not for Jesus' sake only, but that they might see Lazarus also, whom he had raised from the dead. . . . by reason of him (Lazarus) many of the Jews . . . believed on Jesus."

JESUS PERFORMED MIRACLES IN GOD'S NAME TO GLORIFY GOD.

Matthew 15:30-31, "And great multitudes came unto him, . . . and he healed them: Insomuch that the multitude wondered, when they saw the dumb to speak, the maimed to be whole, the lame to walk, and the blind to see: and they glorified the God of Israel."

Mark 2:12, Mark 5:19, "And immediately he arose, took up the bed, and went . . . they were all amazed, and glorified God, . . . Jesus . . . saith unto him, Go home to thy friends, and tell them how great things the Lord hath done for thee . . . "

Luke 9:43, Luke 17:15, Luke 18:43, Luke 19:37, "And they were all amazed at the mighty power of God, . . . And one of them, when he saw that he was healed, turned back, and with a loud voice glorified God, And immediately he received his sight, and followed him, glorifying God: and all the people, when they saw it, gave praise unto God. . . . the whole multitude of the disciples began to rejoice and praise God with a loud voice for all the mighty works that they had seen."

FAITH IN GOD CAUSED HEALING.

Luke 8:48, Luke 17:19, Luke 18:42 (Matthew 9:22) (Mark 5:34) (Mark 10:52), "And he said unto her, Daughter, be of good comfort: thy faith hath made thee whole; . . . And he said unto him, Arise, go thy way: thy faith hath made thee whole. And Jesus said unto him, Receive thy sight: thy faith hath saved thee."

THE UNGODLY ALSO CAN PERFORM MIRACLES.

Matthew 7:22-23 (Luke 13:27), "Many will say to me in that day, Lord, Lord, have we not prophesied in thy name? and in thy name have cast out devils? and in thy name done many wonderful works? And then will I profess unto them, I never knew you: depart form me, ye that work iniquity."

Matthew 24:24, "For there shall arise false Christs, (Messiahs), and false prophets, and shall show great signs and wonders; insomuch that, if it were possible, they shall deceive the very elect."

Acts 8:9-11 (author) "But there was a certain man, called Simon, which beforetime in the same city used sorcery, and bewitched the people of Samaria, giving out that himself was some great one: To whom they all gave heed, from the least to the greatest, saying, This man is the great power of God. And to him they had regard, because of the long time he had bewitched them with sorceries."

MIRACLES CAN BE NATURE'S PROCESS.

John 5:2-4, "Now there is at Jerusalem by the sheep market a pool, which is called in the Hebrew tongue Bethesda, having five porches. In these lay a great multitude of impotent folk, of blind, halt, withered, waiting for the moving of the water. For an angel went down at a certain season into the pool, and troubled the water: whosoever then first after the troubling of the water stepped in was made whole of whatsoever disease he had."

JESUS' FOLLOWERS ALSO CAN PERFORM MIRACLES.

Mark 3:14-15 (Matthew 10:1), "And he ordained twelve, . . . to have power to heal sicknesses, and to cast out devils:"

Mark 16:17-18, "And these signs shall follow them that believe; In my name shall they cast out devils; . . . they shall lay hands on the sick, and they shall recover."

THE HEBREW SCRIPTURES DESCRIBE GOD'S MIRACLES WHICH HUMAN BEINGS PERFORMED.

Exodus 17:5-6, "And the Lord said unto Moses . . . thou shalt smite the rock, and there shall come water out of it, that the people may drink. And Moses did so . . ."

Numbers 11:2, "And the people cried unto Moses; and when Moses prayed unto the Lord, the fire was quenched."

Numbers 21:8-9, "And the Lord said unto Moses, . . . And Moses made a serpent of brass, and put it upon a pole, and it came to pass, that if a serpent had bitten any man, when he beheld the serpent of brass, he lived."

Joshua 10:12-14, "Then spake Joshua to the Lord . . . and he said in the sight of Israel, Sun, stand thou still . . . and thou, Moon . . . And the sun stood still, and the moon stayed . . . And there was no day like that before it or after it, that the Lord hearkened unto the voice of a man . . ."

I Kings 17:1,16, *"And Elijah . . . said . . . As the Lord God of Israel liveth, . . . there shall not be dew nor rain these years, but according to my word. And the barrel of meal wasted not, neither did the cruse of oil fail, according to the word of the Lord, which he spake by Elijah."*

II Kings 1:10, *"And Elijah answered and said to the captain of fifty, If I be a man of God, then let fire come down from heaven, and consume thee and thy fifty. And there came down fire from heaven, and consumed him and his fifty."*

II Kings 2:8, *"And Elijah took his mantle, and wrapped it together, and smote the waters, and they were divided hither and thither, so that they two went over on dry ground."*

II Kings 2:21-22, *"And he (Elisha) went forth unto the spring of the waters, . . . and said, Thus saith the Lord, I have healed these waters; there shall not be from thence any more death or barren land. So the waters were healed unto this day, according to the saying of Elisha which he spake."*

II Kings 5:10,14, *"And Elisha sent a messenger unto him, saying, Go and wash in Jordan seven times, and thy flesh shall come again to thee, and thou shalt be clean. Then went he down, . . . according to the saying of the man of God: and his flesh came again like unto the flesh of a little child, and he was clean."*

HEBREW SCRIPTURE MIRACLES OF REVIVING THE DEAD.

I Kings 17:20-22,24, *"And he (Elijah) cried unto the Lord, and said, O Lord my God, hast thou also brought evil upon the widow with whom I sojourn, by slaying her son? And he stretched himself upon the child three times, and cried unto the Lord, and said, O Lord my God, I pray thee, let this child's soul come into him again. And the Lord heard the voice of Elijah; and the soul of the child came into him again, and he revived. And the woman said to Elijah, Now by this I know that thou art a man of God, and that the word of the Lord in thy mouth is truth."*

II Kings 4:32-35,37, *"And when Elisha was come into the house, behold the child was dead, and laid upon his bed. He went . . . and prayed unto the Lord. . . . and he stretched himself upon the child; and the flesh of the child waxed warm. . . . and the child opened his eyes. Then she went in, and fell at his feet, . . . and took up her son, and went out."*

II Kings 13:20-21, *"And Elisha died, and they buried him. . . . as*

they were burying a man, . . . they cast the man into the sepulchre of Elisha: and when the man was let down, and touched the bones of Elisha, he revived, and stood up on his feet."
COMMENT: Observe that the credit for the miracles performed is given to the Lord God. No one, not Moses, nor Joshua, nor Elijah, nor Elisha, whose miracles are reported, claimed special powers for himself. They merely are said to be men of God through whom God performed the miracles. They functioned for God.

HEBREW SCRIPTURE MIRACLES OF ASCENDING TO HEAVEN.
Genesis 5:24, "And Enoch walked with God: and he was not; for God took him."
II Kings 2:11, ". . . and Elijah went up by a whirlwind into heaven."
COMMENT: This special happening to Elijah can be compared to the account of Jesus allegedly ascending to heaven in *Luke 24:51, ". . . he was parted from them, and carried up into heaven."* Both Enoch and Elijah had special ascents. Our conclusion on this point is that no matter what Christianity makes of Jesus' supposed ascent, he could not be called unique in this occurrence reported in the New Testament.

MIRACLES ARE NOT A SIGN OF JESUS' SPECIAL HEAVENLY NATURE.
Luke 17:5, "And the apostles said unto the Lord (Jesus), Increase our faith."
COMMENT: If the miracles Jesus performed were to prove he had God-like power, as Christianity believes, or that he was the Messiah, which is also their belief, the miracles proved no such thing to his own disciples. This verse relates that all the disciples, whom he taught and who witnessed his miracles, needed more faith in him and his message.
Mark 8:11-12 (Matthew 12:38-39) (Matthew 16:1-4)
(Luke 11:29), "And the Pharisees came forth, and began to question with him, seeking of him a sign from heaven, . . . Why doth this generation seek after a sign? verily I say unto you, There shall no sign be given unto this generation."
COMMENT: Obviously, the people as well as Jesus himself did not believe that the miracles he performed were a sign of his special nature. For a "sign from heaven" is requested and denied, apart from the miracles Jesus had been performing.

JESUS ASKED FOR SECRECY FOR HIS MIRACLES, BUT RECEIVED FAME.
Matthew 9:28-31, ". . . Believe ye that I am able to do this? . . . According to your faith be it unto you. . . . See that no man know it. But they, when they were departed, spread abroad his fame in all that country."

Mark 1:42,44-45 (Matthew 8:2-4) (Luke 5:12-15), "And as soon as he had spoken, immediately the leprosy departed . . . And he saith unto him, See thou say nothing to any man: . . . But he went out, and began to publish it much . . ."

Mark 7:35-36, "And straightway his ears were opened, and the string of his tongue was loosed, and he spake plain. And he charged then that they should tell no man: but the more he charged them, so much the more a great deal they published it;"

COMMENT: Over and over again Jesus admonished the people not to tell others of the miracles he accomplished for them. It is not for us to ascertain why he wanted them to tell no one. In any case, the reports state that he was not obeyed. In addition, he held mass healings in the open which, of course, were not secret. Clearly, the miracles were a great attraction for him and brought multitudes to him.

JESUS PREACHED REPENTANCE FOR THE KINGDOM, NOT VICARIOUS ATONEMENT.

Matthew 6:10,13, (Luke 11:2), "Thy kingdom come, Thy will be done in earth, as it is in heaven. . . . For thine is the kingdom, and the power, and the glory, for ever. Amen."

COMMENT: It is God's earthly kingdom which Jesus preached.

Luke 4:18-19, ". . . he hath anointed me to preach the gospel to the poor; . . . heal the brokenhearted, to preach deliverance to the captives, . . . sight to the blind, . . . liberty (to) them . . . bruised, To preach the acceptable year of the Lord."

COMMENT: Nothing is said about belief in Jesus' dying for mankind's sins in order to make vicarious atonement. The word "gospel" here is associated with Judaism's teachings. And it is Judaism he taught.

Luke 8:1 (Luke 10:9), ". . . he went throughout every city and village, preaching and showing the glad tidings of the kingdom of God . . ."

Mark 1:14 (Matthew 4:23) (Matthew 9:35) (Matthew 10:7), ". . . preaching the gospel of the kingdom of God."

Luke 4:43 (Luke 9:2,11) (Luke 12:31), ". . . I must preach the kingdom of God to other cities also: for therefore am I sent."

COMMENT: His mission was to preach the good news, the glad tidings, the gospel of the kingdom of God. These terms, which Christianity has taken for its meaning of Christology, actually refer to Jesus' preaching of the earthly kingdom of God, the Messianic kingdom. There is not one word said about his message being vicarious atonement, because it was not.

Mark 1:15, Mark 6:12, ". . . the kingdom of God is at hand: repent ye, and believe the gospel. And they went out, and preached that men should repent."

Luke 5:32 (Matthew 9:13) (Mark 2:17), "I came not to call the righteous, but sinners to repentance."

Matthew 4:17, Matthew 6:33, Matthew 10:7, "From that time Jesus began to preach, and to say, Repent: for the kingdom of heaven is at hand. But seek ye first the kingdom of God, and his righteousness; . . . And as ye go, preach, saying, The kingdom of heaven is at hand."

COMMENT: What was Jesus' message? It was that Jews should repent, for the Messianic kingdom was coming soon and return to God was necessary for acceptance into the kingdom. This message is totally within the framework of Judaism as revealed in the Holy Bible. Jesus did not preach Christology. As surprising as this fact may be, Jesus' preaching was of Judaism, as Jews interpret the Jewish religion.

JESUS CONSIDERED HIMSELF A PROPHET AS DID THE MULTITUDES.

Mark 6:4 (Matthew 13:57) (Luke 4:24) (John 4:44), "But Jesus said unto them, A prophet is not without honor, but in his own country, and among his own kin, and in his own house."

Matthew 21:11,46, "And the multitude said, This is Jesus the prophet of Nazareth of Galilee. . . . they feared the multitude, because they took him for a prophet."

Luke 7:16, Luke 13:32-33, Luke 24:19, ". . . they glorified God, saying, That a great prophet is risen among us; And he said unto them, . . . for it cannot be that a prophet perish out of Jerusalem. . . . Jesus of Nazareth, which was a prophet mighty in deed and word before God and all the people:"

John 6:14, John 7:40, ". . . when they had seen the miracle that Jesus did, said, This is of a truth that prophet that should come into the world. Many of the people . . . said, Of a truth this is the Prophet. . . ."

COMMENT: The above passages state that Jesus, as well as his followers, considered that he was in the category of a prophet. Ask this:—Can you envision the person who considers himself sent by God to be the Messiah calling himself merely a prophet? Although both are holy, they are worlds apart in function. And as for God the Son of the Trinity calling himself a prophet—well, you contemplate it.

Acts 3:22 (Acts 7:37) (RE: Deuteronomy 18:15,18), "For Moses truly said unto the fathers, A prophet shall the Lord your God raise up unto you of your brethren, like unto me; him shall ye hear in all things whatsoever he shall say unto you."

COMMENT: So Jesus is supposed to be the special prophet Moses asserted would arise for the people. But is he? First, what are the attributes of a prophet? Jesus, like the prophets, chastised the Hebrew people for not doing God's will, for turning from God's laws. But, the prophets justified their pronouncements on God's Torah, never on their own authority. They always gave to God His supremacy and to God's laws their immutability. Jesus, however, did not follow this tradition of the prophets. His justification seemed to be on his own authority. Also, see here that the special prophet announced by Moses would be "like" Moses, not greater, but just like him. Certainly, this is not Christianity's view of Jesus Christ. Now let's present some other Hebrew Bible verses concerning prophets.

Deuteronomy 18:20, "But the prophet, which shall presume to speak a word in my name, which I have not commanded him to speak . . . even that prophet shall die."

Deuteronomy 13:5, "And that prophet, . . . shall be put to death; because he hath spoken to turn you away from the Lord your God, . . . to thrust thee out of the way which the Lord thy God commanded thee to walk in . . ."

Deuteronomy 18:22, "When a prophet speaketh in the name of the Lord, if the thing follow not, nor come to pass, that is the thing which the Lord hath not spoken . . ."

COMMENT: Jesus? The Law of Moses? The second coming?

THERE WAS GENERAL CONFUSION ABOUT WHO JESUS WAS.

Matthew 13:10-11,13 (Mark 4:11-12) (Luke 8:10), "And the disciples came, and said unto him, Why speakest thou unto them in parables? He answered and said unto them, Because it is given unto you to know the mysteries of the kingdom of heaven, but to them it is not given. . . . they seeing see not; and hearing they hear not, neither do they understand."

Matthew 16:13-16 (Mark 8:27-29) (Luke 9:18-20)

(Mark 6:14-15) (Luke 9:7-8), ". . . Whom do men say that I the Son of man am? And they said, Some say that thou art John the Baptist: some, Elijah; and others, Jeremiah, or one of the prophets. . . . But whom say ye that I am? And Simon Peter answered and said, Thou art the Christ (Messiah), the Son of the living God."

COMMENT: There was confusion and difference of opinion among the people as to who Jesus was. Actually, Jesus said he spoke in parables in order to leave the people bewildered and lacking knowledge of the mysteries of the kingdom. He presumably deliberately kept them in confusion. On the other hand, Jesus said he gave his disciples knowledge of the Messianic kingdom. They should have known he was the Messiah, if he believed he was. This important information would have been part of the mysteries of the kingdom. Yet, they did not know this supposed fact. Peter had to venture an opinion when asked by Jesus who he thought Jesus was. If Jesus had divulged that he was the Messiah, Peter would not have had to be asked to give an opinion.

Clearly, Christianity has a choice here. Either Jesus lied, and did not give his disciples the mysteries of the kingdom, as he said he did, or Jesus did not believe himself to be the Messiah. If you read what Jesus said in *Matthew 16:17*, "*. . . (my Father) hath . . . revealed it (that Jesus is the Christ) unto thee (Peter),*" the conclusion which must be drawn is that Jesus did not include his being the Messiah in his revelation of the secrets of the kingdom. The conundrum is Christianity's.

THERE WERE DIFFERENT OPINIONS ABOUT WHO JESUS WAS, INCLUDING THE MESSIAH.

John 3:2, "*. . . Rabbi, we know that thou art a teacher come from God: for no man can do these miracles that thou doest, except God be with him.*"

COMMENT: Here Jesus is seen as a holy teacher, addressed as "Rabbi." The miracles he performed are seen as evidence of his being close to God.

John 6:68-69, "*Then Simon Peter answered him, . . . And we believe and are sure that thou art that Christ, the Son of the living God.*"

COMMENT: Yet, right after this assurance of belief comes the revelation that Judas Iscariot, one of the disciples, will betray Jesus. There is evidently something missing in the sureness of the disciples' belief.

John 7:41, "*Others said, This is the Christ. . . .*"

COMMENT: We read before that many said he was a prophet. Here, others said he was the Messiah. Opinions did vary.

Mark 11:9-10 (Matthew 21:9) (Luke 19:37-38), "*And they . . . cried, saying, Hosanna; Blessed is he that cometh in the name of the Lord: Blessed be the kingdom of our father David, that cometh in the name of the Lord . . .*"

COMMENT: Some people ventured to think Jesus was the Messiah. However, we have shown that others believed him to be John the Baptist, Elijah, Jeremiah, a prophet, a teacher-rabbi, a miracle worker of God, or even a mad man.

John 1:49, "*. . . Rabbi, thou art the Son of God: thou art the King of Israel.*"

COMMENT: A man here expressed his belief that Jesus was the expected Messiah because of the great things he did. This, of course, was one of the differing opinions about Jesus before the expectation of his Messianic fulfillment collapsed when he was executed by the Romans.

JESUS SEEMED TO BELIEVE HE WAS THE MESSIAH.

Matthew 18:11 (Luke 19:10), "*For the Son of man is come to save that which was lost.*"

John 4:25-26, "*The woman saith unto him, I know that Messiah cometh . . . Jesus saith unto her, I that speak unto thee am he.*"

Matthew 26:63-64, ". . . tell us whether thou be the Christ, the Son of God. Jesus saith unto him, Thou hast said . . ."

John 18:37, ". . . Thou sayest that I am a king. To this end was I born, and for this cause came I into the world . . ."

Luke 7:20,22 (Matthew 11:2-4), ". . . they said, John Baptist hath sent us unto thee, saying, Art thou he that should come? or look we for another? Then Jesus answering said unto them, Go your way, and tell John what things ye have seen and heard . . ."

COMMENT: Jesus, in these passages, seems to avow that he believed he was the Messiah of the Jewish people. In the usage of the term "Son of man" the Messiah could be interpreted, even though in many other passages this term simply means "man." What can be made of this? It is not unimaginable that a man caught up in the extreme Messianism of the times could go one step further and believe he was the man with the Messianic mission from God. He, it seems, had a strong spiritual relationship with God. Others have thought themselves to be the Messiah, why not Jesus? He was unique, however, in that a new religion was built around him as Messiah. His assertion (or perhaps hope) of being the Messiah, nevertheless, was just as invalid as other false Messiahs' claims.

JESUS INFERRED HE WAS NOT THE MESSIAH.

Matthew 20:28, ". . . the Son of man came not to be ministered unto, but to minister . . ."

COMMENT: Remember that it is written that the Messiah is to be ministered unto. For example, read *Psalm 72:11, "Yea, all kings shall fall down before him: all nations shall serve him."* Jesus, therefore, clearly denied having the Messiah's role.

JESUS ASKED SECRECY ABOUT HIS ALLEGED MESSIANIC ROLE.

Matthew 17:5,9 (Mark 9:7,9) (Luke 9:35-36), ". . . a voice out of the cloud, which said, This is my beloved Son, in whom I am well pleased; hear ye him. . . . Jesus charged them, saying, Tell the vision to no man . . ."

Mark 8:29-30 (Matthew 16:15-16,20) (Luke 9:20-21), "And he saith unto them, But whom say ye that I am? . . . the Christ, And he charged them that they should tell no man of him."

Luke 4:41, Mark 3:11-12 (Mark 1:34), "And devils also came out of many, crying out, and saying, Thou art Christ the Son of God. And he rebuking them suffered them not to speak for they knew that he was Christ. And unclean spirits, when they saw him, fell down before him, and cried, saying, Thou art the Son of God. And he straightway charged them that they should not make him known."

Matthew 21:23,27 (Mark 11:28,33) (Luke 20:2,8), ". . . By what authority doest thou these things? and who gave thee this authority?

. . . And he said unto them, Neither tell I you by what authority I do these things."

COMMENT: In these verses, we have acknowledgement together with secrecy of Jesus being Christ. Just as we are at a loss to explain why Jesus said he was the Messiah, when his claim lacked Biblical foundation, we are at a loss to explain why he wished to keep this supposed identity a secret. However, we need not contemplate these puzzles as they belong to Christianity, not Judaism.

We feel there is something we should say concerning this, however. Jesus expressed belief he was a prophet at times. At other times he said he was the Messiah. People were confused as to his identity, including his disciples. It's possible that he meant to have confusion. When he said he was the Messiah, he asked for secrecy. This is our conjecture:—Jesus may have had a pounding beat within him, telling him that he was drumming to the Messiah's tune. He may have felt impending Messianic achievement. But, events of Messianic expectations were lacking. Any announcement by Jesus that he was the Messiah would have been received in disbelief, to say the very least. When he said he was the Messiah, a superlative anticipation must have taken hold of hearts, but the situation called for secrecy in order to prevent general incredulous reaction. In addition to this, secrecy was called for in order to prevent political problems. His execution by the Romans as "king of the Jews (Messiah)" proves this. Therefore, by announcing he was the Messiah, he not only was in error, but he put himself in jeopardy. Word of his claim labeled him a danger to the government, an insurrectionist. Of course, the true Messiah, when he arrives, will have no such problems and will not need to keep his identity a secret.

JESUS' DISCIPLES DID NOT HAVE FAITH AND DID NOT UNDERSTAND.

Mark 7:18 (Matthew 15:17), ". . . Are ye so without understanding also? Do ye not perceive, that whatsoever thing from without entereth into a man, it cannot defile him;"

Matthew 16:8-9, ". . . O ye of little faith, why reason ye among yourselves, because ye have brought no bread? Do ye not yet understand, neither remember the five loaves of the five thousand, and how many baskets ye took up?"

Matthew 14:31, "(to Peter)... Jesus stretched forth his hand, and caught him... O thou of little faith, wherefore didst thou doubt?"

Matthew 17:19-20, "Then came the disciples to Jesus apart, and said, Why could not we cast him out? And Jesus said unto them, Because of your unbelief . . ."

Matthew 21:21 (Luke 17:6), "(to disciples)... If ye have faith, and doubt not, ye shall not only do this which is done to the fig tree..."

Mark 4:39-40 (Matthew 8:25-26) (Luke 8:24-25), "And he . . . said unto the sea, Peace, be still. . . . And the wind ceased, . . . And he said unto them, Why are ye so fearful? how is it that ye have no faith?"

COMMENT: Proximity to Jesus, being those in his chosen group, and being taught by him still left the disciples with doubts about Jesus' power, ignorance of his claimed mission, and general lack of faith.

Mark 8:31-33, Mark 9:31-32 (Matthew 16:21-23) (Matthew 17:22-23) (Luke 9:44-45), "And he began to teach them, that the Son of man must suffer many things, . . . and be killed, and after three days rise again. And Peter . . . began to rebuke him. . . . But . . . he rebuked Peter, saying, . . . thou savorest not the things that be of God, . . . For he taught his disciples, and said unto them, The Son of man is delivered into the hands of men, and they shall kill him: and after that he is killed, he shall rise the third day. But they understood not that saying, and were afraid to ask him."

COMMENT: The above should be read very carefully. The supposed vicarious atonement of the Messiah-Christ is newly taught to the disciples by Jesus. This occurred after the disciples had been with Jesus for quite a while. The Hebrew Messiah they expect is not of this teaching, and they do not comprehend Jesus' description of what is supposed to happen to him. We know this because Jesus is repremanded by Peter who says Jesus should not say he will die. Peter was shocked to be told that Jesus, who he believed was the Messiah and, therefore, should have success and world dominion, instead was to die. Further on, we find that all the disciples are confounded by this new teaching. And well they should have been, for Messianic vicarious atonement has no place in Hebraic Biblical revelation.

John 21:12, ". . . And none of the disciples durst ask him, Who art thou? knowing it was the Lord."

COMMENT: This is a perfect example of non-reasoning within a verse. Why would they "not dare to ask him" unless there was doubt involved. And then it says "knowing it was" which is unbefittingly planted on the first part. Yes, doubt existed even at seeing Jesus after his alleged resurrection.

Matthew 28:16-17, "Then the eleven disciples went away into Galilee, into a mountain where Jesus had appointed them. And when they saw him, they worshipped him: but some doubted."

COMMENT: You have just read another extraordinary passage. At the end of Matthew's writings, some of Jesus' disciples are said to doubt. They saw Jesus after his supposed rising from the dead and did not believe in it. They doubted the resurrection in the same way they could not understand when Jesus told them that he would be killed and rise on the third day. Remember, Jesus said the disciples were given the mysteries of the kingdom. We are left wondering what Jesus' revelations included, if the disciples knew nothing about Christologics. It appears that Jesus' kingdom of God mysteries were not those of Christianity. Even assuming that only then, at the end, were they allowed to know the mysteries, Christianity still has explanation difficulties. For, if they were given the mysteries, why didn't they understand the mysteries given to them?

DISCIPLES EXPECTED A SECOND COMING OF JESUS SO THAT THE MESSIANIC HOPES WOULD BE FULFILLED.

Matthew 24:3, ". . . the disciples . . . saying, Tell us, when shall these things be? and what shall be the sign of thy coming, and of the end of the world?"

Acts 1:6-7, ". . . they asked of him, saying, Lord, wilt thou at this time restore again the kingdom to Israel? And he said unto them, It is not for you to know the times or the seasons, which the Father hath put in his own power."

Acts 3:20-21, "And he shall send Jesus Christ, . . . Whom the heaven must receive until the times of restitution of all things, which God hath spoken by the mouth of all his holy prophets . . ."

COMMENT: From these verses, we grasp the fact that Jesus had not performed as his disciples anticipated he should in the role of the Messiah. Biblical revelation remained unfulfilled. As Jews, the disciples knew that the Messiah must be in an earthly kingdom of God. The Christologics of death—resurrection—vicarious atonement—did not correspond to or satisfy the Messianic expectations. Therefore, in desperation, they reflected on, and took needed comfort from, Jesus returning to earth to complete what must be done.

EXPECTATIONS OF A SECOND COMING ARE UNFULFILLED.

Matthew 16:28 (Mark 9:1) (Luke 9:27), "Verily I say unto you, There be some standing here, which shall not taste of death, till they see the Son of man coming in his kingdom (kingdom of God with power)."

Luke 21:31-32 (Matthew 24:33-34) (Mark 13:29-30), "So likewise ye, when ye see these things come to pass, know ye that the kingdom of God is nigh at hand. Verily I say unto you, This generation shall not pass away, till all be fulfilled (done)."

Matthew 10:23, ". . . for verily I say unto you, Ye shall not have gone over the cities of Israel, till the Son of man be come."

Luke 12:37,40 (Matthew 24:44), "Blessed are those servants, whom the lord when he cometh shall find watching: . . . Be ye therefore ready also: for the Son of man cometh at an hour when ye think not."

Luke 19:11, ". . . they thought that the kingdom of God should immediately appear."

Acts 1:4, "And, being assembled together with them, commanded

*them that they should not depart from Jerusalem, but wait for the
promise of the Father, which, saith he, ye have heard of me."*
   *Romans 16:20, "And the God of peace shall bruise Satan under
your feet shortly. . . ."*
   *I Corinthians 7:29, "But this I say, brethren, the time is short: it
remaineth, that both they that have wives be as though they had
none . . ."*
   *I Thessalonians 4:15, "For this we say unto you by the word of the
Lord, that we which are alive and remain unto the coming of the
Lord . . ."*
   *Hebrews 1:2, Hebrews 10:37, "(God) Hath in these last days spo-
ken unto us by his Son, . . . For yet a little while, and he that shall
come will come, and will not tarry."*
   *James 5:8, "Be ye also patient; stablish your hearts: for the com-
ing of the Lord draweth nigh."*
   *I Peter 4:7,17, "But the end of all things is at hand: be ye there-
fore sober, and watch unto prayer. For the time is come that judgment
must begin . . ."*
   *I John 2:18, "Little children, it is the last time: . . . even now are
there many antichrists; whereby we know that it is the last time."*
   *Revelation 22:(7)12,20, "And, behold, I come quickly; and my
reward is with me, to give every man according as his work shall be.
He which testifieth these things saith, Surely I come quickly. . . ."*
COMMENT: These quotations say it clearly. The second coming was
at hand, coming quickly, within the lifetime of the generation standing
then. Despite *II Peter 3:8, ". . . one day is with the Lord as a thousand years . . ."* the promise was to come within the lifetime of the
living generation at that time, two thousand years ago. This was Jesus'
promise and the understanding and belief of the early followers of
Jesus. But, it did not occur as promised in the New Testament, did it?
The promise, however, did create a spark in the early Church which
must have helped make it dynamic and successful.

SOME JEWS LEFT JESUS AT HIS DEATH—SOME DID NOT.
   Faithful Jews returned to mainstream Judaism after the hopes of
Jesus being the Messiah collapsed when he was put to death by the
Romans. These Jews who returned, it is interesting to observe, were
the only authentic "Jews for Jesus" who ever lived. For they were
truly observant Jews who hoped that Jesus was the Messiah as prophesied in the Hebrew Bible. When they found they were mistaken, they
naturally returned to basic Judaism, waiting for the Messiah. Other
Jews continued in the Pauline-Christologic belief and were the first
converts to the new religion of Christianity. For these converts, a new
interpretation of Jesus' life took precedence over traditional Biblical

Messianic expectations. Hebrew Messianism became Christologic, with expectations delayed, distorted, and demoted in importance.

SOME JEWS LEFT JESUS BECAUSE HE BLASPHEMED AND LED AWAY FROM GOD.

John 5:16,18, "And therefore did the Jews persecute Jesus, and saught to slay him, because he had done these things on the sabbath day. . . . also . . . making himself equal with God."

John 6:54,60,66, "Whoso eateth my flesh, and drinketh my blood, hath eternal life; and I will raise him up at the last day. Many therefore of his disciples, when they had heard this, said, This is an hard saying; who can hear it? From that time many of his disciples went back, and walked no more with him."

John 7:12, "And there was much murmuring among the people concerning him: for some said, He is a good man: others said, Nay; but he deceiveth the people."

John 8:58-59, "Jesus said unto them, . . . Before Abraham was, I am. Then took they up stones to cast at him . . ."

John 9:16, ". . . This man is not of God, because he keepeth not the sabbath day. Others said, How can a man that is a sinner do such miracles? And there was a division among them."

John 10:30-31,33, "I and my Father are one. Then the Jews took up stones again to stone him. The Jews answered him, saying, For a good work we stone thee not; but for blasphemy; and because that thou, being a man, makest thyself God."

John 10:18-20, ". . . I have power to lay it (my life) down, and I have power to take it again. . . . There was a division therefore again among the Jews for these sayings. And many of them said, He hath a devil, and is mad; why hear ye him?"

Luke 5:21 (Matthew 9:3) (Mark 2:6-7), "And the scribes and the Pharisees began to reason, saying, Who is this which speaketh blasphemies? Who can forgive sins, but God alone?"

COMMENT: His followers believed Jesus and his teaching of repentance for the kingdom of God. Repentance, turning back to God, was part of their Jewish heritage. The Scriptures taught them of the earthly kingdom of God and the Day of the Lord, Judgment Day. Jesus, through his miracles, attracted Jews and awakened them to the righteousness required by God for entrance into the kingdom and the immediacy of it! All this his followers could and did accept, as believing Jews.

However, when his teaching turned to breaking the laws of the Torah, even with his religious interpretation of such breaking, the devout Jewish people could follow him no more. He seemed to be teaching the circumventing of the revealed word of God, the law of

Moses, with flimsy reasoning. No matter how many his acts of kindness or his beautiful rabbinical sermons, Jesus was leading the people of Israel away from God's word. He was seen as unacceptably interpreting laws of God. Jews put this above their desire for miracles to cure them and they departed his following.

Furthermore, they left him because he was a blasphemer in their sight. Jesus said he had power that only God possesses. Let it be understood that the Jewish people were happy when they believed he might be the Messiah. This claim was not objectionable. In fact, it offered great hope. What was unacceptable was his claim of having power and authority that only God possesses. Nothing in the Scriptures would allow for such an interpretation of the Messiah's role. The Moshiach was prophesied as a servant of God, not as having the power and authority of God! It may be strange to put it this way, but it's probable that Jeshua ben Joseph would have been among those religious Jews who left Jesus Christ because of blasphemy. This picture is hard to focus, but it is offered as an interesting mind-juggling contemplation.

Now, what about Jesus' seeming switch to Christologics at the end of his ministry? It was a switch, because none of his disciples knew anything about the concept previously and even doubted it after they saw him supposedly resurrected. Jesus' message to them was devoid of Christologics throughout their whole association together, until a certain time at the end, and the Jewish disciples were unable to comprehend it as it was not Biblically based! Let's just say that this is part of Christianity's share of Jesus in the New Testament. It is all theirs and need not be analyzed by Judaism. The Christology is their portion of God's workings in this world. We have the Jewish Jesus with Judaism's God, laws, and salvation.

We have shown you, in this chapter, that Jesus' message was Judaism's and that the miracles he performed were not indicative of any God-like or Messiah-like stature. He did have a special closeness with God. He did God's will in urging Jews to repent, return to God's requirements of us, and be ready for the coming kingdom. His miracles drew people to him and his Judaic message. Hopes that he was the Hebrew Messiah terminated at his death by Roman execution. Christianity takes it from there.

Needless to say, the New Testament is Christianity's Holy Book and is filled with passages of Christologic import:—Jesus Christ's death is the vicarious atonement—Belief in his resurrection is the Christian hope for salvation—Eternal life is offered only through belief in Jesus as Savior—Jesus has God's power and glory. This is incompatable not only with Judaism, but with contradictory passages in the self-same New Testament. In this book, we have presented Judaic layers from the New Testament which conflict with Christologic layers and have given a reverse proof-text understanding of Jesus, returning him to his Judaism! Christianity cannot efface the Judaic Jesus, because he is from the New Testament's written word. They can present their "Christ," but they cannot deny their Jeshua ben Joseph:—He taught Jewish ethics—He believed the law of Moses should be observed eternally—His God is Judaism's God of unity, not Trinity—Personal salvation is obtained through Judaism—Judaism presents God and His Chosen People and the Hebrew Messiah of God's earthly kingdom. When we ask who Jesus was, this is the Jewish advocate's reply.

14

Missionaries' Alleged Proof-Texts

Finally, we come to the so-called proof-texts, which are used by Christian missionaries to the Jews in order to validate Jesus being the Hebrew Messiah. Judaism has no fear of these proof-texts, because they are all erroneous as proofs for Christianity! They are all completely spurious as evidence for their ideas. In this section of our book, we shall analyze, one by one, the primary Hebrew Bible verses utilized by missionaries to point to Jesus. You will learn how they have been misused. Previously, you were shown that Jesus did not function as the Messiah and that the Messianic expectations remain unfulfilled. We have illuminated Hebraic Messianism based on the Scriptures and demonstrated that Jesus' ministry was devoid of any Messianic achievement. And now we complete our study with a survey of the fallacy of Christianity when they claim proof-texts as pointers to their Christ. We explain each of these passages within traditional Judaism.

We have done all of this for Jews who have somehow lost our road, Jews who have need for enlightenment. The person of Jewish heritage who has converted or is contemplating conversion to Christianity will find apostasy a blunder of major proportions and eternal significance!

Both Judaism and Christianity revere the same Hebrew Bible, the "Old Testament" of the Christians, as God's revealed word. The same Bible basically belongs to both mother and daughter religions. However, the verses are as from different books when interpreted by a Jew or a Christian!

Not only was the New Testament added to the "Old Testament" by Christianity, but passages of Judaism's Bible are given meanings which presumably would make them foreshadow the coming of Jesus

Christ! Hebrew Scripture is interpreted as prophetic announcements of events in the New Testament. Conversely, events are written in the New Testament with the intention of showing fulfillment of passages in the Hebrew Bible. Truly natural events are found alongside contrived ones as well as events of doubtful authenticity. They are mixed in the New Testament to achieve the desired results of the emerging Church. Without challenging authenticity, we expose errors involved in the usage of proof-texts. When authenticity is at issue, we present powerful reasons for doubt, reasons based on the verses of the New Testament itself.

Of course, other Hebrew Bible verses, those which give evidence of the eternal nature of Judaism, are ignored or overthrown, using Christianity's viewpoint. Judaism's interpretation of passages is based on meaningfulness in context of God as known and continually revealed in Scripture! Verses are read and understood with connected relevance. God's word is seen as significant, purposeful, and unchangeable. Every word, every detail, every passage is comprehended and expounded within Judaism, and Judaism is certain that the Hebrew Bible has nothing at all to say about Jesus Christ!

If Christianity had nothing to do with Judaism's Bible, we would have nothing to say about Christianity's errors or truths. It simply would be another religion, which we would respect for approaching God. But, when Christianity grew from Jewish roots, it took along our Bible. It misrepresented the Holy Scriptures' meaning, tore down Judaism's legitimacy, and presented itself as the "New Israel." Therefore, we have a need, even an obligation to God and to ourselves, to explain the errors of Christianity when it uses the Hebrew Bible to lay forth its claims. Christology of the New Testament is not our concern. Christology belongs to and is for Christians in their approach to God. However, what is Judaism's concern is Christianity's transformation of the Hebrew Messiah into the Christ of Christianity and its use of Biblical verses as proof-texts to that end!

PROOF-TEXTS ARE FAULTED IN DIFFERENT WAYS.

1—OUT OF CONTEXT—They are taken out of context, so that the authentic, original meaning is lost and isolated ways of interpreting them emerge which are devoid of any in-place connection.

2—TWISTED MEANING—They are read into and misunderstood, so that a new meaning results instead of the meaning which is appropriate for the situation as written.

3—FORCED CONNECTION—They are unnaturally described and contrived to point to Jesus.

4—MISTRANSLATIONS—They are translated wrong.

5—MISQUOTATIONS—They are quoted wrong.

6—SO THAT IT BE FULFILLED—They are connected to created events or "created writings" of such events in the New Testament which explicitely state that the events were made to occur "so that it be fulfilled."

Proof-texts can be understood as such only be someone who knows about Christianity. They are not self-explanatory in relation to Christianity, but must be interpreted from their viewpoint. Jews, both before and after the New Testament, see these verses as only within Judaism. Moreover, many Christian scholars admit that they doubt the validity of many of the proof-texts. The Hebrew Scriptures are clear and comprehensible in Judaic terms to Jews who spend their lives reading and studying them.

We ask this:—Why would the alleged references to the Christian Christ be so masked and hidden to the very people for whom they were supposedly meant? To reply, "because of the Jewish people's blindness," would be expected only from those who have been taught this calumny and are themselves lacking in open-mindedness. Assuredly, God would have made his teaching clear in the Hebrew Scriptures concerning the coming of a new kind of salvation through vicarious atonement, if this were the truth. Yet, He did not say one word about this. Nothing is found out of joint, pointing to a Christologic future. The God of Israel has not disclosed any such thing, nor has He hidden any such thing among His holy words. We know because all Holy Scripture is understood within Judaism, fully understood, within traditional Judaism.

Jews are able to comprehend Christianity's claims. These claims are not a mystery to us. What is a mystery is their use of proof-text explanations which are wrong. Their story is theirs, right or wrong. But, their proof-texts, the explanations they use basing their religion on Hebrew Bible revelation, exposes their vulnerability and their error.

Our survey is comprehensive and fully developed. It proves that Judaism's Holy Scriptures speak only of God as Judaism knows God, and the Messiah, as Judaism knows the Messiah. Keep in mind that our rebuttals are far more acceptable than Christianity's distortions, for we do not make God's word of naught. His words are eternally true in Judaism, His admonitions, His promises, His attachments, and His purposes. You will find our rebuttals substantial and convincing, for they are based on original insider understanding. And our understanding makes the holy word of God fit in place properly, naturally, and reasonably.

Besides our understanding as the people of the Book, we have been given the authority to interpret the Book by God Himself. This comes from *Deuteronomy 17:9-10, "And thou shalt come unto the . . . judge (of Israel) . . . and enquire; . . . and thou shalt observe and do according to all that they inform thee:"* Therefore, the Hebrew Bible and its so-called proof-texts are under the jurisdiction of Jewish judges alone, as designated by God. We are ready now to proceed with the inquiry and rebuttal. Let's go.

15

Proof Texts—Trinity

GOD IS A TRINITY.

Deuteronomy 6:4, "Hear, O Israel: The Lord our God is one Lord:"

COMMENT: Astonishing as it may be to Jews or others, instead of finding God's unity proclaimed here, Christianity finds a proof-text for the Trinity. They say the names for God are used three times and are called one. Therefore, the Trinity is presented in the Shema prayer of Judaism, it is alleged.

REBUTTAL: This, doubtless, is one of the prime examples of forced connection they use. But, let's take it apart logically. First, only two names are given, not three, the "Lord" being repeated. Second, if the number of names of God given in a sentence is indicative of His multiple nature, then God changes from unity, to duality, to trinity, to quadruple essence, etc., throughout the Bible. For example in *Deuteronomy 7:6, "For thou art an holy people unto the Lord thy God . . ."* God would be a duality. While he would be quadruple in *Deuteronomy 7:9, "Know therefore that the Lord thy God, he is God, the faithful God . . ."* It is understood in Judaism that the various terms which are used alluding to God are descriptions of His aspects, not divisions of His essence. Christianity really understands this also, otherwise they would be adding another person to their concept of God when they say, "God is 'love'."

Another pertinent observation is that the correct translation from the Hebrew is, "Hear, O Israel, the Lord is our God, the Lord is One." This itself destroys the proof-text as verification of the Trinity, for it refers to God four times. And one last remark concerning "echad," which is the Hebrew word for "one" here. "Echad" is an equivalent to "alone," not a composite of joined elements. We believe that devout Jews can rest easily when they recite the Shema prayer, daily and on their dying lips, with the knowledge they are affirming God's holy unity as a one-in-one and only God.

GOD IS A PLURALITY.

Genesis 1:1,26, "In the beginning God (Elohim) created the heaven and the earth. And God said, Let us make man in our image, after our likeness: . . ."

COMMENT: Both these verses are used to allude to God being a plurality.

REBUTTAL: These verses, in which God is referred to in the plural, seemingly contradict His oneness and singularity. It must be explained, so that the Trinity is not legitimized due to grammatical expression and misunderstanding of the usage of the plural form. First, you must admit that a rare usage of the plural is a poor way for the Bible to teach the supposed reality of a triune God. And we shall show it actually does not.

The Hebrew word "elohim" is the plural of "eloha" meaning majesty, power, authority, or grandure. It is not used exclusively for God, although it is one of His frequent appellations. It has been used to signify angels and judges in authority. Refer to *Judges 13:21-22, "But the angel of the Lord did no more appear to Manoah . . . And Manoah said, . . . We shall surely die, because we have seen God (elohim)."* Here the plural word refers to a singular angel. Also read *Exodus 22:9, ". . . the cause of both parties shall come before the judges (elohim): . . ."* Elohim clearly signifies judges here.

Another usage of "elohim" which, in addition to being about an entity other than God, gives insignificance to the plural word form is found in *I Samuel 28:13-14, ". . . And the woman said unto Saul, I saw gods (elohim) ascending (plural verb) out of the earth. And he said unto her, What form is he of? And she said, An old man cometh up . . ."* In the passage, important entities (plural) is followed by a plural verb usage, yet the "elohim" refers to a singular old man. This indicates that the plural "elohim" can be used for a singular concept. Furthermore, in *Exodus 7:1,* we read that Moses is an "elohim." Read, *"And the Lord said unto Moses, See, I have made thee a god (elohim) to Pharaoh: . . ."* Again we see the confirmation that the plural "elohim" can refer to a singular entity. And so it does in our subject verse from Genesis.

Let's get to the interesting place where God uses both terms alternately about other powers. We read in *Isaiah 44:6, ". . . and beside me there is no God (Elohim),"* which is followed by *Isaiah 44:8,*

"... *Is there a God (Eloha) beside me?* ..." The significance is that
God has no rival in plural or singular form. God says He is the only
God there is. There is no multiplicity of gods, either dividing His
essence or challenging His sole, unique, alone nature. What is given
for us to know is that only God is God. This is the real issue at hand.
And no Son or Holy Ghost is to be found.

There are very many occurrences of the singular "Eloha" in the
Hebrew Bible referring to God. The usage is presented often, as found
in *Deuteronomy 32:15*, "... *then he forsook God (Eloha) which made
him* ..." and in *Psalm 50:22*, "... *ye that forget God (Eloha)* ..."
That this is so is sufficient refutation of the plural form being indicative of the Trinity. Surely, if God were a triune form, He would not
suggest if fleetingly in grammatical construction. He would proclaim it
openly and abundantly saying, "I am the Lord—your Trinity God."
This is not to be found anywhere in the Hebrew Scriptures or in the
New Testament for that matter.

In fact, the plain language of the Hebrew Bible defies Christianity's triune God concept specifically and strongly. Here are more verses
expressing God's unity, uniqueness, and aloneness. God is described as
one-in-one. Any other interpretation would be obviously lacking in
objectivity. Read, "none else," "none beside me," "no god with me,"
"Lord (God) alone," "alone . . . by myself," and "no savior beside
me." Could anything be clearer than what these quotes say in the
denial of a three-in-one God!

Deuteronomy 4:35, "... *the Lord he is God; there is none else
beside him.*"

Deuteronomy 4:39, "... *he is God in heaven above, and upon
the earth beneath: . . . there is none else.*"

Deuteronomy 32:39, "*See now that I, even I, am he, and there is
no god with me: . . . neither is there any that can deliver out of my
hand.*"

I Chronicles 17:20, "*O Lord, there is none like thee, neither is
there any God beside thee . . .*"

Nehemiah 9:6, "*Thou, even thou, art Lord alone;*"

Psalm 86:10, "... *thou art God alone.*"

Isaiah 43:10-11, "... *I am he: before me there was no God
formed, neither shall there be after me. I, even I, am the Lord; and
beside me there is no savior.*"

Isaiah 44:24, "... *I am the Lord that maketh all things; . . .
alone . . . by myself;*"

Isaiah 45:5-6, "*I am the Lord, and there is none else, there is no
God beside me: . . . there is none beside me. I am the Lord, and there
is none else.*"

Isaiah 45:21-22, ". . . and there is no God else beside me; . . . Look unto me, and be ye saved, all the ends of the earth: for I am God, and there is none else."
Hosea 13:4, ". . . for there is no savior beside me."

God has many names in the Scriptures. Some names are given in the plural, but are singular in essence and actuality. We have shown this Biblical manner of presentation. "Elohim" is used expressing the majestic Creator of unfathomed multiple abilities. "Elohim" does not reveal the secret triune nature of God, but the magnificence of qualities and characteristics of a God of unity.

Now let's proceed to the rebuttal to *Genesis 1:26* meaning a plural god in, *"Let us make man in our image, . . ."* We offer the verse right after it. In it God is described as follows, *"So God made man in his own image, in the image of God created he him:"* Yes, there is a seeming contradiction between "our image" and "his own image," but this is explained within Judaism very comfortably.

In regard to "us—our," Judaism offers a double explanation. First, we certainly can be reading the "royal—we" which is used for grand emphasis. Those in power, having high esteem and lofty qualities, are entitled to the "royal—we." The Bible can be using this special application of the plural here. Assuredly, it befits God above all others to be referred to with this respectful grammatical effect.

A second way of looking at this is that the plural signifies that the angels, who were with God at creation, were atttending God. While God was creating, His angels were aiding. In this interpretation, God created with His power, having helping angels at His side. And God made man in their likeness, which must have a similarity of condition that could be transmitted to human beings.

No matter which Judaic explanation is selected (or both), it is far better than the Christian one. Judaism's interpretations are acceptable because they agree with God's words about Himself, while Christianity's views do not.

LET US GO DOWN.
Genesis 11:7, ". . . let us go down, and there confound their language . . ."
COMMENT: This verse's use of "us" is explained as God's plurality.
REBUTTAL: Although God says "us," it is the Lord in the singular in verse 9 who actually did the confounding, And it is the Lord in the singular in verse 5 who "came down." Although obscured by the changing from singular to plural, and then back again to singular, the oneness of God is not challenged by this use of "us." It is either a grammatical turn of expression, as explained in the foregoing analysis

of Genesis 1:1,26, signifying the "royal—we" or it refers to God's helping angels.

GOD, LORD, GOD (EL—ADONAI—ELOHAYNU).

II Samuel 22:32, "For who is God (El), save the Lord (Adonai)? and who is a rock save our God (Elohaynu)?

COMMENT: These three appellations together indicate the existence of the Trinity, it is said.

REBUTTAL: Whenever three names of God occur together like this they indicate a naming of His diversity of attributes, not a division of His entity. Here "El" means God Almighty. "Adonai" means Merciful God. And "Elohaynu" means Our God. Here, as well as everywhere else where more than one appellation of God is presented together, it is to bring about a crescendo of appreciation for the Lord God of Israel. No triune God is disclosed in the expression of these words.

YE ARE GODS.

Psalm 82:6, "I have said, Ye are gods; and all of you are children of the most High." (SEE John 10:34).

COMMENT: The Psalm is used by John in Jesus' refutation of blasphemy. The reasoning goes that if the Psalm says we are all god-like creatures (elohim—angels) then it is not blasphemy for Jesus to say he is the Son of God.

REBUTTAL: The argument used is devious. Although we are all made in God's image and are thereby lofty creatures of His creation, Jesus' claim was to a special status between God and himself. He seemed to claim a status set apart, one of special messenger sent by God. See *John 10:36, "Say ye of him, whom the Father hath sanctified, and sent into the world, Thou blasphemest; because I said, I am the Son of God?"* We humans cannot have a pretension to a "special" holiness without passing across a separation line, which is blasphemy.

Nevertheless, this Psalm is actually welcomed as a reverse proof-text. John's verse, argument aside, quotes the Psalm as being true in relation to Jesus' understanding of himself. Therefore, looked at this way, Jesus does not claim to be anything other than what we all are, creatures near angelic stature.

CREATOR, LORD GOD, SPIRIT.

Isaiah 48:16, "Come ye near unto me, hear ye this; I have not spoken in secret from the beginning; from the time that it was, there am I: and now the Lord God, and his Spirit, hath sent me."

COMMENT: This shows the Trinity, they say. The Creator "I" and the hath sent "me" are the same, with this "I—me" saying the Lord God and His spirit sent the "I—me." So, here are supposedly three entities of God which form the triune God.

REBUTTAL: There are many fallacies to Christianity's claim that this presents the Trinity. The first rejoinder is that it simply makes no sense. The Creator is not known in Judaism or Christianity to be sent by another. The Creator is in charge of the world. The verses in Isaiah chapter 48 show Him creating, declaring, showing, choosing, doing, speaking, commanding, teaching, etc., all of which are in the Creator's power. All of a sudden in verse 16 He presumably loses His stature as God and a different Lord God "sends" Him. There is no mystery here, for it is pure error. Something is amiss in the words. There are two possible explanations for the perplexity of words. We give both because either fits properly and both could be considered correct.

First, the "me" at the end is not the Creator "I" at the beginning. The "come ye near unto me" is the same as the "me" of "hath sent me," both being Isaiah himself. Verse 16 improperly incorporates at its end the prophetic introduction by Isaiah of God's words in verse 17. Thus, this is how it should read. *Verse 16, (Isaiah says) "Come ye near unto me, hear ye this; (God says) I have not spoken . . . there am I: (Isaiah ends) and now the Lord God and His spirit hath sent me." Verse 17, (Isaiah continues) "Thus saith the Lord, . . . I am the Lord thy God . . ."* This explanation fits.

A second explanation is that the verse is improperly translated and should read as follows. *Verse 16 reads, "And now the Lord God has sent me and his spirit."* What is sent is "me and his spirit." There are Biblical parallels for this kind of grammatical turn of words, usually in poetic passages. So, here we have God sending Isaiah, together with the prophetic spirit of God. Of course, it is the spirit of prophesy, not the Trinity's third member, which is with Isaiah.

Now let's continue to other fallacious aspects. If it were to be taken as proof of the Trinity, it would lack Jesus Christ, who is God the Son. The three entities, if you read them again, are the "Lord God," "his spirit," and "I—me (Creator)." All right, we have God the Spirit. But, this leaves us with a "Lord God" and an "I—me (Creator)." Jesus has to take one of these appellations, doesn't he? Which one? We think it would be impossible for Christianity to claim the "I—me (Creator)," because this is the Father, without a doubt. Therefore, by the process of elimination Jesus is the "Lord God." Yet, this also cannot be, for it is the name which always refers to the Father. What happened to God the Son, Jesus? The New Testament calls Jesus "Lord," which is a term of dignity. But, Jesus is never called "Lord God." In fact, we have shown that in all the New Testament Jesus is not termed "God." But, getting back to our subject here, something is wrong with the Christian Trinity, for Jesus is missing.

If the number of names in a passage is the key to God's constitution, then Christianity has a lot to figure out. First, in most of the Bible sentences God is alone, making for uncontestable monotheism. In other sentences, He is given duality, such as "Lord God, Savior." Still elsewhere, we find a multiple-named God. For example in this *Isaiah 48, in verse 17*, we see, *"Thus saith the Lord, thy Redeemer, the Holy One of Israel; I am the Lord thy God . . ."* Add these to the other designations of God which are found in this chapter of Isaiah, "Lord of Hosts," "Spirit," "first," and "last," and you see how ludicrous pursuing this becomes. The synonyms for God describe Him, they do not divide Him. The counting of the Trinity is very troublesome for Christianity using this kind of approach, don't you agree?

One last point, if the "sent me" refers to Jesus here, as Jesus is repeatedly described as being sent in the New Testament, then what is he being sent to do? What is the sending all about? There is absolutely nothing said about a vicarious atonement mission for the "sent me" entity.

Our analysis makes it clear that Christianity is in error using this verse to indicate the Trinity. We have shown that there are many faults in their claim. We have given you explanations which fit properly into the Jewish understanding of a God of unity. And thus it stands.

THE LORD SAID TO MY LORD. (MELCHIZEDEK).

Psalm 110:1, "The Lord said to my Lord, sit thou at my right hand, until I make thine enemies thy footstool." (SEE Matthew 22:44) (Mark 12:36) (Luke 20:42-43).

COMMENT: This is used to show that the Lord God and the Lord Jesus are in some close supernatural relationship.

REBUTTAL: These words are from God to the human "lord" of this Psalm, who is none other than David himself. It is necessary to read at the beginning of this Psalm that it says in the Hebrew that it is "concerning or about" David. The translation of the second "lord" is the equivalent of "master." No capitalization should exist, as it is not a reference to God. The reading more properly is, "A psalm concerning David, God said to my master (David) . . ." Jesus as Lord is not alluded to here at all.

Through inspirational prophesy, the psalm writer gives King David (himself) the assurance of victory over the enemies of the Jewish people. He is to be protected by God's power, as shown in the special phrase "at my right hand." This special phrase is repeated elsewhere, for instance in *Psalm 118:16, "The right hand of the Lord is exalted: the right hand of the Lord doeth valiantly."* The figurative expression denotes a place of importance and special care. The expression "footstool" denotes defeat and completes the picture.

Now, note the past tense of the verb, which reads "said." It means that God already had presented His remarks to this "lord." Yet, Jesus was to be born much later in history. God certainly would not be talking Lord-to-Lord to Himself in the same Godhead. He could not in any rational manner, could He? It is inconceivable and absurd. Any thoughts of Christologic findings in this Psalm must be dismissed.

However, an important comment on the New Testament's verses concerning this Psalm is in order. It says in *Matthew 22:45 (Mark 12:37) (Luke 20:44),* that Jesus asked how the Messiah (Christ) can be David's son when David himself called the Messiah "Lord." So, here we have the origination of the error. Jesus asked a very perplexing question. It is a question, which if taken at face value, would devastate the New Testament's texts on the subject of the Messiah. Pay attention to this. If Jesus did not believe the Messiah is to be a descendant of David, then he denied the necessity for all the validation of the Messiah from Davidic ancestry. This contradicts Christianity's own claim that Jesus, through his ancestry, has Messianic pretensions and is fulfilling Scripture prophesy. It cannot be both ways. We leave the pondering of this dilemma to those it concerns, Christians.

MELCHIZEDEK, JESUS' PRE-FORM. (THE LORD SAID TO MY LORD).
Psalm 110:4, ". . . Thou art a priest for ever after the order of Melchizedek." (SEE Hebrews 7:1-3).
COMMENT: This verse continues after "The Lord said to my Lord," and is used to tie in with Jesus being the incarnation of God. Somehow, Jesus' pre-existence in Melchizedek's form is given credence by this.
REBUTTAL: The Psalm speaks of Melchizedek from *Genesis 14:18-19,* which is the only other mention of him in the Hebrew Bible. Read, *"And Melchizedek king of Salem . . . was the priest of the most high God. And he . . . said, Blessed be Abram . . ."* Paul in *Hebrews 7:1-3,* fabricates a base for the misconception that Melchizedek and Jesus are interconnected in some way. Paul relates the happening from Genesis 14:18-19 correctly. But, then he relates the following, which is entirely unsubstantiated about Melchizedek, *"Without father, without mother, without descent, having neither beginning of days, nor end of life; . . ."* Unless Paul had information the Bible did not tell, Paul's presentation is baseless. In any event, it is not holy writing information.

Then Paul ends with, *". . . but made like unto the Son of God; abideth a priest continually."* Look here, if Melchizedek were "made," then he is not what Christianity claims for Jesus. If he were "like unto" the Son of God, then he was similar to, but not actually, the Son of God. Jesus is Christianity's special Son of God in actuality, not "like unto." And remember that Jesus was born very many years after Melchizedek. Therefore, someone predating him could not be made like him. Each point made is sufficient alone to make Christianity's concept of this crumble. The idea is preposterous and groundless.

The only connection that might be appropriate between Jesus and Melchizedek is that both could be considered special priests of God. "Continually" could be taken to mean in the lifetime of the priest in this case. But, there is no substantiation of any connection between the two in any supernatural manner. Why Paul wrote this misinformation is not our concern.

This is what we would find if we were to take Paul's words as true. "Without father, without mother," does not describe Jesus, who had both, in one sense or another. "Neither beginning of days, nor end of life," does not fit him either, as he had a birth in Bethlehem and a death in Jerusalem. So, where is there any legitimate association?

Now, we submit the real meaning of Psalm 110:4. This Psalm is dedicated as "a psalm to David" in the original Hebrew. It is David, himself, who is being likened to a priest during his lifetime, a priest of the stature of Melchizedek the priest of God. Both men ruled as kings and, yet, performed priestly functions. This explanation fits very comfortably, especially in contrast to the forced one of Christianity.

I AM THE FIRST, AND I AM THE LAST.

Isaiah 44:6, Isaiah 48:12, "Thus saith the Lord the King of Israel, and his redeemer the Lord of hosts; I am the first, and I am the last; and beside me there is no God. . . . I am he; I am the first, I also am the last." (SEE Revelation 1:17).

COMMENT: It is claimed that Jesus said he is God when in John's Revelation Jesus said he is the first and the last.

REBUTTAL: Jesus stated he is the first and the last resurrected by God in the manner the New Testament states. He is in *Revelation 1:5,* ". . . *the first begotten of the dead . . .*" Hence, if it is God in Isaiah who is the first and the last, and Jesus in Revelation is laying no such claim, we can end our examination here. Of course, we need not concern ourselves with the actual assertion of Jesus or the truth of the resurrection, because both belong to Christianity.

One last note is that "and his redeemer" means Israel's redeemer, where "his" signifies "Israel." We see this multiple designation elsewhere in *Isaiah 54:5, "For thy Maker is thine husband; the Lord of hosts is his name; and thy Redeemer the Holy One of Israel; the God of the whole earth shall he be called."*

I WILL SAVE THEM BY THE LORD.

Hosea 1:7, "But I will have mercy upon the house of Judah, and will save them by the Lord their God . . ."

COMMENT: This is used to show there are two parts of the Trinity here, one promising and one doing.

REBUTTAL: It is found in many other places that God speaks of himself in the third person. It is a manner of expression common in the Scriptures. It has nothing whatsoever to do with God being multiple entities. Here is an example which should end any further questioning in this area. It deals with Moses and the laws, with which neither the Son nor the Holy Ghost of Christianity is associated. See *Numbers 19:1-2, "And the Lord spake unto Moses and unto Aaron, saying, This is the ordinance of the law which the Lord hath commanded . . ."*

THE ANGEL OF THE LORD.

Judges 6:12, "And the angel of the Lord appeared . . ."

COMMENT: When the angel of the Lord is mentioned it is considered Jesus.

REBUTTAL: Of course, there are many angels in heaven, who are spiritual beings. See *Psalm 8:5, "For thou hast made him (man) a little lower than the angels . . ."* The Hebrew word "malach" which is translated "angel" means messenger. So, angels are God's messengers. Moreover, the article can be translated "the" or "an" at various times according to context. For example, look at *Judges 6:11-12, "And there came an angel of the Lord . . . And the angel of the Lord appeared . . ."* We plainly see that "the angel" and "an angel" are referring to the same angel, just one of a group of angels. Therefore, "the angel of the Lord" is just one of many angels and does not refer to Jesus.

Let's go further. In *Judges 13:17-18,* when the angel is asked his name so he could be honored, he answers that his name is a secret. Thereby, he indicates that his status does not deserve or require recognition. Jesus, surely, is not lacking identity.

Also, the angel of the Lord has one purpose, which is to be God's messenger or helper. He relates exactly the words and desires of God to Biblical people, aiding God in His work. God Himself is heard when the angels talk, the words being directly attributed to God. The angel and prophet have the same function of quoting God. Read *Genesis 22:15-16, "And the angel of the Lord called unto Abraham . . . And said, By myself have I sworn, saith the Lord . . ."* Besides quotations, even a blending of the words of God and the angel occur. In *Judges 2:1-4* we read, *"And an angel of the Lord came up . . . and said, I made you to go up out of Egypt, . . . and I said, I will never break my covenant with you. . . . And it came to pass, when the angel of the Lord spake these words . . ."* Also see *Judges 6:12-14, "And the angel . . . said unto him, . . . And the Lord looked upon him, and said . . ."* Here we learn that unnamed angels of the Lord function as holy messengers who aid God. Christianity's Jesus, however, is personalized and supposedly has the distinct function of offering vicarious atonement through his death. He does not act like an angelic messenger, one who aids God's work, but Jesus takes over God's functioning. In Christianity, Jesus assumes God's power.

Just to make sure it is understood that the angel of the Lord is in no way synonomous with God or in any way part of the Godhead of Christianity, we read in *I Chronicles 21:18,27, "Then the angel of the Lord . . . And the Lord commanded the angel . . ."* As God cannot command himself in any reasonable manner, we know from this that He and the angel are distinct from each other.

Finally, let's not neglect to mention that the New Testament recognizes archangels, which are angels of the highest order. If Jesus were the angel of the Lord, wouldn't it be appropriate for him to be titled the special archangel of the Lord at least?

SAVIOR, ANGEL OF HIS PRESENCE, HOLY SPIRIT.

Isaiah 63:7-9,11, "I will mention the lovingkindnesses of the Lord . . . Surely they are my people . . . so he was their Savior. . . . and the angel of his presence saved them: . . . Where is he that brought them up out of the sea . . . where is he that put his holy Spirit within him (Moses)?"

COMMENT: The passage is taken to signify the Trinity.

REBUTTAL: This passage must be read in context in order for it to be properly interpreted. Note that at the beginning it states that the mercies, the lovingkindness, of the Lord God to His people is the subject being mentioned. First, He is called "Savior," the redeemer of Israel, savior being one of God's appellations. Then mentioned is "angel of His presence," which is to say the angel chosen to be God's messenger. In this case, it is to bring help to Israel. Last, we encounter God putting "His holy Spirit" into Moses as part of His mercies to His people Israel. It should be comprehended that the holy spirit here is not a division of God, but an emission which can be dispensed to humanity. Properly interpreted, Isaiah is in no way divulging a triune God, as this explanation makes clear.

THREE MEN (ANGELS) ARE THE TRINITY.

Genesis 18:1-4, "And the lord appeared unto him (Abraham) . . . and, lo, three men stood by him: . . . he ran to meet them . . . and bowed himself . . . And said, My Lord, . . . Let a little water . . . be fetched, and wash your feet, and rest yourselves . . ."

COMMENT: Supposedly, the three men who appeared to Abraham were the Trinity, as Abraham calls them "My Lord."

REBUTTAL: This is a difficult passage to analyze, because it is unclear. Nevertheless, it will not reveal the Trinity. Two things are happening at the same time. One, God appears. And two, three men-angels stand by. Abraham chooses to attend to the men-angels in his hospitality. He bows to them and speaks to the leader of the three calling him "my lord" and asking him and the others to wash their feet and rest. We see that it is the leading angel, the one who delivers God's message to Abraham, who is addressed as "my lord." No Lord God is being spoken to here. This is very plain, because God need not have his feet washed, as he is never seen and is incorporeal. Read *Exodus 33:20, "And he said, Thou canst not see my face: for there shall no man see me, and live."* Even *John 1:18, John 5:37,* and *I John 4:12,20* state that God is never seen. But, Abraham sees these three.

The passage continues with all three men-angels asking where Sarah is and then we read, "And he said, I will certainly return . . . Sarah thy wife shall have a son, . . ." The "he" of "he said" is the man-angel selected by God to give Abraham the news. But, the "I" of "I will" is the direct quotation from God, as angels are capable of presenting. In the next verses it is hard to say with certainty if God spoke directly or through one of the men-angels. But, it is of no importance to know this. What is important is that we find no Trinity. The three men-angels are not the Trinity. Only the language problems make it possible for Christianity to grasp at this. But, for those who know the manner of analysis necessary for this kind of passage, Christianity's introduction of the triune God formulation cannot succeed.

In *Genesis 18:22* we read, *"And the men turned their faces from thence, and went to Sodom: but Abraham stood before the Lord."* And Abraham talks to God, alone, with the three men-angels gone. Isn't this clear proof that the three men-angels were not God incarnate, as puzzlingly proposed. And to conclude this, in *Genesis 18:33,* we read, *"And the Lord went his way, as soon as he had left communing with Abraham . . ."* So, we see that God left separately and is not in any way a combination with the three men-angels.

It is interesting to note the functions of the three men-angels. One completed the task of announcing the birth to Abraham and did not continue to Sodom. See *Genesis 19:1, "And there came two angels to Sodom . . ."* Also in *Genesis 19:13* we read, *"For we will destroy this place . . ."* And in *Genesis 19:15* we see, *". . . then the angels hastened to Lot, saying, Arise, take thy wife . . ."* So the function of the other two men-angels was to destroy Sodom and save Lot. In all this there is no Trinity.

FROM EVERLASTING.

Proverbs 8:22-23, "The Lord possessed me in the beginning of his way, before his works of old. I was set up from everlasting, from the beginning, or ever the earth was."
COMMENT: It is seen that this refers to Jesus.
REBUTTAL: This must be put back in context. The Proverb is speak-

ing of "wisdom" in a Biblically personified manner. Representing wisdom as a person is Biblical poetic form, nothing more. Furthermore, in that wisdom was "set up" or created, the possibility is eliminated that Jesus could be called wisdom and thereby be designated as God. Let's read some verification of the personification of wisdom. In *Proverbs 8:12,14* read, *"I wisdom dwell with prudence . . . I am understanding; . . ."* Moreover, in *Proverbs 8:15-16* read, *"By me kings reign, and princes decree justice. By me princes rule, and nobles, even all the judges of the earth."* As you see, wisdom's function is not that of Jesus' Christologics at all. And one last refutation comes from *Luke 2:52, "And Jesus increased in wisdom . . ."* which proves he is not the personification of wisdom as presented in these verses.

WHAT IS HIS SON'S NAME? (BEGOTTEN SON).

Proverbs 30:4, ". . . who hath established all the ends of the earth? what is his name, and what is his son's name . . . ?"
COMMENT: Christianity says the answer is God the Father and God the Son.
REBUTTAL: We can both agree that "His name" is the Creator, the Lord God, the Father of us all. However, the latter question of "His Son's name" is answered in Judaism as the "people of Israel." We have evidence that the collective people of Israel can be termed "God's son" from the following verses, among others. See *Exodus 4:22, ". . . Thus saith the Lord, Israel is my son, even my firstborn."* Also see *Jeremiah 31:9, ". . . for I am a father to Israel, and Ephraim is my firstborn."* And read *Deuteronomy 14:1, "Ye are the children of the Lord your God . . ."* Also read *Hosea 1:10, ". . . Ye are the sons of the living God."*

In addition to the children of Israel, the Davidic line in particular is also referred to as "God's son." Read the following, where the Davidic line, symbolic of the Israel people, is called by God "son." See *Psalm 2:7, "I will declare the decree: the Lord hath said unto me, Thou art my Son: this day have I begotten thee."* Also see *Psalm 89:20, 26-27, "I have found David my servant; with my holy oil have I anointed him: He shall cry unto me, Thou art my father . . . I will make him my firstborn . . ."* And read *I Chronicles 22:10, "He (Solomon) shall build an house for my name; and he shall be my son, and I will be his father . . ."* Last, see *II Samuel 7:14, "I will be his (Solomon's) father, and he shall be my son . . ."* So, we see that the Davidic line, which is the Messiah's heritage, is metaphorically the son of God also.

Let's go further into the Messiah being the special son of God. The holy figure who fulfills the wonderful Messianic expectations will claim the title of the son of God. Jesus did not fulfill the expectations of the Hebrew Scriptures. If he were to do this in a "second coming," he would have the right to that name at that time. At this time, Christianity has no right to claim the designation for Jesus in anticipation of something still to be accomplished. Christology is another story, of course, and it is not of relevance here.

We offer one last thought. Jesus' lifetime was much after the time Proverbs were written. Hence, the early people reading Proverbs, and being asked the questions posed, had no conception of the Christologic Jesus as God the Son of the Trinity. Consequently, they could not be expected to answer anything other than the replies of Judaism, which makes the Judaic reply the only proper one.

(ONLY) BEGOTTEN SON. (WHAT IS HIS SON'S NAME?).

Psalm 2:7, "The Lord hath said unto me, Thou art my Son; this day have I begotten thee." (SEE Hebrews 1:5).

COMMENT: This is taken to mean Jesus is the only begotten Son of God as stated in *I John 4:9.*

REBUTTAL: The fact is that this is about David, the anointed king. Look at the verse before it which says, ". . . *I set my king upon my holy hill of Zion.*" Certainly, this does not refer to Jesus who was not king of Jerusalem, but to David who was set as king. Also, a direct parallel exists in *Psalm 89:20,26-27,* which mentions David by name and gives credence to David being the subject of this Psalm. Read again the rebuttal for the preceding *Proverbs 30:4* for statements of pertinence here. We know that Jesus was not the only begotten Son of God, because the Scriptures show us others begotten of God. Whatever he may be to Christianity, he cannot be legitimately called the only son of God.

As a parting observation, we offer you refutations of Jesus being the subject of this verse by studying the very following verse, *Psalm 2:8.* This reads, *"Ask of me, and I shall give thee the heathen for thine inheritance, and the uttermost parts of the earth for thy possession."* The Psalm is speaking of King David and Messianic Israel. Observe how unbefitting it is to consider Jesus here.

1—One part of the Trinity cannot "beget" another part (a Son).

2—One part of the Trinity cannot (need not) ask for something of another part.

3—Jesus never ruled an earthly kingdom.

4—Jesus not only was not in possession of the heathen, but they killed him.

16

Proof-Texts—General Messiah

RIGHTEOUS BRANCH—THE LORD OUR RIGHTEOUSNESS.
Jeremiah 23:5-6, ". . . I will raise unto David a righteous Branch, and a King . . . shall execute judgment and justice in the earth. In his days Judah shall be saved, and Israel shall dwell safely: and this is his name . . . The Lord Our Righteousness."
COMMENT: This is said to refer to Jesus, the branch of David who is the righteous Lord.
REBUTTAL: Yes, the Davidic Messiah is to come. But, where is there any pointing to Jesus in this passage? Except in the specificity forced in the backward look of Christianity there is absolutely no connection to Jesus here. Moreover, we shall show that Jesus did not fulfill the salient requirements of the Messiah as propounded in this Hebrew Scripture. Connection and fulfillment are lacking.

1—NO KINGDOM. Jesus, never was a king in an earthly kingdom, which the Bible says the Messiah is to be. He did not rule a prosperous land, where he judged and imparted justice in the earth. Note that it says, "in the earth," which is not the heavenly kingdom of Christianity.

2—ISRAEL NOT SAVED. In his days, Judah and Israel shall be saved and safe. This eliminates Jesus as the "righteous branch," because Israel remained troubled in his days. The Jewish people did not have safety. The Romans continued their cruel occupation. Indeed, the Second Temple was destroyed by the oppressors just forty years after Jesus' lifetime.

3—SECOND COMING INVALID. If the "second coming" is when Jesus is to fulfill Jeremiah's writing, then the "first coming" of someone else would be just as proper to identify as pre-Messianic. The only consideration needed is the fulfillment of the Messianic expectations, not what happened before. Remember also, we have exposed the lack of validity of a return by Jesus, which is Christianity's answer to Jesus' non-accomplishment as presumed Messiah.

4—JESUS NAMED JESHUA. Jesus' name was not "The Lord Our Righteousness," but Jeshua. The symbolic name could have been given to Jesus. Names associated with aspects of God are given to people as well as objects as a sign of respect to God. "Immanuel" (God is with us) is in this category and will be discussed later. Note the following example in *Exodus 17:15, "And Moses built an altar, and called the name of it Jehovahnissi: (the Lord is my Banner)."*

5—THE LORD "IS" OUR RIGHTEOUSNESS. The correct translation reading is, "The Lord Is Our Righteousness," with the verb included properly from the Hebrew rendering in which it is understood. Therefore, the symbolic name of righteousness belongs to God, and the words actually do not describe the Messiah king.

One further observation is that, very strangely, in *Jeremiah 33:16* we find, *"In those days shall Judah be saved, and Jerusalem shall dwell safely: and this is the name wherewith she shall be called, The Lord our righteousness."* It appears that the holy city of Jerusalem is to have the same name as the Messiah of the righteous branch of David. This should fully end speculation that the Messiah is equated with God any more than Jerusalem would be God Himself.

THE MIGHTY GOD.

Isaiah 9:6-7, "For unto us a child is born, unto us a son is given: and the government shall be upon his shoulder: and his name shall be called Wonderful, Counsellor, The mighty God, the everlasting Father, The Prince of Peace. Of the increase of his government and peace there shall be no end, upon the throne of David . . ."

COMMENT: Christianity puts forward that this speaks of Jesus.

REBUTTAL: In reality, this passage is of King Hezekiah of Judah, born to King Ahaz. By miraculous intervention, God defeated the Assyrians who attacked Judah during King Hezekiah's rule. Hezekiah was a great religious reformer who removed idolatry and reinforced pure monotheism. The series of appellations is intended by Isaiah to describe God's characteristics in relation to the extraordinary happenings to be accomplished in Hezekiah's reign.

We must first correct the translation from the Hebrew. The translation projects to the future incorrectly and gives the names to the child improperly. This is how it should read to be accurate, "And the Wonderful Counselor, the mighty God, the everlasting Father, he called the child born the Prince of Peace. . . ." It is quite clear, even from the verse given, that the child had been born. The confusion arises concerning whether the appellations are God's or are for the child. The names are God's, as clarified here.

However, it really is of no consequence in our inquiry whose names they are, because they are not of Jesus, who was born many hundreds of years later. With expanded imagination, the names could be made to suit Hezekiah, but never the unborn Jesus. Hezekiah did have a government. He was a wonderful religious leader. He could be likened to displaying the mighty power of God which destroyed the enemies miraculously. As a religious purifier, he assisted God's everlasting watchfulness. And his reign did have peace after the enemies were defeated. The peace could be described as abundant, therefore with no end in the Biblical sense. Even though this explanation is not smoothly fitted, you can see that it has all the elements to be considered correct. Christianity's explanation lacks all the elements necessary. But, because the names are God's, the appropriateness of them for Hezekiah is of no concern to us.

Furthermore, it should be understood that names which reflect God are given to human beings. For example, we have "Elihu" (my God is He). Also, people can be called god-like in many ways, none of which means the person is believed to be God.

Let's get to the heart of the matter and summarize the substantial ways in which Jesus is proved absent from this passage from Isaiah.

1—Jesus was not born at the time described.

2—Jesus never headed a government. He never was an earthly king of the land. We have presented the functions of the Messiah in the chapter entitled, "The Hebrew Messiah."

3—Jesus was not called these names, even in the New Testament. So, how can Christianity appropriate them for him?

4—Jesus never thought himself God the Father, nor does the New Testament indicate that others thought him the heavenly Father. It is not his role in Christianity. He is called the Son of God, never "mighty God" or "Father." We have shown all pertinent information concerning this in the chapter called, "His God Is Not a Trinity."

5—Jesus was not mighty. We offer the following verses from the New Testament to prove this. Read *Matthew 20:23 (Mark 10:40), ". . . but to sit on my right hand, and on my left is not mine to give . . ."* And see *Matthew 26:39, ". . . O my Father, if it be possible, let this cup pass from me: nevertheless not as I will, but as thou wilt."*

6—Jesus might be referred to as the prince of peace, if the Sermon on the Mount were his only sayings. But, we expose in a later chapter, "Proof-Texts—No Violence, No Deceit," that he said and did many things which had elements which would disqualify him from the title of champion of peace. For example, read *Matthew 10:34 (Luke*

12:51), "Think not that I am come to send peace on earth: I came not to send peace, but a sword." Also see *Matthew 10:35 (Mark 13:12) (Luke 12:52-53), "For I am come to set a man at variance against his father, and the daughter against her mother . . ."*

7—Jesus may be a wonderful counselor to Christians, but Jews have another opinion about his counseling. Christians have had poor instruction as to how to treat their fellow human beings, the Jews. We do believe that this is in spite of his advice, yet it shows his counseling did not capture the hearts of his followers and, therefore, cannot be considered superior or wonderful in effect.

NAME GREAT AMONG GENTILES.

Malachi 1:11, ". . . my name shall be great among the Gentiles; and in every place incense shall be offered unto my name, . . . saith the Lord of hosts."

COMMENT: Christianity is the name made great among the Gentiles, they say.

REBUTTAL: In this chapter of Malachi, God reprimands the people for imperfect offerings. He sees the heathen, although approaching idols, performing their religious duty purely and laudably. It can be interpreted to mean that to the extent Gentiles search for the Divinity they make the name of God great. In addition to this meaning, we have presented in the chapter, "Scriptural Messianic Expectations," that Israel will be a light to the nations and that Gentiles will convert to Judaism and the Lord God of Israel. Either way, Christianity is not in the picture here.

A ROD OUT OF JESSE.

Isaiah 11:1, "And there shall come forth a rod out of the stem of Jesse, and a Branch shall grow out of his roots:"

COMMENT: This rod of Jesse is supposed to mean Jesus.

REBUTTAL: Christianity is entirely without substantiation that this refers to Jesus. It does speak of the Hebrew Messiah, but there is no connection to Jesus presented in this verse from Isaiah. They make this forced connection prompted by their viewpoint, but lacking any evidence. Moreover, further on in this chapter of our book, we demonstrate that Jesus' genealogy disqualifies him from being a descendant of King David and Jesse, David's father. Certainly, he also is disqualified from being a descendant of King David if he were conceived by the Holy Ghost instead of by his father, Joseph.

Furthermore, *Isaiah 11:1-16* deals fully with the glorious Messianic expectations, which are not fulfilled. Some very general verses possibly could be conceived to be about Jesus. But, they are too vague and could be applied to many others, not specifically to Jesus alone. Generalities prove nothing. Indeed, specificity in many verses concerning the Messiah destroys the Christian contention that Jesus fills the role of the Hebrew Messiah.

No "second coming" for this rod of Jesse is alluded to, because Isaiah says the stem of Jesse will be functioning in the Messianic times, not before. Read *Isaiah 11:10-11, "And in that day (Messianic Era) there shall be a root of Jesse . . . And it shall come to pass in that day, . . ."* Nowhere does Isaiah imply a "first" and than a "second" arrival. Nowhere is a "this now" and a "that later" stated or inferred. All will be "in that day." Isaiah's prophesy cannot be separated into a first coming, a leaving, and a return for completion. However, Christianity has done just this in its message of Jesus Christ as Messiah.

SEED OF ABRAHAM.

Genesis 17:8, "And I will give unto thee, and to thy seed after thee, the land . . . for an everlasting possession; and I will be their God." (SEE Galatians 3:16).

COMMENT: The seed of Abraham refers to Jesus Christ and Christians, according to their interpretation.

REBUTTAL: Paul in *Galatians* says, *"Now to Abraham and his seed were the promises made. He saith not, And to seeds, as of many; but as of one, And to thy seed, which is Christ."* Paul's mistake is so glaring that it is obvious to all using their reasoning. The "seed of Abraham" has meant, and will continue to mean, the people of Israel. Invariably, when future generations are referred to Biblically it is as "seed," not as "seeds" in the plural. Scripture uses the singular "seed" to mean descendants consistently. This makes Paul's remarks very puzzling, because it is simply wrong. Note that in this Genesis we read, ". . . to thy seed . . . and I will be their God." "Seed" here is connected to "their" in the plural. Let's read some more examples. *Genesis 13:15-16* says, *". . . to thy seed for ever. And I will make thy seed as the dust of the earth: . . . be numbered."* *Genesis 15:13* reads, *". . . thy seed shall be a stranger in a land that is not theirs . . ."*

Not only was Paul in complete error when he claimed "seed" is singular in meaning and thereby connected to the individual Jew, Jesus, but he then turned around and made a flip-flop total reversal of his claim. It is singular for Jesus, but plural again for Christians, as it suits him. Read *Galatians 3:29, "And if ye be Christ's, then ye are Abraham's seed, and heirs according to the promise."* See how easy it is for Christians to be plural descendants, but not the Jews. This is Paul's devious way of sending the mother away out the back door and bringing the new baby in the front. Of course, keep in mind that Christianity is based on being the "New Israel," supplanting the People of the Book as well as their religion. As Christianity's beliefs are not our concern, our valid objection here is to their falsification of

Hebrew Scripture in making their claim.

One more observation is due. In *Genesis 22:18* see, *"And in thy seed shall all the nations of the earth be blessed; . . ."* Christianity usurps this for themselves also. They make themselves the base of the world blessing through Jesus the seed. They do this without any Biblical verification. In the Hebrew Scriptures God's great promise is to the children of Abraham, the people of Israel. There is clarity in the words of God's promise, and there is no other legitimate interpretation of these eternally valid words.

LATTER TEMPLE GREAT BECAUSE OF JESUS.

Haggai 2:9, "The glory of this latter house shall be greater than of the former, saith the Lord of hosts: and in this place will I give peace..."

COMMENT: This is interpreted by them as Jesus' glory.

REBUTTAL: There was no glory in the Second Temple, because it lacked the fullness of the First Temple, materially without the holy Ark of the Covenant, etc., and spiritually without the special holy presence of God, the Sechinah. See *Ezekiel 43:7, ". . . the place of my throne, . . . where I will dwell in the midst of the children of Israel for ever . . ."* Unmistakably, this verse is not about the Second Temple, because, in addition to lacking fullness it lacked peace. Indeed, the Second Temple was destroyed by Israel's enemies in 70 C.E.. The forced connection between this verse and Jesus is without justification. We do know, however, that the latter house will be the Temple of the Messianic Era, and that it will be greater than the former, the First Temple.

LAW FROM JERUSALEM.

Isaiah 2:3 (Micah 4:2), "And many people shall go. . . to the house of the God of Jacob; and he will teach us of his ways. . .for out of Zion shall go forth the law, and the word of the Lord from Jerusalem."

COMMENT: Christianity says there will be a law of Jesus from Jerusalem which will replace the law of Moses from Sinai.

REBUTTAL: The verse does not have to do with a new legality to be promulgated, but a new instruction of the immutable law to occur in the "last days," the Messianic times. This new instruction of the word of God will be accomplished from Jerusalem. The Hebrew word which is translated "law" often is correctly translated "instruction," which is the meaning in this instance. Keep in mind that we have demonstrated that Jesus is not the awaited Hebrew Messiah. So, if the Messiah is to be involved in the instruction, it is not Jesus who is to teach God's unchangeable law from Jerusalem.

CHRIST IS END OF THE LAW.

Leviticus 18:5, "Ye shall therefore keep my statutes, and my judgments: which if a man do, he shall live in them . . ."

Deuteronomy 30:9-14, "And the Lord thy God will make thee plenteous in every work of thine hand, . . . If thou shalt harken unto the voice of the Lord thy God, to keep his commandments and his statutes which are written in this book of the law, and if thou turn unto the Lord thy God with all thine heart, and with all thy soul . . . But the word is very nigh unto thee, in thy mouth, and in thy heart, that thou mayest do it." (SEE Romans 10:4-8).

COMMENT: Paul uses the passages to present Christianity's view that Christ has ended the need for the law.

REBUTTAL: Paul distorted these passages so thoroughly that there is no original meaning left. No meaning of the Hebrew Scriptures finds its way to his words in Romans. If you have read the Leviticus and Deuteronomy verses you see that they uphold the value of the law. Not the slightest intimation of the law being valueless appears here, or elsewhere. Yet, Christianity uses distortions and misquotations as their basis for abandoning the law. Those who have knowledge of the misapplication of Scripture, involving the twisting of God's word as Biblically revealed, have a duty to recognize the error and reject the unfounded teaching. Christians who are open-minded can see that the law's holiness, value, and eternal nature are upheld in the Hebrew Bible. They need not accept the law, but they should respect those who do. And Jews, knowing the immutability of the law, should remain steadfast to Judaism's eternal link to God.

Look at what Paul says in *Romans 10:4, "For Christ is the end of the law for righteousness to every one that believeth."* The Hebrew Bible's verses are contradicted, as well as Jesus' own pronouncements. This book's chapter, "Laws Are Good for Salvation," gives a full survey of Jesus' positive attitude to the law and other New Testament quotations in support of the law of Moses. Remember this for example? *Matthew 5:17-19, "Think not that I am come to destroy the law, or the prophets: I am not come to destroy, but to fulfill. For verily I say unto you, Till heaven and earth pass, one jot or one tittle shall in no wise pass from the law, till all be fulfilled."*

Jesus goes on to say, *"Whosoever therefore shall break one of the least commandments, and shall teach men so, he shall be called least in the kingdom of heaven; but whosoever shall do and teach them, the same shall be called great in the kingdom of heaven."* Without delving into Jesus' actual treatment of the laws in practice, we have substantiation of his belief in the eternal validity of the law as God's word. He treated the law with respect, even though he may not have followed a straight course in the execution of specific commandments. Jesus never said the law of Moses was not God's word and will. He never said the law was ineffective. His pronouncements were quite the reverse, asserting that the law offers eternal life.

It was Paul who overturned the law's validity. It was Paul who broke the laws and taught others to do so. Seemingly, if you believe Jesus, Paul "shall be called least in the kingdom of heaven." For Jesus' words against this arrogation of authority read *Matthew 10:24 (Luke 6:40) (John 13:16), "The disciple is not above his master, nor the servant above his lord."*

One last thought is offered concerning the twisting of the original meaning in Deuteronomy. Paul in *Romans 10:8* says, *". . . The word is nigh thee, even in thy mouth, and in thy heart: that is, the word of faith, which we preach;"* This is Paul's assault on God's holy words in Deuteronomy. For, in the Hebrew Scriptures we read it is "commandments and statutes" which are not far off, but in our mouth and heart that we may "do them." Paul, the organizer of Christianity, replaces Moses' laws of God with Christian faith, misusing and subverting the Scriptures. With no Biblical foundation, faith is made the successor to God's laws. We challenge the thinking person to find anything in the Hebrew Scriptures which lends credence to Paul's statements here. Nothing is to be found.

ASCENDED ON HIGH.

Psalm 68:18, "Thou hast ascended on high, thou hast led captivity captive: thou hast received gifts for men; yea, for the rebellious also, that the Lord God might dwell among them."

COMMENT: It is supposedly Jesus the Messiah who will ascend into heaven.

REBUTTAL: This Psalm, written in the past tense, is not a prophesy. It relates a past event, which is the ascending Mount Sinai by Moses who received the gift of the Torah which brings God to mankind through Judaism. This is one of those verses which Christianity uses inappropriately in order to serve its own purpose.

GOD'S SERVANT.

Isaiah 49:1,3,5-6, "The Lord hath called me from the womb . . . And said unto me, Thou art my servant, O Israel, in whom I will be glorified. And now, saith the Lord that formed me from the womb to be his servant, to bring Jacob again to him, Though Israel be not gathered, yet shall I be glorious in the eyes of the Lord, . . . I will also give thee for a light to the Gentiles that thou mayest be my salvation unto the end of the earth."

COMMENT: It is supposedly Jesus who is the servant and light to the Gentiles.

REBUTTAL: In verse 3, the servant is explicitly stated as "Israel." Consequently, without question, the people of Israel are those called from the womb as God's servant. But, the servant in verse 5 is the terminology used for Isaiah himself. We see this clearly because the prophet's function is to call Jacob to God while Israel is still not redeemed. The indication of the servant is once again returned to Israel in verse 6, where Israel is described as a light to the Gentiles, as it often is in Scripture. Due to transfer of appellation "servant," this might be confusing to the unlearned in Biblical passage structure. But, once viewed correctly, the literary style presents no obstacle for Judaic understanding. Israel, as well as Isaiah, is God's servant. Jesus' name is surely not "Israel," is it? So, he is not the subject of this passage, is he?

Another point to be made here is that Christianity claims Jesus is God. God cannot be made in the womb to be a servant of Himself, can He? It's not a mystery. It's just irrational and absurd. Also, he cannot be given status as servant from birth, when he is God eternal in Christianity. Once again, the comfortable fit is Judaism's explanation. It fits because it is true.

THE HOLY ONE.
Isaiah 49:7, (SEE Rebuttal following).
COMMENT: The Holy One of Israel is Jesus, they say.
REBUTTAL: Due to awkwardness of literary presentation, ambiguities are present. But, when interpreted properly everything falls in place with ease as in the preceding verses from Isaiah 49. Just read the verse as indicated to comprehend its meaning. It says, *"Thus saith the Lord, the Redeemer of Israel, and his (Israel's) Holy One, to him (Israel) whom man despiseth, to him (Israel) whom the nation abhorreth, to (Israel) a servant of rulers, Kings shall see and arise, princes also shall worship (God), because of the Lord that is faithful, and (is) the Holy One of Israel, and he (God) shall choose thee (Israel)."* As you see, the Holy One of Israel is none other than God.

GARDEN OF EDEN DAMNATION—ORIGINAL SIN.
Genesis 2:17, "But of the tree of the knowledge of good and evil, thou shalt not eat of it: for in the day that thou eatest thereof thou shalt surely die."
(SEE I Corinthians 15:22, Romans 5:12).
COMMENT: From this we are all hell-bent, it is said, except for the intervention of Jesus. Paul said, ". . . in Adam all die, . . ."
REBUTTAL: This passage says Adam will die that very day, which did not happen. Thus, clearly, God did not mean the immediate physical death of Adam. But, God also did not mean the future spiritual death of Adam's descendants, mankind. Read *Ecclesiastes 12:7, "Then shall the dust return to the earth as it was: and the spirit shall return unto God who gave it."* Consequently, we know the spirit lives after physical death. Further, read *Leviticus 18:5, "Ye shall therefore keep my statutes, and my judgments: which if a man do, he shall live in*

them . . ." Therefore, we learn that the spirit lives in keeping the commandments. And we know that perfection is not required, for God forgives our trespasses. See *Micah 7:18, "Who is a God like unto thee, that pardoneth iniquity . . ."* and *Jeremiah 31:34, ". . . for I will forgive their iniquity . . ."* and also *Isaiah 1:18, ". . . though your sins be as scarlet, they shall be as white as snow . . ."* Thus, we know that by keeping the laws even imperfectly, because God forgives the repentant sinner, souls earn eternal life. Refer back to, "Personal Salvation Through Judaism."

Humanity is not being put to spiritual death by Adam's actions. Read *Deuteronomy 24:16, ". . . neither shall the children be put to death for the fathers: every man shall be put to death for his own sin."* The same message is conveyed in Ezekiel chapter 18, for example *Ezekiel 18:20, "The soul that sinneth, it shall die. The son shall not bear the iniquity of the father, neither shall the father bear the iniquity of the son . . ."*

So, we discover that Adam's death was not his immediate physical death, nor was it the spiritual death of his descendants, humanity. No, Judaism knows from the Hebrew Bible that man's spiritual life or death depends on his own actions in following God's pathway. What we have occurring in the Garden of Eden is Adam losing immortality in his physical existence on earth and his descendants inheriting physical mortality. Man is to have physical death, after his lifetime is spent.

GENEALOGY OF MESSIAH FROM DAVIDIC ANCESTRY.

Psalm 89:3-4,35-36, ". . . I have sworn unto David my servant, Thy seed will I establish for ever, and build up thy throne to all generations. . . . I will not lie unto David. His seed shall endure for ever, and his throne as the sun before me." (SEE *Matthew 1:1-17, Luke 3:23-38, Acts 2:30*).

COMMENT: Judaism and Christianity agree that the Messiah will be a descendant of King David. Jesus' genealogy is traced back to King David in the New Testament.

REBUTTAL: Two different and conflicting genealogies are offered by Matthew and Luke. If a genealogy is given to prove descent from David, then it should be faultless and true. Instead, we find multiple difficulties exist which make both enumerations highly suspect due to inconsistencies and questionable presentations. We have outlined points of irregularity, each a formidable challenge to Christianity's claim of Jesus being descended from David. Read and see.

1—Matthew lists 42 generations between Abraham and Jesus, while Luke has over 10 more generations listed between them.

2—In Matthew, David's son Solomon is the ancestor of Joseph, while Luke has David's son Nathan as Joseph's ancestor.

3—Matthew places 18 generations from David to Zerubbabel, while Luke has 23 generations between them.

4—After Solomon and Nathan, the enumerations differ until Shealtiel and his son Zerubbabel.

5—The most recent ancestors of Joseph, which should be the ones easiest to substantiate by Matthew and Luke, are given as completely different. Matthew lists Eliud, Eleazar, Matthan, Jacob, and then Joseph. Luke, in contrast, lists Melchi, Levi, Matthat, Heli, and then Joseph.

6—Matthew omits three generations listed after David in *I Chronicles 3:11-12,* which are Ahaziah, Joash, and Amaziah.

7—Luke lists Cainan two times, not found in the Hebrew Scriptures.

8—Biblically, Luke's genealogy is disqualified because the ancestral line does not include Solomon, but David's son Nathan instead. See *I Chronicles 28:5,7, ". . . he hath chosen Solomon my son to sit upon the throne of the kingdom of the Lord over Israel. Moreover I will establish his kingdom for ever . . ."*

9—Scripture also disqualifies Matthew's genealogy because any descendant of Jehoiakim cannot be the Messiah. Read *Jeremiah 22:30* concerning this, *". . . for no man of his seed shall prosper, sitting upon the throne of David . . ."* Continue with *I Chronicles 3:16-17, "And the sons of Jehoiakim: Jeconiah his son, . . . And the sons of Jeconiah: Salathiel . . ."* This matches *Matthew 1:12,* and we find Jehoiakim belongs in this genealogy.

Some of these errors appear to have been caused by the use of the Greek translation, rather than the original Hebrew, and the New Testament writers copying the listing of the generations from there. But, in any case, the contradictions and faults are beyond any attempt at reconciliation or explanation. In *I Timothy 1:4* warning is given against trying to use confusing genealogy tables in, *"Neither give heed to fables and endless genealogies, which minister questions . . ."* This probably alludes to this present problem, as *Titus 3:9* seems to do also. Nevertheless, the proof of ancestry is given twice in the New Testament and creates a quagmire for Christianity.

In desperation, Christianity attempts to resolve these problems with weak and inadequate explanations, such as the following. First, Matthew is alleged to list Joseph's ancestors, while Luke lists Mary's. She presumably is descended from King David also. The trouble with this is that it is not Biblically stated, and the evidence is against it. See in *Matthew 1:16* it reads, *"And Jacob begat Joseph the husband of Mary, of whom was born Jesus, . . ."* And in *Luke 3:23, "And Jesus . . . the son of Joseph, which was the son of Heli,"* is read. Thus, that explanation is disproved. In addition, in Scripture maternal ancestors are never used for succession to thrones. Only paternal ancestors, using male figures of heritage, are used.

Another explanation Christianity tries to have accepted concerns Joseph as a son-in-law. But, this has no validity as to succession. It has been conceived that Heli was Mary's father, not Joseph's. But, by no stretch of the imagination can a father-in-law be given credibility as a named father in Biblical writing. Yet, even with this twisted reasoning, we still would find the female genealogy lacking in importance. For, Mary as a female is not an heir.

One other idea which has been devised is that Mary had two different husbands called Joseph, both married to her at the time of Jesus' birth. What do you think of that one?

Now consider this:—How many people can trace their ancestry even one or two hundred years, no less the approximate one thousand years between King David and Jesus? Men in those days had many children from several mates, and no official birth records were kept. How could any genealogy for this number of years in this primitive society be valid?

And remember the New Testament shocker that Jesus himself even denied that the Messiah would be descended from King David. In *Matthew 22:45 (Mark 12:37) (Luke 20:44)* he said, *"If David then call him Lord, how is he his son?"* We have analysed this in our previous chapter, "Proof-Texts—Trinity." Now, we are interested in the denial that the Messiah will be descended from David. In spite of this, Christianity tries to prove descent from King David for Jesus. Two genealogies are offered in the New Testament, because they know the Bible has requirements of lineage for the Messiah to come.

In conclusion, with all that we have presented, we believe we have disposed of the so-called proof of Jesus being the Messiah through Davidic descent. However, now we must ask the fundamental question of why should we bother to do so when Christianity says Joseph was not the natural father of Jesus? Read *Matthew 1:20, ". . . the angel of the Lord appeared . . . saying . . . fear not to take unto thee Mary thy wife: for that which is conceived in her is of the Holy Ghost."* Whether this actually happened or not is not pertinent to our subject. What is of interest is that in Christianity Jesus is not the natural son of Joseph. Therefore, Joseph's heritage is not Jesus'. Adopted sons or step-sons do not receive paternal lineage. They are not as *Acts 2:30* states the Messiah should be, ". . . *the fruit of his loins, according to the flesh . . ."* So, if Jesus was not the physical son of Joseph, why the two genealogies? But, if he was the physical son, he cannot be described as conceived by the Holy Ghost as presented in the New Testament. It cannot work both ways. It is quite a dilemma for Christianity. But, it is theirs to resolve as they wish. What Judaism's advocate wants understood is that keeping the supernatural conception, as Christianity must, we arrive at the conclusion that Jesus has no claim to Davidic heritage on any grounds whatsoever.

VIRGIN BIRTH.

Isaiah 7:14, ". . . a sign; Behold, a virgin shall conceive and bear a son, and shall call his name Immanuel." (SEE Matthew 1:23).

COMMENT: Jesus was born of a virgin, supposedly his Messianic sign.

REBUTTAL: The Hebrew word used here is "almah" which should be properly translated as "young girl," with her state of virginity unspecified. In *Exodus 2:8*, for example, we meet this general term for youthful maiden, *"And the maid went and called the child's mother."* Clearly no indication of the maiden's state of virginity is made or intended here. A different word, the Hebrew word "betulah," is the word used specifically and exclusively to denote virginity. And "betulah" is not the word Isaiah used. We see the term of virginity used in *Deuteronomy 22:28, "If a man find a damsel that is a virgin, which is not betrothed . . . and lie with her . . ."* The Scriptures often use this double verbage in order to make emphatic statements, such as in *Genesis 24:16, ". . . a virgin, neither had any man known her: . . ."* To clarify its usage in *Joel 1:8,* the word "betulah" is used in a simile and refers to a woman in extreme sorrow, having lost her husband before marriage consummation. It is used for dramatic effect. Read, *"Lament like a virgin girded with sackcloth for the husband of her youth."* Even recognizing the translation error, Christian theologians still cling to the claim for the virgin birth, due to reverence for the New Testament.

Let's add one more comment on linguistic error. The Hebrew "almah" became the Greek "parthenos" in translation. Yet, "parthenos" is used for a girl who certainly is not a virgin in *Genesis 34:2-3* which reads, *". . . he took her, and lay with her, and defiled her . . . and he loved the damsel . . ."* So, we find the Greek word "parthenos" is not used solely for a virgin. This compounds Christianity's problem here.

Now, there is an important point to be made apart from linguistics. Notice that if we were to use the translation "virgin" it reads, "a virgin shall conceive," not "a virgin shall give birth." Think of the words. It doesn't signify that the virgin remains virginal after conception. In other words, it simply means a woman who never before had intercourse shall conceive at this her first intercourse. Christianity has made this their story, and so a jump to the conclusion is made on reading Isaiah that this "virgin" is virginal after conception. No such idea is given in Isaiah.

At this point, we shall explain the real meaning of Isaiah's passage. Isaiah is telling King Ahaz of Judah not to fear, because God will not allow the invading armies to succeed against Jerusalem. There will be a sign. A young woman will have a son she will name Immanuel, which means "God is with us." He will be the assurance to Ahaz that the enemies will be defeated. In *Isaiah 8:8,10,* the name "Immanuel," God is with us, again is used as comfort.

A Biblical sign is something God gives to be helpful for the events under consideration. A sign to be given to King Ahaz must be for his time and his circumstance. Jesus, who was born over five hundred years later, cannot be the sign of comfort for King Ahaz in his troubles then, could he? Christianity's virgin birth is not the subject of this prophesy. In fact, the Messiah is not in this prophesy in any way.

Although we have disproved the so-called proof-text referring to the birth of Jesus, let's pursue this subject in order to offer answers to the puzzle of whose birth is being prophesied. Who is the man connected to the sign for King Ahaz?

First, it is possible it is King Ahaz's own son Hezekiah. Refer to *Isaiah 9:6-7,* "The Mighty God," analyzed earlier in our present chapter. By miraculous intervention, God defeated the Assyrians who attacked Judah during King Hezekiah's rule. Certainly, he could be designated "Immanuel," because during his reign God was with us in helping the Jewish people.

Another possibility is that it is Isaiah's own son. See *Isaiah 8:3-4,8,* "And I went unto the prophetess (Isaiah's wife); and she conceived, and bare a son. Then said the Lord to me, . . . For before the child shall have knowledge to cry, . . . the spoil of Samaria shall be taken away before the King of Assyria, . . . and . . . his wings shall fill . . . thy land, O Immanuel." This is a remarkable parallel to Isaiah 7:16, "For before the child shall know to refuse the evil, and choose the good, the land that thou abhorest shall be forsaken of both her kings."* A thought is offered here about Christianity's Jesus being in a position to refuse evil and choose good. Isn't Jesus sinless in Christianity? He could not, therefore, be the child spoken of in this verse or be the Immanuel of Isaiah's alleged virgin birth passage. Whether the verse under discussion is about Hezekiah, or Isaiah's own son, or anyone else is not of importance for our purpose. What is of importance is that we know the subject of Isaiah is assuredly not Jesus.

Of pertinence here are observations about Biblical supernatural birth. We are not alluding to God the Creator, by whom all things are. We do mean God the intervener, who miraculously circumvents the natural process to produce human birth. In the Hebrew Scriptures, we discover that God has intervened, but He never did so without a male seed, except at creation. Observe *Genesis 18:11,13-14, "Now Abraham and Sarah were old . . . and it ceased to be with Sarah after the man-*

ner of women . . . Shall I of a surety bear a child which am old? Is any thing too hard for the Lord? . . ." Here, by the way, is a very strange similarity to Elizabeth's conception in the New Testament. Read *Luke 1:36-37, ". . . Elizabeth, . . . also conceived a son in her old age: . . . her, who was called barren. For with God nothing shall be impossible."* Another intervention is disclosed in *Judges 13:3,(5), "And the angel of the Lord appeared unto the woman, and said unto her, Behold now, thou art barren, and bearest not: but thou shalt conceive, and bear a son."*

Thus, although no birth without male impregnation is ever reported in the Hebrew Bible, God has made special sons through unnatural means in cases of infertility. Stop and think. Doesn't this mean that Jesus, even if we were to accept the alleged virgin birth as true, is not a unique miraculously born being? Isn't he merely one among others, such as Isaac, Samson, and even John the Baptist? Elizabeth's conception is even likened to Mary's by the angel. Read the angel's words in *Luke 1:36, "And, behold, thy cousin Elizabeth, she hath also conceived a son . . ."* So barrenness and virginity are comparable barriers to conception in the New Testament it seems. Keep in mind that it is not the possibility of God's intervention which is at issue in our inquiry. What is being challenged is the situation as described in the New Testament.

Here is something else to think about. Why didn't Mary tell her husband of the special way the angel said she would conceive? It wasn't a secret. Elizabeth apparently knew. Yet, Joseph is said to have almost "put her away" believing her unfaithful. It is quite understandable that he should believe his wife was adulterous, because she conceived without him ever touching her. Furthermore, why didn't the angel tell Joseph about Mary, like he told Zacharias before the miraculous conception of Elizabeth? Instead, Joseph is left uninformed of the supposed special way Mary was made pregnant, until an angel in a dream tells him. The angel tells him so that Joseph should not believe Mary is unworthy of being his wife. This is really very peculiar. It is never said that Mary thinks Joseph would not believe her. She just neglects to tell him what obviously would be of great importance to him, as it is to her. It is a wonder, isn't it?

And now, we go on to another point. Observe in *Matthew 1:18,24-25, ". . . When as his mother Mary was espoused to Joseph, before they came together, she was found with child . . . Then Joseph . . . did as the angel of the Lord has bidden him, and took unto him his wife: And knew her not till she had brought forth her firstborn son . . ."* We learn that Joseph did not touch Mary, not only at the wedding time but throughout his whole marriage to her until Jesus was born. Strange, but as it is Christianity's narrative, it does not concern us. What is of concern is that the New Testament clearly relates that Joseph did have conjugal relations with Mary after Jesus was born. This is told plainly by the words "knew her not till." Yet, Christianity claims her perpetual virginity. In addition, we are told that Jesus was "firstborn," which implies that Mary had other children. This is corroborated by other verses, as discussed in our previous chapter, "His Family and Lack of Holy Awe," which divulge his siblings' names.

Our last remarks about this alleged virgin birth deal with its conceptual roots, which probably were found in pagan religions. For example, the pagan god Attis was written as born of a virgin. Many other pagan ideas are in the background of Christian worship, even though Christianity insists they have been elevated to true religious heights. However, our subject here is not paganism's expression in the Christian religion, but pandering to pagans. The virgin birth story appears to be an intrusion of a blatant pagan concept in order to make pagans feel at home in Christianity. Be that as it may, our inquiry should put the story under a very heavy cloud of disbelief.

HIS NAME IMMANUEL.

Isaiah 7:14, ". . . a virgin shall . . . call his name Immanuel." *(SEE Matthew 1:23)*

COMMENT: It allegedly is Jesus who is Immanuel, God is with us.

REBUTTAL: The verse in Isaiah says "she" shall call him. Matthew changes this to "they," without justification. Isaiah's reading is that the child is to be specifically named "Immanuel," while Matthew misdirects the emphasis from an actual name to a general designation. Biblically, humans or objects can have appellations or a series of appellations descriptive of God. Earlier in this chapter we have written of this in "The Lord Our Righteousness" and "The Mighty God." "Immanu-el" is to be a real name like "Samu-el" or "El-iezer," having a connection to "El" or God. People do get these names without being considered part of the essence of God in a special and different way from other human beings. The name is bestowed in respect of God.

Now, look at this twist of Scripture. Isaiah says his name shall be "Immanuel." Yet, in *Matthew 1:21-23 (Luke 1:31)* we read that an angel tells Joseph, ". . . thou shalt call his name Jesus: . . . Now all this was done, that it might be fulfilled which was spoken of the Lord by the prophet (Isaiah), saying, . . . they shall call his name Emmanuel, . . ."* We ask, how could the naming him "Jesus" fulfill Isaiah saying his name will be "Emmanuel," which Matthew correctly quotes from the prophesy? Remember, Isaiah says, "she shall call his name Immanuel," not, "they shall consider him to be Emmanuel." Paranthetically, his name should have been "Jeshua," which is what a child of the Hebrew people would be called, not "Jesus," a Greek language translation of Jeshua.

In any case, Matthew is not correct in believing Isaiah 7:14 is about the Messiah, the Christ of Christianity. As we have shown in the explanation of "Virgin Birth" preceding, Isaiah is speaking of someone who will be a sign so that King Ahaz has assurance the enemies will be defeated. This sign is not Jesus.

SPIRIT OF GOD UPON ME.

Isaiah 61:1-2, "The Spirit of the Lord God is upon me; because the Lord hath anointed me to preach good tidings ... To proclaim the acceptable year of the Lord, and the day of vengeance of our God ..." (SEE Luke 4:17-21).

COMMENT: Jesus saying, "This day is the scripture fulfilled in your ears," supposedly announces he is the Messiah in Luke.

REBUTTAL: Actually, Jesus just said that he is a prophet like Isaiah. He did not claim to be the anointed Messiah, but an anointed prophet. Continue reading *Luke 4:24 (Matthew 13:57) (Mark 6:4) (John 4:44)* where Jesus says plainly, ". . . *No prophet is accepted in his own country."* He even adds his own qualifications in *Luke 4:18, ". . . recovering of sight to the blind . . ."* The subject he is preaching is the kingdom, the time of God's Messianic kingdom and Day of Judgment. In these verses, the prophet Isaiah is speaking about his being anointed by God to prophesy, giving good tidings of the Messianic expectations to the Hebrew people. Note that the words "gospel" and "good tidings" pertain to news of the Messianic kingdom, not Jesus' alleged vicarious atonement. Jesus' preaching was of the kingdom, not his future death. Read *Luke 8:1, ". . . showing the glad tidings of the kingdom of God: . . ."* Also see *Mark 1:14, ". . . preaching the gospel of the kingdom of God."* The very same deliverance is preached by Isaiah and Jesus. It is Judaic. What Christianity has made of Jesus' preachings is another story.

SPIRIT OF GOD UPON HIM.

Isaiah 11:2, "And the spirit of the Lord shall rest upon him, the spirit of wisdom and understanding," (SEE Luke 3:21-22 (Matthew 3:16-17) (Mark 1:10) (John 1:32)).

COMMENT: This, in Christianity's viewpoint, was fulfilling the Messiah's obtaining God's spirit at Jesus' baptism.

REBUTTAL: Isaiah speaks here of the special qualities the Hebrew Messiah will have, which include God's spirit of wisdom and understanding. Christianity claims that Jesus received this special spirit of God at his baptism by John. They assert this, seemingly, with no substantiation. Moreover, if this assertion were to be accepted as fact, it would completely shatter Christianity's teaching that Jesus is God.

If there had been such a dramatic baptismal event, as reported in the New Testament, with a multitude of people seeing the descending dove and hearing the voice from heaven as Luke reported, they would surely have known they were looking at the special Son of God, presumably the Messiah. This fabulous news would have been spread far and wide, don't you think? Yet, there is no mass knowledge of this astounding event. If the occurrence at Jesus' baptism were true, the very many people viewing it would have made secrecy impossible. Think of the incredibility of anyone, no less "all the people," not passing along the word of what he had seen to the whole countryside. The people supposedly heard God's voice from heaven saying to Jesus, "Thou art my beloved Son; in thee I am well pleased." Nevertheless, we are shown that throughout his ministry people questioned who he was. The New Testament discloses that when Jesus asked who people thought he was in *Matthew 16:14 (Mark 8:28) (Luke 9:19), "And they said, Some say that thou art John the Baptist: some Elijah; and others, Jeremiah, or one of the prophets."* Refer to this book's previous chapter, "Jesus Was Not the Messiah—Who Was He?" for more.

We also add that the supposed miracle of the Christmas story is completely unknown to the people. It is as if the news of Jesus being the born Messiah had never been announced. The New Testament tells that shepherds knew of the birth and spread the news revealed to them by the angels. Kings from the east came to give him gifts. Still, now it is unknown. Read the analysis of "Bethlehem Birth" following for details.

Further, let's look into the knowledge of John the Baptist, the man who performed the baptism for Jesus and who presumably saw and heard everything, as reported in all accounts. Keep in mind that the baptism was a water cleansing ceremony for spiritual repentance. It had nothing to do with Christian baptism. It was Judaic. And Jesus participated in it.

Read this surprising revelation in *Matthew 11:2-3 (Luke 7:19-20), "Now when John (the Baptist) had heard in the prison the works of Christ, he sent two of his disciples, And said unto him, Art thou he that should come, or do we look for another?"* From this we learn John the Baptist did not know Jesus was the Messiah. These words surely prove false the alleged baptismal scene for Jesus, as depicted in the New Testament, especially as presented in John's version. The question, coming from John the Baptist, simply means he did not witness God's voice from heaven calling Jesus His "beloved Son." If John the Baptist didn't hear it, who did? John the Baptist's question also throws great suspicion on the following remarks by him that Jesus was greater than he. Read *Matthew 3:14, "I have need to be baptized of thee, and comest thou to me?"*

On the other hand, if the baptismal story were to be believed, very serious faults would result in the depiction of Jesus as God the Son of

the Trinity. Can God send Himself His own spirit? And, although it
might be possible to describe God as being pleased with Himself, God
cannot be described as being pleased with His Son, if His Son is Himself. It just doesn't make sense. The Trinity concept is in difficulty
here. However, with Judaism's interpretation of Isaiah, we comfortably
find God's "spirit of wisdom and understanding" resting on the
Hebrew Messiah, who in no way is God Himself.

SPIRIT OF GOD UPON MY SERVANT.

*Isaiah 42:1,6, "Behold my servant, whom I uphold; mine elect, in
whom my soul delighteth; I have put my spirit upon him: he shall bring
forth judgment to the Gentiles. I the Lord have called thee . . . and
will keep thee, and give thee for a covenant of the people, for a light of
the Gentiles;" (SEE Matthew 12:18).*

COMMENT: The servant is supposed to be Jesus with God's spirit.
REBUTTAL: The "him" of Isaiah is God's servant Israel. Note that
God has already put His spirit upon "him," so that Israel will be a
light to the nations. The fruition will occur in Messianic times, with
Messianic judgment. The following is verification of the servant representing the people of Israel. In *Isaiah 49:3,6* read, *". . . Thou art my
servant, O Israel, in whom I will be glorified. . . . I will also give thee
for a light to the Gentiles, that thou mayest be my salvation unto the
end of the earth."* Christianity's assertion for Jesus notwithstanding,
Israel is plainly the servant presented. Who is the light to the Gentiles?
Israel. Who gives salvation to the whole world for God? It is Israel,
the Chosen People.

BETHLEHEM BIRTH.

*Micah 5:2, "But thou, Bethlehem Ephratah, though thou be little
among the thousands of Judah, yet out of thee shall he come forth unto
me that is to be ruler in Israel; whose goings forth have been from of
old from everlasting." (SEE Matthew 2:5-6).*

COMMENT: Jesus was born in Bethlehem and fulfills this prophesy
for the Messiah. He, as well, is described as being in existence before
his earthly birth, Christianity says.
REBUTTAL: Micah is stating the Davidic heritage of the Messiah.
"Out of thee" is not the same as "born in." It merely means that the
Messiah's Davidic ancestors are from Bethlehem. We see this in
*I Samuel 17:12, "Now David was the son of that Ephrathite of Bethle-
hem-judah, whose name was Jesse . . ."*

Even if the passage were inferring that the actual birth of the Messiah would occur in Bethlehem, it still would not signify it was Jesus
being described by Micah. Many thousands of births over the many
centuries have occurred in Bethlehem since Micah. Even though the
New Testament went into special detail to describe Jesus birth in Beth-

lehem, it proves absolutely nothing. The Messianic function will indicate the Messiah, not his birthplace.

If the Messiah is to have a birth connection to Bethlehem, he also has to be a ruler, as indicated in the verse. But, we know that Jesus never ruled the land of Israel. Christianity cannot pick and choose. All verses pertaining to the Messiah's qualifications and activities have to become reality. See *Micah* verse *3* following, *". . . the remnant of his brethren shall return unto the children of Israel."* The ingathering of the dispersed Jewish people to the Holy Land did not occur in Jesus' time. The opposite happened when the Temple was destroyed, about forty years after his death. Also, see *Micah* verse *5* following, *"And this man shall be the peace when the Assyrian shall come into our land: . . ."* Jesus did no such thing. Fulfilling one verse out of context does not a Messiah make or prove. His birthplace is inconsequential when viewed against his non-performance in Messianic matters and the non-occurrence of Messianic expectations in Jesus' lifetime. The so-called second coming Judaically was not to happen and Christologically did not happen as specified, in the lifetime of the generation then alive.

Christianity's miracle birth in Bethlehem was not hidden. The New Testament states that three wise men came from the east. Did they say nothing of their remarkable journey? The New Testament reports that King Herod killed many Bethlehem children under the age of two because the Messiah was rumored to have been born there then. Did not all Bethlehem shake from this? The Christian Scriptures tell that Elizabeth, the mother of John the Baptist, knew of Mary's miraculous baby. Was nothing said by Elizabeth of this to others? She was not asked to keep this a secret. Also, shepherds knew of the birth. They even are said to have told people. In *Luke 2:17-18*, *". . . they made known abroad the saying which was told them concerning the child. And all they that heard it wondered . . ."* Still, the multitudes following Jesus' ministry were totally unaware of his miraculous birth as related. Finally, Jesus' family should have known of his miraculous birth. Nevertheless, with all this disclosure and lack of secrecy, the population of the Holy Land knew nothing.

What can be made of this seeming ignorance of the Christmas birth? The important supernatural event of Christianity is unknown to the people of Israel. It is even specifically stated that the people were still awaiting the Messiah while Jesus was among them. Read *John 7:41-42*, *". . . But some said, Shall Christ come out of Galilee (Nazareth)? Hath not the scripture said, That Christ cometh of the seed of David, and out of the town of Bethlehem, where David was?"* Look here. If the Christmas story were true, the people would be seeking him who was already born, not waiting for him who was still to come. Certainly, the fabulous news of the birth of the Messiah would quickly have been passed from village to village, had the Christmas story been true.

One last explanation is given now concerning, "whose goings forth have been from old, from everlasting." The Messiah is not from everlasting. It is God's preparing for the coming of the Messiah which is from everlasting. Messianic expectations are in this manner described as being his plans eternally. Any other explanation of this phrase would be lacking Biblical basis. Judaism's understanding of this verse by Micah is comfortable and meaningful in context.

OUT OF EGYPT.

Hosea 11:1, "When Israel was a child, then I loved him, and called my son out of Egypt." (SEE Matthew 2:14-15).

COMMENT: Jesus' Egypt journey was the fulfillment of Hosea's words about the Messiah, they say.

REBUTTAL: It can be said that the trip to Egypt is highly questionable. Luke omits it entirely. Read *Luke 2:22, ". . . they brought him to Jerusalem, to present him to the Lord:"* And then see *Luke 2:39, "And when they had performed all things according to the law of the Lord, they returned into Galilee, to their own city Nazareth."* There is no fleeing to Egypt in Luke. We ask why they would have to flee to Egypt when they were not residents of Bethlehem, where Herod supposedly was a danger? Nazareth was a safe place from Herod's reported murders of the children. Yet, Matthew has them fleeing on a long and difficult journey into Egypt and then going to Nazareth, while Luke has them sensibly going directly from Jerusalem to Nazareth.

The other point to be made here is that the "son" being spoken of is the Biblical "Israel." Read Hosea in context and you will clearly see the exodus from Egypt of the Israel people is the subject. This "son" is the loving term God uses for His Chosen People. Whether Christianity will accept it or not, the term "son" refers to Israel here, and we will corroborate this fact with the Scriptural verses of *Exodus 4:22-23, "And thou shalt say unto Pharaoh, Thus saith the Lord, Israel is my son, even my firstborn: And I say unto thee, Let my son go, that he may serve me: . . ."* Do we have to relate the Passover story concerning God's miraculous rescue of the Israel people from the oppressors in Egypt? Also, note that Hosea used the past tense, "called my son." Jesus was not in this time frame, surely. The Messiah is nowhere in Hosea's verses. No fulfillment was required by the Messiah, because the call out of Egypt was for Israel and had been accomplished.

RACHEL WEEPING FOR HER CHILDREN.

Jeremiah 31:15, ". . . Rachel weeping for her children refused to be comforted for her children, because they were not." (SEE Matthew 2:16-18).

COMMENT: Rachel, it is said, wept for the children Herod allegedly killed at Bethlehem at the time Jesus was born.

REBUTTAL: This is a prime example of a verse being taken out of context. The story of Rachel weeping has to do with the captive children of the tribes of the Jewish people in exile. It has nothing to do with Herod's supposed slaying of children. Just continue reading the next two verses, *"Thus saith the Lord; Refrain thy voice from weeping . . . they shall come again from the land of the enemy . . . thy children shall come again to their own border."* Rachel is weeping for the missing Jewish children who had not returned from exile. God promised that they would all return.

Also, if this were about Bethlehem, it should have been Leah who was weeping, not Rachel. For this region was occupied by the tribe of Judah, and Leah was the foremost female ancestor of note here. Rachel was a primary ancestor of Ephraim's tribe. The name Ephraim often was used as the collective name of the Jewish people. So, this fits the Jewish understanding completely.

Here is a historical question. Why was Herod's terrible deed of mass murder of infants never reported other than in the New Testament? Information of this magnitude and importance certainly should have gotten into Josephus' writings, as he was a major historian who was writing about this area in those days. Not a word is found about Herod's slaying of Bethlehem's infants, which leaves a cloud of doubt about it having happened at all.

DWELT IN NAZARETH.

Judges 13:5, ". . . for the child shall be a Nazarite unto God from the womb . . ." (SEE Matthew 2:23).

COMMENT: Jesus was a fulfillment of this, according to Matthew.

REBUTTAL: There is no such statement as Matthew claims. The passage from Judges concerns a barren woman, who through God's intervention, will give birth. It is announced by an angel of the Lord that she will have a child, one who belongs to the Nazarite sect. In the original Hebrew the words Nazarite and Nazarene are not the same or even similar, being Nazir and the other Notsri. There is obviously a name mix up. But, more than this, the son is to "begin to deliver Israel out of the hands of the Philistines," which Jesus never did.

NAZARETH TO CAPERNUM.

Isaiah 9:1-2, "Nevertheless the dimness shall not be such as was in her vexation, when at the first he lightly afflicted the land of Zebulum and . . . Naphtali (Capernum's borders), and afterward did more grievously afflict her (Israel). . . . The people that walked in darkness have seen a great light: they that dwell in the land of the shadow of death, upon them hath the light shined." (SEE Matthew 4:13-16).

COMMENT: Christianity says these two verses show that Jesus was referred to in prophesy in this when Jesus went to Capernum.

REBUTTAL: That Jesus went to Capernum and that Christianity calls him the "light" has no bearing on Isaiah. First, it should be noted that the New Testament incorrectly places these verses together. They really are verses 8:23 and 9:1, separated in style of writing, one prose and one poetry, as well as in subject matter. Reading the original Hebrew makes this quite clear. Verse 8:23 is in a chapter which is about the recent destruction by the Assyrians, at first lightly and then grievously afflicting Israel. The second verse, the beginning of the next chapter 9, concerns the deliverance of the people that were walking in darkness, meaning suffering destruction. They that were in the "shadow of death" were saved from Assyria's victory by the miraculous intervention of God.

The word "light" used in this context by Isaiah means deliverance, not enlightenment. Another Scripture verse which uses "light" in this same way is *Esther 8:16, "The Jews had light, and gladness, and joy, and honor."* And even if it were the meaning of enlightenment, it is the nation of Israel which is the "light" God has given to the world. For example read *Isaiah 49:3, 6, ". . . Thou art my servant, O Israel, in whom I will be glorified. . . . I will also give thee for a light to the Gentiles, that thou mayest be my salvation unto the end of the earth."*

We have disclosed earlier in this chapter that Isaiah 9:6-7 under title "The Mighty God" is about King Hezekiah, who ruled during this miraculous deliverance. He is the deliverer who brought safety to the people of Israel, defeating the enemy with God's help. Capernum, except for bordering on the land under discussion, and Jesus, except for having gone to Capernum in the New Testament, have nothing to do with the passage from Isaiah.

ON AN ASS.

Zechariah 9:9-10, "Rejoice . . . thy King cometh unto thee: he is just, and having salvation; lowly, and riding upon an ass, and upon a colt the foal of an ass. . . . and he shall speak peace unto the heathen: and his dominion shall be from sea to sea . . ." (SEE Matthew 21:2-5 (Mark 11:2-7) (Luke 19:30-35) (John 12:14-15)).

COMMENT: It is Jesus the Messiah who has come in this manner, Christianity claims.

REBUTTAL: There is an important aspect of this which should be examined, because it exposes the term "fulfillment" in Christianity's alleged proof-texts. We find that in the New Testament it is admitted that fulfillment is post-arranged. There is no casualness of linkage to Hebrew Bible passages. Boldly, the New Testament asserts there is manipulation of the situation in order to "fulfill." Just what is suspected about many proof-texts is openly reported in this one. There is a forced connection of situation to fit prophesy. An open mind should look more skeptically at other proof-texts which also could have been manipulated. Here is what is said which exposes the false fulfillment in *Matthew 21:2,4, ". . . Go into the village . . . find an ass tied, and a colt with her: loose them, and bring them unto me. All this was done, that it might be fulfilled which was spoken by the prophet, saying, . . . thy King cometh unto thee . . ."* Couldn't anyone have done this? What kind of proof is that?

Matthew makes an error in reading *Zechariah 9:9.* Because of his misreading he has Jesus asking for two animals to be brought to him, and he rides them, in whatever strange manner, into Jerusalem. The other gospel writers knew that, *"upon an ass, even upon a colt the foal of an ass,"* was the proper rendering, double designation being Biblical style. They have Jesus coming on a single colt correctly. Now, keep in mind that riding on a donkey was a common occurrence there and then. It still is done there. Thousands of people could be included in this manner of coming to Jerusalem. Therefore, the passage does not point to Jesus alone and is valueless as proof for Christianity.

If Jesus were the Messiah, he wouldn't be so concerned about how he rode into Jerusalem, but how he would fulfill the next verse in *Zechariah 9:10* which reads, *". . . and he shall speak peace unto the heathen: and his dominion shall be from sea even to sea, . . ."* Once again we state that Jesus never had dominion and never was a king from sea to sea. Moreover, we have New Testament verses in *Matthew 15:24* and *Matthew 10:6* which say that Jesus' message was not for the heathen, which contradicts Zechariah's prophesy for the Messiah. Jesus says, *". . . I am not sent but unto the lost sheep of the house of Israel. But go rather to the lost sheep of the house of Israel."* As for speaking peace, read *Matthew 10:34 (Luke 12:51), "Think not that I am come to send peace on earth: I came not to send peace, but a sword."* We conclude with an explanation of "having salvation." It has nothing to do with vicarious atonement. "Having salvation" simply means giving help and escape from earthly troubles, which is the Messianic expectation for Israel.

WITH CLOUDS OF HEAVEN.

Daniel 7:13-14, "I saw in the night visions, . . . one like the Son of man came with the clouds of heaven, and came to the Ancient of days, and they brought him near before him. And there was given him dominion, and glory, and a kingdom, that all people, nations, . . . should serve him: his dominion is an everlasting dominion . . ." (SEE Matthew 24:30).

COMMENT: This shows that Jesus has God-like qualities, as he is the

Messiah, so they say.

REBUTTAL: This is Daniel's dream. It is a vision. He saw someone like a human, enveloped in clouds, approach God and brought closer to God, perhaps by angels. There, before God, this human was given the Messiah's glorious role. Note that this is not an appearance on earth, but a heavenly one. He does not appear on earth enveloped in clouds, but is thus in heaven before God. Therefore, no conflict exists between Zechariah's Messiah given before this and Daniel's Messiah. Also, understand that the Messiah is given his role by God. He is not described as part of God in any way. And know that the Messiah is to function as the ruler on earth for God in the Messianic times.

Now proceed to *Daniel 7:26-27*, "*. . . they shall take away his dominion . . . And the . . . dominion . . . shall be given to the people of the saints of the most High. . . .*" In the continuation of Daniel's vision, it seems the Messiah is only temporarily in charge, after which the Messianic Era will continue everlasting with the dominion given to the entire people of Israel as a whole. Our final remark is that there is nothing whatsoever that points to Jesus as the Messiah. Anyone might be the ruler Daniel saw in a dream.

JOHN THE BAPTIST IS ELIJAH

Malachi 4:5 (Malachi 3:1), "*Behold, I will send you Elijah the prophet before the coming of the great and dreadful day of the Lord:*" (*SEE Matthew 11:10 (Mark 1:2) (Luke 1:17)* and also see *Matthew 11:14 (Matthew 17:10-13) (Mark 9:11-13)*).

COMMENT: John the Baptist is supposed to be Elijah, the precursor of the Messiah. Jesus the Messiah must come after John the Baptist who is Elijah in Christianity.

REBUTTAL: Judaism and Christianity agree that Elijah the prophet is to return before the Messiah comes. Let's see if John the Baptist was Elijah. Elijah was a real human being, and he is to return, not someone "like" him. See *I Kings 18:21*, and *II Chronicles 21:12* for Elijah's identification as a person. Then see *II Kings 2:11* where Elijah is taken "*by a whirlwind into heaven.*" Therefore, he should return in bodily form, not as expressed in *Luke 1:17*, "*. . . in the spirit and power. . .*" It is explicitly said by Jesus that Elijah has returned and is John the Baptist in person. For instance, in *Matthew 11:14* we read, "*. . . this is Elijah, which was for to come.*"

Let's examine what John the Baptist says about himself. He should know who he is, don't you think? Read *John 1:19-21*, "*And this is the record of John, . . . And he confessed, . . . I am not the Christ. And they asked him, What then? Art thou Elijah? And he saith, I am not. Art thou that prophet? And he answered, No.*" This is a forthright, clear denial. He twice answered, denying he was Elijah, after denying he was the Messiah. A prophet would not lie in a confession. A prophet would not hide his mission. Malachi says Elijah is to be a messenger to prepare the people for the Lord. John the Baptist, if he were Elijah, would not deny, but would communicate, his mission. Consequently, we must accept as true his denial.

John the Baptist says in *Matthew 3:11*, "... *he that cometh after me is mightier than I* ..." But look again. You find he is modestly saying he is not anyone other than a baptizer, of lesser importance than the one who follows later.

What, then, is John the Baptist's function? You find in *Mark 1:3-5 (Matthew 3:1-6) (Luke 3:2-4)*, "... *Prepare ye the way of the Lord, make his paths straight. John did baptize in the wilderness, and preach the baptism of repentance for the remission of sins. . . . all baptized of him in the river of Jordan, confessing their sins.*" Thus we learn that people came to John the Baptist for confession and repentance of transgression. They performed a ceremony of spiritual cleansing in water. It was Judaism in ancient form. Take a good look at this question:— Why would John the Baptist be engaged in helping people rid themselves of sin if he were awaiting the Christ of vicarious atonement to take away sin? Read everything in the New Testament about John the Baptist and you will find nothing Christologic whatsoever. He preached repentance for the forgiveness by God of sin, not vicarious atonement.

Moreover, Jesus preached this very same message, the necessity of repentance for the remission of transgression. Both Jesus and John the Baptist preached repentance for entrance into the coming Messianic kingdom of God on earth and Judgment Day. Jesus said in *Mark 1:15*, "... *the kingdom of God is at hand: repent ye, and believe the gospel.*" And this "gospel" was before his supposed sacrificial death. It was Judaism's teaching of repentance, Judaism's good news. Refer back to our chapter, "Jesus Was Not the Messiah—Who Was He?" for other verses revealing Jesus' preaching of Judaism's message.

What specifically is Elijah to do? In *Malachi 4:6* we read, "*And he shall turn the heart of the fathers to the children, and the heart of the children to their fathers* . . ." In other words, peace and harmony are to follow his arrival. Alas, we still await this beautiful prophesy's fulfillment.

Last, we shall analyze *Luke 7:19-20,22 (Matthew 11:2-4)* in regard to John the Baptist. Look at, "*And John calling unto him two of his disciples sent them to Jesus, saying, Art thou he that should come? or look we for another? . . . then Jesus answering said . . . tell John what things ye have seen . . .*" This demonstrates that he was not aware who Jesus was. Well, if John the Baptist were Elijah the prophet returned to earth, wouldn't he have special knowledge of the Messiah and no need to inquire? After all, they both supposedly were sent from heaven and should know of each other. You discover that not only does John the Baptist deny he is Elijah and not achieve the results of Elijah's mission, but he also displays lack of knowledge which Elijah must have concerning the Messiah. Therefore, no forerunner arrived before Jesus, as required Biblically for the Messiah's coming.

SHEPHERD AND SHEEP.

Zechariah 13:7, "Awake, O sword, against my shepherd, and against the man that is my fellow, saith the Lord of hosts; smite the shepherd, and the sheep shall be scattered: and I will turn mine hand upon the little ones." (SEE Mark 14:27 (Matthew 26:31)).
COMMENT: It is said that Jesus is the shepherd, while the disciples are the sheep.
REBUTTAL: Jesus may have used these words to make a point to his disciples, but Zechariah meant no such thing. The verse pertains to the kings (shepherd) and princes (little ones) who mistakenly think they are special creatures of God. The sheep are the people of Israel who will be freed from the foreign rulers' domination as God promised. This difficult verse can be explained no better. A forced usage of shepherd and sheep by Jesus has no connection to the original meaning by Zechariah.

JESUS BRUISED THE DEVIL'S HEAD.

Genesis 3:15, ". . . it shall bruise thy head, and thou shalt bruise his heal." (SEE Romans 16:20).
COMMENT: Christianity's Jesus is to destroy the Devil.
REBUTTAL: This is taken as a prophesy concerning Jesus and the Devil, in the guise of the serpent. It isn't. This interpretation is so forced that it is obviously false to all except those whose purpose it serves. But, even if it were to be interpreted as having reference to Jesus bruising the Devil, it can be shown erroneous, in that Jesus' alleged sacrificial death did not defeat evil on this earth.

The New Testament states that the Devil lives and has power, even over Christian believers. Read *I Thessalonians 2:18, "Wherefore we would have come . . . but Satan hindered us."* Also see *I John 1:8, "If we say we have no sin, we deceive ourselves . . ."* But, if Jesus were the subject of Genesis here, at his death the Devil's power would have lost its sway. In addition, Paul himself contradicts the forced interpretation being about Jesus in these words, *". . . shall bruise Satan under your feet shortly."* He admits the Devil is not yet defeated, that he will be bruised "shortly." According to Christianity the "shortly" is now expanded in time two thousand years. According to Judaism, a second coming has no basis in Hebrew Scripture, whether shortly or otherwise. This point has been made elsewhere in our book.   Additionally, the verse contains within itself the proof of the falseness of the interpretation by Christianity. If you read the words, we see "It (Jesus) shall bruise thy (Devil's) head, and thou (Devil) shalt bruise his (Jesus') heel." So, we find that after having been bruised on the head by Jesus the Devil still is able to do injury to Jesus' heel. No matter how this verse is twisted, it cannot be made to fit Jesus conquering the Devil.

Finally, we remind you that Jesus was even tempted by the Devil in the wilderness. This, of course, disqualifies him from being part of God in the Trinity, for God cannot be tempted by the Devil. Read *James 1:13, ". . . God cannot be tempted with evil . . ."* But, it further shows that Jesus was so weak he could be tempted by the very essence he is supposed to defeat.

A STRANGER IN THE LAND.

Jeremiah 14:8, "O the hope of Israel, the savior thereof in time of trouble, why shouldest thou be as a stranger in the land . . . ? "

COMMENT: Because it was said that Jesus had no where to lay his head in *Matthew 8:20,* Jesus is the savior of Jeremiah's verse, as they see it.

REBUTTAL: This verse is taken out of context, where it is referring to God, who is the hope of Israel. It is God who is our Savior in time of trouble. In context, it is a plea to God to help Israel in its famine. Asking God why he is "a stranger in the land" is actually a way of asking Him to help his people in their trouble. Anthropomorphic expressions alluding to God's doings are common in the Scriptures. Moreover, God is Israel's Savior. See *Hosea 13:4, "Yet I am the Lord thy God . . . there is no savior beside me."* A final point is if Jesus were the subject of this verse it would make him other than God. For we read in *Psalms 24:1, "The earth is the Lord's, and the fulness thereof . . ."*

TWO COMINGS.

Zechariah 9:9-10, ". . . thy King cometh . . . lowly, and riding upon an ass, . . . and shall speak peace unto the heathen: and his dominion shall be from sea to sea . . ."

Daniel 7:13-14, "I saw in the night visions, . . . one like the Son of man came with clouds of heaven, and came to the Ancient of days . . . And there was given him dominion . . ."

COMMENT: On these two verses rest Christianity's basis in the Scriptures for two comings of Jesus.

REBUTTAL: Zechariah and Daniel have different descriptions of the Messiah, but they are explained comfortably within Judaism. There is only one coming of the Messiah. Refer to "On an Ass" and "With Clouds of Heaven" earlier in this chapter. Daniel is describing his dream. He saw someone approach God in heaven enveloped in clouds who was given the Messiah's glorious role. It is not an earthly appearance as in Zechariah.

It is very important to understand that there is no Hebrew Scripture basis for two comings of the Messiah, none whatsoever! This lack of foundation coupled with non-appearance as promised in the New Testament in the lifetime of the generation then alive presents us with justification in asserting that two comings is a false teaching of Christianity. Often, when Christianity is at a loss to reply about an unaccomplished fulfillment, they utilize the two comings for their reply. Of course, they may do so as they are in charge of formulating their own religion. But, their claim has no basis in the Hebrew Bible and no completion as indicated in the New Testament. Judaism's advocate answers, "False teaching," when a second coming is put forward to solve Christianity's quandaries.

A SECOND COMING.

Hosea 5:15, "I will go and return to my place, till they (Ephraim and Judah) acknowledge their offence, and seek my face . . ."

COMMENT: According to Christianity, Jesus is to come a second time as told in this verse.

REBUTTAL: Hosea is discussing repentance being needed before God gives His salvation. It is acknowledgement of error and drawing near to God's holy laws which will help the Jewish people and bring God back to closeness to His Chosen People. This is Hosea's message. Paul, in opposition to Hosea, says salvation will come through a Deliverer's intervention taking away sins. Although Paul says "as it is written," it is not at all written in Hosea or anywhere else in the Hebrew Bible. But, returning to thoughts of a second coming for the Messiah based on this verse from Hosea, we find there is nothing of the kind propounded. The "return" is by God, not the Messiah, for reasons of proper repentance for transgression.

RESURRECTION, SOUL IN HELL.

Psalm 16:9-10, "Therefore my heart is glad, and my glory rejoiceth: my flesh also shall rest in hope. For thou wilt not leave my soul in hell; neither wilt thou suffer thine Holy One to see corruption. (SEE Acts 2:27, 31).

COMMENT: Here is Biblical back-up for Jesus' presumed resurrection, it is said.

REBUTTAL: The Psalm is an expression of the supreme joy the psalmist feels in having hope of eternal life. The translation incorrectly uses "Holy One" for what simply is "godly one" in the Hebrew original, thus being misleading. We have shown in this book's chapter, "Personal Salvation Through Judaism," that Judaism does, indeed, offer eternal life to devout Jews.

The proper translation from the Hebrew is, ". . . my flesh also dwelleth in safety;" which is not true about Jesus in the literal sense. We know he died on the cross with wounds in his body. So, as this is false about Jesus in one area, it just as well could be false in supposedly alluding to the future event of Jesus' resurrection in Christian belief. Furthermore, if Jesus were part of God, how could he as God ever go to hell? And if he got to hell, how could God the Father give help to God the Son to remove him from the Devil's home? It is a nonsensical picture.

Now we shall study the New Testament's disclosure of the resurrection. We are not interested in discussing the resurrection as a happening or non-happening, per se. It is certainly beyond proving either way. In any case, it is Christianity's bedrock and has no relevance to Judaism. However, we are justified in inquiring into the substantiation of the resurrection because, as Paul admitted in effect, without the resurrection there is no Christianity. If we can bring to light and properly expose the doubt of the resurrection to those Jews who have converted or may be considering conversion to Christianity, Judaism's truth should take hold and prevail for all thinking persons. The thinking God-given mind should be able to capture the God-given heart and return it to its home in Judaism.

There is an astonishing lack of harmony and many conflicting details in the renderings of the four Gospel stories concerning the resurrection of Jesus from death. Why, if it were true, is there such an abundance of incompatable evidence about this most important event in Christianity? Why, if it were true, are there such inconsistencies in the documentation, with as many as four different accounts of the same happening being related? Christianity may be certain of the resurrection, but it would be in spite of, not because of, the Gospel stories which contradict each other in substantial ways. At best, the stories make for much confusion and justifiable lack of trust. At worst, they demonstrate that the resurrection is a deception.

Let's look at some contradictory areas which lay open the resurrection as likely contrived, rather than a true happening. In *Matthew chapter 28,* an angel descends during an earthquake, rolls back the stone closing the tomb, and sits on it. The angel shows the empty sepulcher to Mary Magdalene and another Mary, saying Jesus is risen from the dead and is on his way to Galilee. The angel says the women will meet Jesus on the road as they go to tell the disciples. They do meet him and hold his feet, and he tells them to continue on their way. The eleven disciples see Jesus. We are then presented with this perplexing verse concerning his disciples' doubts, even after supposedly seeing him alive, resurrected. Read *Matthew 28:17, "And when they saw him, they worshipped him: but some doubted."* Some "doubted" his return from the dead. Moreover, there is absolutely no reference to any ascension to heaven by Jesus in Matthew's version.

Now let's see *Mark's chapter 16.* There are three women, not two. Mary Magdalene, Mary the mother of James, plus Salome. They arrive at the tomb, with the stone already rolled away. When they enter the tomb, they see a young man sitting. He tells them what in Matthew the angel tells them. Jesus appears to Mary Magdalene alone, not to anyone else as in Matthew, and she tells his disciples. Again, we have complete doubt by his disciples. Read *Mark 16:11, "And they, when they had heard that he was alive and had been seen by her, believed not."* They did not believe Jesus was resurrected. Even more disbelief is found in *Mark 16:12-13, "After that he appeared in another form unto two of them, . . . And they went and told it unto the residue: neither believed they them."* It is perfectly clear from this that the disciples were not prepared to believe in Jesus coming back to life. We add this plain statement in *Mark 9:10, "And they kept that saying with themselves, questioning one with another what the rising from the dead should mean."* This is even more extraordinary in that it comes allegedly directly after a voice from out of a cloud tells the disciples that, *"This is my beloved Son."*

We must reflect on all this disbelief by Jesus' disciples. One can ask, what was all the master to disciples talk about? A disciple is someone who learns from his teacher. Jesus' ministry is over, and yet his disciples understand nothing of Christianity's vicarious atonement. He obviously taught nothing to his disciples of death, resurrection, and vicarious atonement for mankind's sin. They weren't taught this. They didn't believe or understand anything about this. Their lack of knowledge is verified earlier in the Gospels when he told that he must "suffer, die, and the third day rise." Doesn't this confirm our understanding of Jesus the Jew and the Messianic message he preached of repentance for the forgiveness of sins?

Jesus displays annoyance at his disciples' lack of understanding. In *Mark 16:14* we read, *"Afterward he appeared unto the eleven as they sat at meat, and upbraided them with their unbelief and hardness of heart, because they believed not them which has seen him after he was risen."* It seems Jesus' own close disciples, whom he taught, had to see him personally and did not believe second-hand reports of his resurrection. In Matthew we are told that some doubted even after viewing him supposedly risen from the dead. The question we ask here is:—Why should untold millions of nonbelievers, who also never saw and never touched, believe something his own disciples did not believe without firsthand experience, and some not even then? Put another way, there is New Testament justification for people not believing the unbelievable, for his disciples did not either.

Returning to Mark, we have a flimsy statement of his ascending to heaven. We have this verse in *Mark 16:19*, *"So then after the Lord had spoken unto them, he was received up into heaven, and sat on the right hand of God."* What did the eleven see, if anything? Note that there is nothing written of how he was lifted from the earth or the disciples' seeing anything. We read of what the disciples surely did not have the capability to see, his being received into heaven. Certainly, no one actually saw Jesus being received and seated on the right hand of God. The verse is obviously a belief, not a verification of his ascension.

Let's compare *Luke's chapter 24* rendering with Matthew and Mark. Here we have the women expanded to Mary Magdalene, Joanna, Mary the mother of James, and other women that were there. The women find the stone already rolled away and the tomb empty. Two men standing by the women tell them what in Matthew the one angel and in Mark the one sitting man tells. All the women tell the disciples, while in Matthew only the two Marys tell and in Mark only Mary Magdalene tells. Jesus does not appear to Mary Magdalene at all in this version.

Luke, alone, tries to convince that Jesus had made a Christology message known to these women previously. The two men in *Luke 24:6-8* say, *". . . remember how he spake unto you when he was yet in Galilee, Saying, the Son of man must be delivered into the hands of sinful men, and be crucified, and the third day rise again. And they remembered his words."* Our opinion is that this was added by Luke to lend credence to Christology. And our opinion is based on the evidence in the New Testament concerning this. Read *Matthew 13:10-11 (13-14) (Mark 4:11-12) (Luke 8:10)*, *". . . Why speakest thou unto them in parables? . . . Because it is given unto you (disciples) to know the mysteries of the kingdom of heaven, but to them (others) it is not given."* Only Jesus' disciples were told whatever the mysteries were, and they were perplexed by what they heard. They were "to know," but they did not understand what was said to them. More later on this. But, our point here is that only they, not the women, were told.

Now we return to disbelief in *Luke 24:11*, *"And their words seemed to them as idle tales, and they believed not."* Two followers meet Jesus, in hidden form, and tell him the story of how Jesus, a mighty prophet, was condemned to death. They then confirm that they believed he would fulfill the Messianic expectations. Read *Luke 24:21*, *"But we trusted that it had been he which should have redeemed Israel: . . ."* They say plainly they had believed Jesus was the Hebrew Messiah, and we gather that they were disappointed by his death. Then they recognize they are with Jesus, and Jesus speaks Christologically. The two followers go to Jerusalem to find the eleven disciples, while the other Gospels place the disciples in Galilee. They tell the disciples that Jesus rose from the dead and they saw him alive. Jesus then appears in their midst, but the disciples do not believe they are seeing Jesus alive until he shows them his body and tells them to touch him so they know he is not a vision.

In the last verses of Luke, Jesus seems to make the point that the Hebrew Scriptures have Christologics. No one appears to have had comprehension of this previously. Read *Luke 24:45, "Then opened he their understanding, that they might understand the scriptures."* Whether these words were actually Jesus' is not of consequence, for it surely is what Christianity believes, as opposed to Jesus' pro-Judaism quotations. Notwithstanding the Christologics, these words are seen by Judaism's advocate as a reverse proof-text, for they implicitly state that the Scriptures were Judaically interpreted by Jesus' disciples throughout his ministry. Jesus taught what the disciples learned, and they learned the Hebrew Bible in Judaism's terms.

Moreover, why his disciples never knew of Christologics before is baffling. He supposedly did tell them all previously, as written in *Matthew 16:21-23 (Mark 8:31-33) and Luke 9:22,44-45 (Matthew 17:22-23) (Mark 9:31-32).* For example read *Luke 9:22,45, ". . . the Son of man must suffer many things, . . . and be slain, and be raised the third day. But they understood not this saying, and it was hidden from them, that they perceived it not: and they feared to ask him of that saying."* The disciples were given "to know" the mysteries, were told the happenings, and yet only at the end of the Gospel, after Jesus' death, was their understanding opened. This lacks logic. Because they were "to know," they should have understood and should not have been "afraid to ask." Also, we know their understanding was not to be delayed until after Jesus' alleged resurrection. We have just read that they were to understand during Jesus' ministry, while the others were spoken to in parables so they did not comprehend.

Jesus' disciples seem totally unaware of his supposed mission. This is incomprehensible, because a disciple's function is to learn his master's teachings. Why possess disciples at all if no one understands what is being taught? Why have a message at all that is not fully grasped? We offer the following in answer which solves the riddle:— The disciples did, indeed, understand Jesus' teachings to them, for he taught Judaism's Messianic message. Christianity changed Jesus, the Jewish Messiah, into Jesus, the Christ of Christianity, when expectations of Messianic fulfillment in Judaic terms collapsed. Consequently, his message changed from Judaic to Christologic. The new layers conflict with the older layers. Confusion and multiple interpretation are the result, as found in the verses of the New Testament. We need not pursue this as a study, because it cannot be proved, yet neither can it be disproved. It is submitted as a reasonable consideration.

Back to Luke, we finally have a verse about ascending in *Luke*

24:51, ". . . he was parted from them, and carried up into heaven."
Yet again, here is really an unsubstantiated belief, lacking in credence.
We read a "carried up," which is an acceptable detail. But, this detail
is accompanied by "into heaven," which is not possible in any firsthand report by the disciples.

Now we arrive at *John's* story in *chapter 20*, which is very different again from the other Gospels. Mary Magdalene, with no other
woman, sees the stone removed. She does so before dawn on Sunday,
which differs from the other reports of early morning. No angel or
man-form was present, and she did not go inside the tomb. All of this
deviates from the other three Gospels. She then goes to Peter and
another disciple to tell them of the stone and tomb. They go to the
tomb to see for themselves that it was empty.

Here again we have corroboration of the fact that the disciples
were totally uninformed of Christology. Read *John 20:9, "For as yet
they knew not the scriptures, that he must rise again from the dead."*
As Jews, they knew of no such Scripture, of course. Christianity has
made the forced, erroneous connections. It can be discerned that the
words in the New Testament, even those ascribed to Jesus, which seem
to say that the Hebrew Scriptures are Christologic are merely the
expression of the early Church trying to validate itself. Although the
New Testament uses alleged proof-texts, they are just as false as the
ones not written there. Judaism's advocate is not challenging Christianity, but challenging their use of the Hebrew Scriptures. Moreover, we
have shown in this book that the New Testament itself possesses a layer
which is totally Judaic. We have shown that Jesus interpreted the
Hebrew Scriptures as a Jew for Judaism would.

Returning to John's story, Mary Magdalene then looks into the
tomb and sees two angels sitting inside. They do not tell her anything
about Jesus' supposed resurrection. We know this because she thinks
Jesus has been hidden elsewhere. When she turns, she sees Jesus in an
unknown form. She does not know him until he speaks, and then we
read in *John 20:17, "Touch me not; for I am not yet ascended to my
Father: . . . and your Father . . ."* In this version, Mary Magdalene is
told not to touch Jesus, while elsewhere she is permitted to do so.
Note also that God is described as the Father of us all, which destroys
the concept of the special Father relationship Christianity bestows on
God for Jesus.

Continuing, she goes and tells the disciples about Jesus. The same
evening, Jesus goes to the disciples and shows them his body to prove
himself. Thomas was absent at the time Jesus appeared, and he says he
would not believe the happening unless he himself touches Jesus' body.
In the other Gospels, Thomas was not absent, because Jesus is
reported to appear to all eleven disciples (minus Judas, the twelfth)

later in the day of the alleged resurrection. Eight days later Jesus reappears and Thomas touches him and is convinced. We read in *John 20:29, "Thomas because thou hast seen me, thou has believed: blessed are they that have not seen, and yet have believed."* But, recall that Thomas' doubting is not any different than the doubting of the other disciples, who also needed to see and touch in order to believe. It is emphasized here, for Christianity's purpose of making doubt unacceptable and reproachful. John omits verification of the supposed ascending to heaven, as did Matthew. Another difference in John's Gospel is that he has Jesus returning three times to his disciples and doing what is not reported elsewhere.

The disciples doubted, some even after viewing Jesus alive after death. Therefore, why should the story of the resurrection have any believability to others who, in addition to not having firsthand proof, have been presented with flimsy and contradictory reports of this very central event for Christianity? Why should the story of the resurrection be believed by those who, in addition, see no fulfillment of God's Scriptures in its unfolding? Plainly, the result of the Gospel stories of the resurrection is that those who believe will believe in spite of lack of proper substantiation. For Paul says in *I Corinthians 15:17, "And if Christ be not raised, your faith is vain . . ."* On the other hand, those who do not believe are justified in their non-belief because of the questionable presentations of what very well may be a non-happening. The post-resurrection appearances whether real, or imagined, or contrived could be explained, in one way or another, as developed from emotional yearning by Jesus' followers for his death to signify success, not defeat. Christianity has achieved its goal of wresting success from the jaws of death. But, this achievement does not make for the confirmation of its truth.

Before we leave this interesting and important study, let's fill in some other details, after which we shall discuss the ascension, a subject of parallel significance.

THREE DAYS AND THREE NIGHTS. In *Matthew 12:40* Jesus says, *"For as Jonas was three days and three nights in the whale's belly; so shall the Son of man be three days and three nights in the heart of the earth."* Actually, no evidence exists for the time Jesus was entombed. No one relates he was seen exiting the tomb. Therefore, any time from minutes to days is possible. We have reports of when the tomb was found empty, not anything else. However, in all four Gospels the three days are definitely shortened, especially in John's story, making for this factual discrepancy. Between Good Friday and Easter Sunday morning, we do not have three days and three nights.

TOMB EMPTY. There are so many possibilities of how the tomb was empty, all at this point in time conjecture. But, balanced against the questionable and contradictory reports of the resurrection, theorizing of any nature takes on weight. One explanation could be that the tomb was already empty when the guards arrived. Another could be that the guards were bribed to allow the body to be taken away after they arrived on their watch, bribed by the followers of Jesus. *Matthew 28:11-15* gives another explanation, albeit Matthew makes it seem a fabrication. He has the soldiers on watch reporting to the Jewish priests and elders that they found the tomb empty. Their statement is accepted as if it were miraculous and fact, because that is what Christianity propounds. That the soldiers might have been derelict in their duty is not even considered. The priests and elders are then depicted as conniving with the watch, bribing them to say, *"(Jesus') disciples came by night and stole him away while we slept."* Thus, a very reasonable explanation is undercut by the budding Church. Watchers asleep are not unknown, are they? The probability of this having occurred is so great that a story is presented to label it a lie. Of course, the stone closing the tomb was rolled away by human effort, similar to the human effort used in putting the stone in place originally.

A reason for the empty tomb may be that Jesus' followers took and hid his body and then created the impression by rumors that he was risen from the dead in order to lend stature to their belief that he was the Messiah. This might have been done while they disappointedly pressed forward with their hope of a second coming after his death. Is this a wild conjecture? Yes, but not as wild as Christianity's story. Nevertheless, the specific conjecture is not of importance. What is important is that it is clear that many possibilities exist to explain the empty tomb besides Christianity's claim.

SHROUD WRAPPINGS. That there were linen wrappings found in the empty tomb in some of the Gospel versions is inconsequential and valueless as proof of Jesus rising from the dead. Why should the shroud be removed anyway? And this leads us to wonder what he was wearing in his post-resurrection appearances. How did he get the apparel he wore? This very minor point might lead us to the conclusion that others furnished him with clothing. A whole line of theorizing is opened up with this minor inquiry. In any case, the shroud wrappings certainly could have been placed there. This leaves us with certainty of nothing.

NO EYEWITNESSES. Of all the events in the New Testament, the supposed resurrection is the most important to Christianity, yet it has absolutely no human witness. Not one person is written to have seen Jesus revive from the dead and leave the tomb. In Matthew we have an angel. In Mark we have an unknown man-form clothed in a long white garment. In Luke two men-forms in shining garments attest to Jesus having risen from the dead. All these, we are given to believe, are

non-human beings. In John's account the two angels do not tell anything about Jesus being risen. We lack a human witness to this, the one
happening on which Christianity rests.

There is no eyewitness confirmation of his coming alive when it
supposedly occurred. The New Testament reports post-resurrection
appearances, but we have presented their many conflicting details and
untrustworthy nature. Also Paul in *I Corinthians 15:6* claims Jesus was
seen by over five hundred at one sighting after his resurrection. Where
did Paul get this information? He was not there, and it was not
reported in the Gospels. Paul has admitted that he uses guile to persuade in *II Corinthians 12:16*, "*. . . being crafty, I caught you with
guile.*" Why should anyone believe his tale, which Paul very well could
have concocted to persuade?

SURVIVED CRUCIFIXION. It is not beyond physical possibility that
Jesus did not have a complete cessation of life processes and revived
after the crucifixion. He was entombed above ground, and therefore
breathing was possible. His followers might have sensed this, in some
way, and come for him at the proper time. This thought is offered to
counterbalance any necessity to accept as truth Jesus' resurrection
from death.

RUMORS OF RESURRECTION. Talk of resurrection was not
unknown there in those days. Read *Luke 9:7-8 (Mark 6:14-15) where it
says,* "*Now Herod . . . was perplexed, because it was said of some,
that John was risen from the dead; And of some, that Elijah had
appeared; and of others, that one of the old prophets was risen again.*"
Thus we know that speculation on resurrection was not limited to
Jesus' alleged resurrection. In this instance, John the Baptist and others
were thought possibly to be raised from the dead in the person of
Jesus. It seems that in those days this kind of thought could take hold.

OTHER RESURRECTIONS. What is so extraordinary about a person
being revived from death? Why should a religion be based on revival
from death as Paul indicated? The Bible tells of many revivals to life.
Look at these in the New Testament. Jesus was able to bring Lazarus
to life after Lazarus was dead four days as recorded in *John 11:39-44*.
In *Luke 7:12-15* and *Luke 8:49-55 (Mark 5:35-43)* he also brought a
boy and a girl to life again. In addition, these resurrections are shown
in the Hebrew Scriptures. Elijah brought a boy back to life in *I Kings
17:20-24*. Elisha raised to life a boy and also a man in *II Kings 4:32-37*
and *II Kings 13:20-21*. That's a lot of revival to life.

THIS DAY IN PARADISE. In *Luke 23:43* Jesus promises the criminal
on the crucifix next to him on Friday, "*. . . To day shalt thou be with
me in paradise.*" Yet, in *John 20:17* Jesus announces to Mary Magdalene on the Sunday following, "*. . . I am not yet ascended to my
Father: . . .*" In fact, in John's account, although no ascension is

reported, Jesus was found on earth at least more than a week after his resurrection. *Acts 1:3* even states he remained on earth for forty days after his resurrection. This contradicts Jesus' promise to the thief.

THE ASCENSION OF JESUS. Jesus, in Christianity, is reported to have ascended to heaven in *Mark 16:19, Luke 24:51,* as well as *Acts 1:9-11.* It is omitted in Matthew and John, not written of whatsoever, which indicates its level of believability. A miraculous mind-boggling event is left out, just as if it never happened, or perhaps because it never happened. In *Mark* we merely read, *". . . he was received up into heaven and sat on the right hand of God."* Who saw that? In *Luke* we read, *". . . he was parted from them and carried up into heaven."* Again, we know it is impossible for the disciples to have seen Jesus in heaven's reaches. In *Acts* the author made matters easier for us to picture by writing, *". . . he was taken up; and a cloud received him out of their sight."* We have a cloud detail, and a rising to the cloud, and then a losing sight of Jesus. It is expressly said he was "out of their sight," so what really did they see? Certainly they didn't see him in heaven. This is Christianity's miraculous ascent. We can't disprove it, However, neither can they prove it.

Nevertheless, we are able to expose conflicting details in the relating of the rising to heaven in the New Testament. Note that in all three accounts Jesus supposedly was lifted from the earth immediately after he spoke to the disciples of certain things. Yet, it is written that he spoke of different things in the three versions. In *Mark* he spoke, *". . he that believeth not shall be damned. And these signs shall follow them that believe; . . ."* In *Luke* he said nothing like that but spoke, *". . repentance and remission of sins should be preached . . . blessed them."* In *Acts* he spoke, *". . . It is not for you to know the times (to restore again the kingdom to Israel) . . . ye shall be witnesses unto me . . ."* So, in all three accounts the last remarks of Jesus are different. Therefore, if the reports of his last words lack evidential reliability, the words of his ascending to heaven also may be emotional belief, rather than factual reports. After all, only those who were there know what he said and reported his ascension. So, why do we have contradictory stories of what his last remarks were?

Remember that Jesus promised the crucified thief that he would be in heaven with him that very Good Friday. In opposition, the author of Acts said it was forty days after the resurrection that Jesus ascended. It doesn't matter which, if either, is wrong or right. What is seen is conflicting statements which bring the ascension into troublesome doubt.

Furthermore, why weren't the multitudes who followed Jesus and viewed his miracles in attendance when he supposedly ascended? They witnessed his earthly miracles, why not his heavenly rise? They did not do so, and therefore made doubt far more acceptable and reasonable. At Sinai all the people were there and trembled. Yet, the people were absent at Christianity's momentous happening.

Just as an interesting observation here, not as a challenge to Christian belief, we show that even before the alleged rise to heaven Jesus taught Judaism. As the New Testament is Christianity's, we make no further comment.

1—*Matthew 28:20, "Teaching them to observe (do) all things whatsoever I have commanded you: . . ."* (Not vicarious atonement).

2—*Mark 16:15, ". . . preach the gospel (Messianic kingdom) to every creature . . ."* (Not vicarious atonement).

3—*Luke 24:47, ". . . repentance and remission of sins should be preached."* (Not vicarious atonement).

4—*Acts 1:6-7, ". . . wilt thou at this time restore again the kingdom to Israel? . . . It is not for you to know the times or the seasons . . ."* (Not heavenly, but earthly kingdom.)

Let's introduce here the Biblical stories of Enoch and Elijah. They both were taken directly to heaven by God, making such a supposed occurrence lacking in uniqueness for Jesus. And if the ascension is not unique for Christianity, even if it were true, it loses its stature as a pillar of basic belief for a new religion.

1—*Genesis 5:24, "And Enoch walked with God: and he was not; for God took him."*

2—*II Kings 2:11, ". . . and Elijah went up by a whirlwind into heaven."*

The truth of the resurrection, ascension, and vicarious atonement rests in the faith of the believing Christian. Faith overcomes questioning, but does not create fact. It has been demonstrated here that there is much justifiable doubt about Christianity's basics. However, this is not our main purpose. The purpose of Judaism's advocate is showing that the Hebrew Scriptures do not support Christianity's claims. There is no vicarious atonement, only personal repentance in the Holy Bible of Judaism. Our final thought here is that whatever might be Christianity's share of God's workings, the written Holy Word has revealed that Judaism's place in the eternal plan of God is loving, important, and certain!

17

Proof Texts—
Crucifixion Related

THIRTY PIECES OF SILVER.

Zechariah 11:12, "And I said unto them, If ye think good give me my price; and if not, forbear. So they weighed for my price thirty pieces of silver." (SEE Matthew 26:14-15).

COMMENT: The thirty pieces of silver Judas got for betraying Jesus supposedly is connected to this verse.

REBUTTAL: The thirty pieces of silver, given for whatever reason, is a proper payment asked for in Zechariah. There is no hint of underhandedness or evil in the money transfer. Matthew clearly misuses the verse, which has no connection to betrayal. Further remarks are unnecessary.

BETRAYED.

Psalm 41:9, "Yea, mine own familiar friend, in whom I trusted, which did eat of my bread, hath lifted up his heel against me. (SEE John 13:18).

COMMENT: Judas Iscariot is the friend who betrayed Jesus, so it goes.

REBUTTAL: Jesus supposedly knew he was to be betrayed by Judas. He said so. We will not challenge this on a factual level, although many discrepancies to the validity of the story exist. However, if it were known, how could Jesus call Judas a trusted friend? Furthermore, it is very difficult to contemplate betrayal in something which was preordained. Read *Matthew 26:24 (Luke 22:22), "The Son of man goeth as it is written of him: but woe unto that man by whom the Son of man is betrayed! It had been good for that man if he had not been born."* If it was meant to be that Jesus was exposed to disloyalty, then how could

187

Jesus display such extreme anger and condemn Judas who was just a figure of fate? Indeed, what happened to "turning the other cheek," especially when the person is only doing what has to be done in the eternal plan of Christianity? Last, if this verse concerns Jesus, then *Psalm 41* verse *4* must also. It reads, *". . . Lord, be merciful unto me: heal my soul; for I have sinned against thee."* This, of course, contradicts all of Christianity's teachings concerning Jesus, who is free of sin and is God Himself in the Trinity.

OPENETH NOT HIS MOUTH.

Isaiah 53:7, "He was oppressed . . . yet he opened not his mouth: he is brought as a lamb to the slaughter, and as a sheep before his shearers is dumb, so he openeth not his mouth."
(SEE Matthew 27:11-14 (Mark 15:2-5)).
COMMENT: Jesus did not answer in his trials, and is spoken of by Isaiah, they say.
REBUTTAL: The Gospels' reports of Jesus' sedition hearing before Pilate appear to be "made to fit." But strangely, even so, they do not fit Isaiah. It is reported in the inquiry about whether Jesus claimed to be "King of the Jews" that "he answered nothing." That fits. However, it is also reported that when Pilate asked him, "Art thou the King of the Jews?" Jesus surely did open his mouth saying, "Thou sayest." But, that is not all Jesus said. In John's account of the high priest's questioning of Jesus concerning his teachings, Jesus is found to have said much, and in no modest manner. Far from being a quiet lamb, he was very verbally assertive. He was so aggressive in his reply that we read in *John 18:22, "And when he had thus spoken, one of the officers which stood by struck Jesus with the palm of his hand, saying, "Answerest thou the high priest so?"* Then in the following verse, *John 18:23*, we read, *". . . why smitest thou me?"* which certainly is opening his mouth. But, it really is inconsequential whether he spoke or not. The story details could have been contrived, as they appear to have been, and can prove nothing, especially when viewed against the total absence of fulfillment of Hebrew Messianic expectations.

There is a truly amazing contradiction to the "lamb to the slaughter" comparison in *Mark 15:34 (Matthew 27:46), "And at the ninth hour Jesus cried with a loud voice, saying, "Eloi, Eloi, lama sabachthani? which is, being interpreted, My God, my God, why hast thou forsaken me?"* This quoting of *Psalm 22:1* conflicts with the alleged Messiah of Isaiah who "opened not his mouth." However, here we have far greater implications. For what he cried is contrary to all that Christianity teaches about the inevitability and unavoidability of Jesus' supposed sacrificial death. We can understand what Jesus said in only one way, that he believed he had been abandoned by God his Father.

How can the Messiah, sent by God, exclaim that he has been abandoned by God, when in the Christologic interpretation of his life he came for the purpose of sacrificing his life for mankind's sins? Christianity is in a tight corner when it seeks a proper explanation for this. It is Christianity's befuddling outcry, but Judaism has a claim on the answer. For here, the basis of the Christologic sacrificial atonement is implicitely denied by Jesus as he was in the act of performing this supposed self-sacrifice.

It is of interest to note that in *Luke 23:34* this is said instead, *"Then said Jesus, Father, forgive them; for they know not what they do. . . ."* This is befitting Jesus' good character, don't you think? It also is in agreement with Christianity's basic tenets. The tragedy is that the Christian has refused, throughout the ages, to do that which Jesus asked of God.

SPIT UPON, SMITE THE JUDGE.

Isaiah 50:6, "I gave my back to the smiters, and my cheeks to them that plucked off the hair; I hid not my face from shame and spitting."

Micah 5:1, ". . . they shall smite the judge of Israel with a rod upon the cheek."

(SEE Matthew 26:67 (Matthew 27:30) (Mark 15:19) (Luke 18:32)).

COMMENT: Christianity claims this describes Jesus before his crucifixion.

REBUTTAL: Actually these verses have no direct application to Jesus as can be ascertained by simply reading their words. The spitting and smiting in the New Testament are force connected to the Hebrew Bible's verses. Look here. If the "spitting" happened, did the plucking of his hair also occur? And was Jesus in shame of himself? Certainly not. This kind of follow-up questioning exposes the worthlessness of this kind of forced proof-text. Concerning Micah's verse, Jesus, of course, was not a judge and said in *John 12:47, ". . . I came not to judge . . . "*

DESPISED, MOCKED, PIERCED, CAST LOTS FOR GARMENTS.

Psalm 22:6-7,16,18, "But I am . . . despised of the people. All they that see me laugh me to scorn: . . . they pierced my hands and my feet. They part my garments among them, and cast lots upon my vesture." (SEE Matthew 27:30-31,35 (Mark 15:17-20) (Luke 18:31-33) (John 19:1-3)).

COMMENT: These lines of Psalm 22 are interpreted by Christianity as foretelling of Jesus' demise.

REBUTTAL: There are several ways of challenging this. First, let's interject that the onus is clairly on the Romans, not the Jews, for the despising, mocking, crucifying, and parting of garments of Jesus. It is the Jewish people who have been suffering throughout the Christian Era for deeds perpetrated by the Roman people. No parallel vilification is given to the Romans for their forefathers' actions. All injurious hatred and wrongful blame is spewed upon the people of Israel.

Second, continue reading *Psalm 22:1,3,8,10,19,21,27-28, "My God, my God, why hast thou forsaken me? . . . But thou art holy, . . . He trusted on the Lord that he would deliver him: . . . thou art my God from my mother's belly. But be not thou far from me, O Lord: O my strength, haste thee to help me. Save me from the lion's mouth: . . . all the kindreds of the nations shall worship before thee. For the kingdom is the Lord's; and he is governor among the nations."* These are words of solid Judaism. Jesus spoke Psalm 22 verse I when he was dying, as we have discussed under, "Openeth Not His Mouth." The verse, which is a deeply human expression, connotes that God has the power, not the person praying.

Look what happens if it is assumed Psalm 22 is about Jesus.

1—Jesus is not the Hebrew Messiah, because the Messiah is not a powerless, endangered being.

2—Jesus is not part of God in a Trinity, because he speaks to God with no intimation or possibility that he is talking to himself as part of the Divinity.

3—Jesus is not the Christ of Christianity, because his sacrificial death was part of the scheme of vicarious atonement from which deliverance would not be requested, expected, or desired.

What do we see of Jesus' thoughts concerning God if he were the subject of Psalm 22? He calls God holy, his maker, and his helper. He says the world will worship God, whose kingdom it is and who is ruler of the world. Read it again. It's all there. And its all fundamental Judaism.

Now let's proceed and ask what you could assume is meant by the whole of Psalm 22 if it does not have relevance to Jesus? Wouldn't the nation of Israel fit comfortably? The Hebrew Bible often uses the figurative description of a lone servant to identify the Jewish people. For example in *Ezekiel 37:25* read, *". . . I have given unto Jacob my servant . . ."* And read *Isaiah 49:3, ". . . Thou art my servant, O Israel . . ."* We Jews have been scorned, abused, murdered, and our belongs diveded among our killers. Any one of millions, including our martyred six million, would have the right to say, "It is I." Certainly, the collective suffering servant of Israel could rightfully assert, "It is I, My God, why hast thou forsaken me?"

But, what of the specific quote, "they pierced my hands and my feet?" This seems descriptive of the crucifixion marks with specificity pointing to Jesus. It could be called figurature speech, but in this case it is not. However, it is not in any way about Jesus either. The answer is that there is a mistranslation of the Hebrew. The proper rendering of the original Hebrew is, ". . . Like a lion they are at my hands and my feet." No "piercing" is to be found, when correctly translated.

Finally, let's look at this in regard to parting of garments and casting of lots. It really does not matter whether it happened or not, because casting of lots for ownership of articles belonging to those condemned is not uncommon in certain areas. Therefore, it has no significance when fulfillment is being discussed.

VINEGAR TO DRINK.

Psalm 69:21, "They gave me also gall for my meat; and in my thirst they gave me vinegar to drink." (SEE Matthew 27:34 (Mark 15:36)).

COMMENT: Jesus' Messianic fulfillment includes this specificity, it is thought.

REBUTTAL: This is one of the many ways Biblical expression is given to the great miseries of the people of Israel in exile. Read the entire *Psalm 69* and see. Keep in mind if verse 21 is about Jesus then *verse 5* also must be about him. It reads, *"O God, thou knowest my foolishness; and my sins are not hid from thee."* Does Jesus have foolishness and sins in Christianity? Of course not. So verse 21 is not referring to him either. Christianity cannot pick and choose to suit their aims.

Matthew says, *"They gave him vinegar to drink, mingled with gall: . . ."* This seems to be one of those verses of the New Testament inserted so that it might be considered fulfillment, rather than based on an actual happening. Note that in *Mark* we have *"wine mingled with myrrh"* being given, not vinegar and gall. Hence, Mark's version casts doubt about Matthew's. It is really superfluous to add that the Psalm is also translated erroneously. The original Hebrew is, "They put poison into my food." Needless to say, Jesus was being killed, not fed, at his crucifixion.

GRAVE WITH THE WICKED, NUMBERED WITH TRANSGRESSORS.

Isaiah 53:9,12, "And he made his grave with the wicked . . . and he was numbered with transgressors . . ." (SEE Mark 15:27-28 (Matthew 27:38) (Luke 23:32-33) (John 19:18)).

COMMENT: The Messiah, they claim, was to be counted with criminals who break the law, and this description fits Jesus.

REBUTTAL: *Mark* says, *"And with him they crucify two thieves; the one on his right hand, the other on his left. And the scripture was fulfilled, which saith, And he was numbered with transgressors."* The trouble here for Christianity is that Isaiah is speaking of the tribulations of the people of Israel, which had already occurred. Observe that it says he "was" numbered. Isaiah could not have been referring to Christianity's Christ who was not born for about another eight hundred years. But, Isaiah surely could be alluding to the Jewish nation which continues to be treated in exile as transgressors and wicked by the Gentiles. Furthermore, countless people have made their graves with the wicked and been numbered with transgressors. Where's specificity?

Concerning "grave with the wicked," we ask whether Christianity believes Jesus is buried in a grave? If so, then the resurrection is denied. If not, this verse is not about him. Moreover, the original Hebrew is properly translated, "And they made his grave with the wicked, . . ." Or it could be, "And his grave was set with the wicked, . . ." These correct translations signify that others had control over this, and that it was not of his own volition. Therefore, it is contrary to the teachings of Christianity. In actuality, the expression is metaphorically describing Israel's exile. We can find a similar usage in *Ezekiel 37:12*, where it is clearly depicting the condition of exile from the Holy Land. Read, *". . . I will open your graves, and cause you to come up out of your graves, and bring you into the land of Israel."*

LET THE LORD DELIVER HIM.

Psalm 22:8, "He trusted on the Lord that he would deliver him: let him deliver him, seeing he delighted in him." (SEE Matthew 27:43).
COMMENT: Jesus is connected to this verse, as they interpret it.
REBUTTAL: *Matthew* reads, *"He trusted in God, let him deliver him now, if he will have him: for he said, I am the Son of God."* There's the copying. But, looking at the entire Psalm 22, we can easily discern that, in context, it is a cry from the depths for relief from terrible troubles. You remember this starts, *"My God, my God, why hast thou forsaken me?"* Matthew reports that Jesus was mocked for God not delivering him. Actually, it is the whole people of Israel who through the centuries have been open to the ridicule of the nations on this account. He who has trusted in the Lord is none other than the collective Chosen Hebrew People. Psalm 22 continues in praise of God, who is trusted to turn away Israel's despair and who will be worshiped by all the nations.

NO BONES BROKEN.

Psalm 34:20, "He keepeth all his bones: not one of them is broken." (SEE John 19:33,36).
COMMENT: Christianity says Jesus is the unblemished lamb offering.
REBUTTAL: This verse is not specific, referring to no one in particular and certainly not to the expected Messiah. It is very odd of John to match the non-breaking of Jesus' bones by the soldiers to this quotation. It is odd because right before it we read in *verse 19, "Many are the afflictions of the righteous: but the Lord delivereth him out of them all."* Thus, we find that this verse is speaking of God's servants who

will be afflicted, but saved, who will be hurt, but not broken. Was Jesus delivered as his bones were not broken? No. He died at the hands of the Romans. In fact, in Christianity Jesus was not to be delivered from affliction, for his crucifixion death was meant to occur. And it did occur, as reported. Yet, in Psalm 34, God promises deliverance. Consequently, any way you look at it, this verse is not of Jesus. Figurative language out of context, as found here, is no basis for a legitimate proof-text. If we refer to *Exodus 12:46* and *Numbers 9:12,* we see the Passover rules concerning unbroken bones, which has nothing to do with prophesy concerning the Messiah. See the next analysis.

BURNT OFFERING OF LAMB.

Genesis 22:8, "And Abraham said, My son, God will provide himself a lamb for a burnt offering: . . ." (SEE John 1:29).

COMMENT: The "lamb for a burnt offering" sacrifice is Jesus and is seen to be connected to the "no bones broken" of John 19:33,36 as well.

REBUTTAL: This fundamental of Christianity has no confirmation in the Hebrew Scriptures. Although *John* writes, *"(Jesus is) the Lamb of God, which taketh away the sin of the world,"* the concept is without foundation Biblically. Let's check this out.

In a burnt offering, the lamb has requirements which must be met for God's acceptance. It is written in *Leviticus 22:19,22,24, "Ye shall offer . . . a male without blemish, . . . of the sheep, or of the goats. . . . an offering by fire of them upon the altar unto the Lord. . . . not . . . bruised, or crushed, or broken, or cut . . ."* Therefore, if Christianity claims Jesus is the substitute sacrificial lamb of God which is put forward by his bones not being broken, he must also be unblemished, free of bruises, crushing or cuts. It is not Judaism, but Christianity, which testifies to the contrary. We learn in *Matthew 27* and *John 19* that the Romans maimed Jesus with a crown of thorns, beat him on the head, and whipped him. In crucifixion his hands and feet were pierced through. Instead of breaking his bones, the Roman soldiers pierced his side so badly that blood and water flowed out. So, Jesus did not fit the requirements of a sacrificial lamb. Also, his supposed sacrifice was not on an altar as required. It was not a burnt offering, as he was crucified. And additionally, obviously Jesus was not an animal (sheep or goat) as the laws of God stipulate.

Let's now check the Passover lamb. In *Exodus 12:46* and *Numbers 9:12* we see, *". . . neither shall ye break a bone thereof."* Here again, we find the blemish-free requirement eliminating Jesus. The words in *Exodus 12:5-8,13* are, *"Your lamb shall be without blemish, a male of the first year: . . . sheep . . . goats: . . . take the blood, and strike it on the two side posts . . . of the houses, . . . And they shall eat the flesh in that night, roast with fire, and unleavened bread; . . . when I see blood, I will pass over you, when I smite the land of Egypt."* This concerns the miraculous event in the Jewish people's escape from Egyptian bondage. The lamb offered had its blood used to mark sideposts. No sacrificial purpose is indicated here. If Jesus' death had a relevance to atonement, it surely should have been associated with the Day of Atonement, Yom Kippur, instead of Passover, which is a day of remembrance. At the Feast of Passover the lamb is eaten in remembrance of the wondrous deeds of God in freeing the Israelites from Egyptian slavery. The Pascal lamb is commemorative in Judaism, not atonal.

Thus, you see there is nothing on which Christianity can base its claim of Jesus being the "lamb" of God if it looks for foundation in the Hebrew Bible. Assuredly, Jesus' appellations in Christianity are of no concern to Judaism, but there is no legitimate assertion that the designation "lamb" arises from Judaic roots.

What is the real meaning of Genesis 22:8? The words are quite straightforward. God has tempted Abraham to show his faith in Him by sacrificing his only son Isaac. We do not have a sin-offering, but a demonstration of faith only. Therefore, even if Christianity wants to call Jesus the sacrificial lamb as demonstrated by Isaac, it still is not in the category of sin-absolver, because that is not what this verse in Genesis is about.

BLOOD OFFERING NEEDED.

Leviticus 17:11, "For the life of the flesh is in the blood: and I have given it to you upon the altar to make an atonement for your souls . . ." (SEE Hebrews 9:13-14,22).

COMMENT: Without blood sacrifice, Jews have no forgiveness of sins, while Christians believe they have Jesus' blood which took the place of such sacrifices.

REBUTTAL: There have always existed two aspects of forgiveness of sin in Judaism. One is the material sacrifice of an offering. The other is the spiritual repentance of the heart in atonement. The spiritual factor has always had ascendancy, although the material factor has been meaningful. Repentance, alone, offers the complete and satisfactory means of atonement and forgiveness, needing no supporting material sacrifice. Although animal offering is a highly regarded adjunct to repentance of the heart, it is not a substitute for it. Judaism's understanding of sacrifice as Biblically required has been to accept its usage and desire its availability. But, when it is unavailable, we rely totally on the surety of repentance for God's forgiveness of transgression.

The Hebrew Bible states the means of sacrificial atonement. For example see *Leviticus 1:1-4,* where unblemished male cattle are to be accepted as an offering. Or read *Leviticus 4:2-3, 20* where it says,

". . . If a soul . . . sin through ignorance . . . let him bring . . . a young bullock without blemish for a sin offering . . . and the priest shall make an atonement for them, and it shall be forgiven them." Clearly, sacrifice is acceptable by God's laws for pardon of sin. Note though, it is for unintentional sins. Scripture does not record acceptance of blood offerings for intentional transgressions except once. Only once in *Leviticus 6:5-7* is an intentional sin of swearing falsely to thievery given an animal sacrificial means for forgiveness. But, it is understood that this must be offered hand in hand with repentance, for only then would Judaism's principles be upheld. See *Numbers 15:29-30* where it is plainly stated that deliberate transgressions are not in the same category as those which are unintentional. It reads, *"Ye shall have one law for him that sinneth through ignorance . . . But the soul that doeth ought presumptuously, . . . shall be cut off . . ."*

Sacrifice was eliminated from Judaism's practice when the two Temples were destroyed. While in exile in Babylon no blood offering was possible. And since 70 C.E., when the Second Temple was destroyed, for almost two thousand years now Biblically based animal sacrifice has been an impossibility. The Temple's rebuilding, remember, is one of the expectations of the Messianic times. The prophets wrote of the rebuilding of the Temple when sacrifices will again be offered to God. No other substitute sacrifice was presented in prophesy, none at all! For example read *Malachi 3:1,4, ". . . and the Lord, whom ye seek, shall suddenly come to his temple . . . Then shall the offering of Judah and Jerusalem be pleasant unto the Lord, as in the days of old . . ."* Continue and read *Hosea 3:4-5, "For the children of Israel shall abide many days . . . without a sacrifice, . . . Afterward shall the children of Israel return . . ."* Temple altar sacrifice is anticipated, nothing else.

An odd claim of Christianity is that because of Jesus' alleged sacrifice the Temple was destroyed, as it no longer was necessary. There was a First Temple which was destroyed many hundreds of years before Jesus was born. Certainly, no connection to Jesus can be forced in that occurrence. Similarly, because of Jesus' death approximately forty years before the destruction of the Second Temple, no cause and effect relationship can be manipulated in this happening either. The Second Temple's blood offering functioning continued for approximately four decades after his crucifixion. The same forces that crucified Jesus brought destruction to the Temple.

Biblically acceptable sacrifice has requirements. It must be done in the Temple where certain unblemished animals must be ritually killed by the priests, with blood sprinkled round the altar. This ceremony is expressed in *Leviticus 1:2-5* and elsewhere. The human being Jesus did not fit the sacrificial description Biblically required, of course. In Christianity he may be considered a sacrifice, but this has no association to Judaism's Biblically based sacrificial offerings.

Moreover, human blood sacrifice is not permissible in Judaism. God forbade it in *Leviticus 18:21*, *"And thou shalt not let any of thy seed pass through the fire to Molech (pagan God) . . ."* And He abhors the drinking of blood as described in *Leviticus 17:10*, *"And whatsoever man there be . . . that eateth any manner of blood; I will even set my face against that soul that eateth blood . . ."* It was strictly in the pagan cults that human sacrifice was practiced.

The one instance of human sacrifice asked by God in the Scriptures was a unique request intended to test religious faith. It never was accomplished or intended to be done by God. Take a good look at this. The offer of sacrifice of Isaac by Abraham, his father, was a special situation which never was to have been completed. It was a test in which God had to intervene. If Abraham had not set up Isaac for sacrifice, no blood offering would have resulted. Abraham would have failed his test of faith. In that Abraham did offer Isaac, God was ready to stop the hand of Abraham on his son, and he did. Consequently, no human sacrifice was to happen. It was merely God's way of putting Abraham, Judaism's father, on special trial of soul.

Observe that Jesus' death in Christianity cannot be considered a Biblical sacrifice at all, because he was a self-appointed volunteer. Put aside that he was a human, blemished, and not ritually acceptable or presented as a sacrifice. Think of this. Jesus gave up nothing to die, as he simply was to return to his place with the other parts of the Trinity, in Christianity's teachings. Therefore, what sacrifice was made in coming to earth, doing what must be done, and returning to heaven? Everything was pre-arranged, according to Christianity. In projecting Jesus as a savior of souls, Christianity is in its own arena. But, to call his crucifixion a sacrificial death and liken it to a blood offering is completely contrary to logical reasoning.

It is true that animal blood offerings are stipulated as proper sacrifices in the Holy Scriptures. But, blood sacrifices are not essential, as other offerings have also been acceptable to God for forgiveness of sin. For example, in *Numbers 31:50* jewelry is offered. In *Isaiah 6:6-7* it is live coal. And in *Leviticus 5:11-13* fine flour is the offering for God's forgiveness. Of course, sacrifices were made for reasons other than forgiveness also, but that is not our subject.

Judaism possesses the sacred act of repentance which is fully efficacious for the remission of sin. Through "teshuvah" we return to God and are at-one. Here is Scriptural verification of this magnificent and beautiful concept which is at the heart of Judaism. Read *Deuteronomy 30:9-10*, *". . . for the Lord will again rejoice over thee . . . if thou turn unto the Lord thy God with all thine heart, and with all thy soul." Also read Psalm 32:5, ". . . I said, I will confess my transgressions unto the Lord; and thou forgavest the iniquity of my sin. Selah." Isaiah 55:7 says, ". . . let him return . . . to our God, for he will abundantly pardon." More is in Jeremiah 36:3, ". . . return every man from his evil way; that I may forgive their iniquity and their sin." Ezekiel 33:19 reads, "But if the wicked turn from his wickedness . . . he shall live thereby." And Hosea 14:1-2,4 says, "O Israel, return unto the Lord thy God: . . . Take with you words, and turn to the Lord: say unto him, Take away all iniquity, and receive us graciously: . . . I will love them freely . . ." Last, we present Zechariah 1:3, ". . . Turn ye unto me, saith the Lord of hosts, and I will turn unto you . . ."*

All of these above quotations express that repentance of the heart is that which is necessary for God to accept us and forgive our transgressions. However, many verses are found which show that repentance goes hand in hand with fulfilling of God's laws to be truly effective and acceptable. Read *Ezekiel 18:21, "But if the wicked will turn from all his sins that he hath committed, and keep all my statutes, and do that which is lawful and right, he shall surely live, he shall not die." Jonah 3:10 reads, "And God saw their works, that they turned from their evil way; . . . and he did it not (destroy)." Also in Micah 6:8 we see, "He hath showed thee, O man, what is good; and what doth the Lord require of thee, but to do justly, and to love mercy, and to walk humbly with thy God."* Hence, deeds of the law of God are a concomitant to repentance.

Let us now show that it is written that sacrifice is not primary in Judaism. In *Psalm 51:16-17 we have, "For thou desirest not sacrifice; else would I give it: thou delightest not in burnt offering. The sacrifices of God are a broken spirit: a broken and a contrite heart . . ."* Also we read in *Psalm 69:30-31, "I will praise the name of God with a song, and will magnify him with thanksgiving. This also shall please the Lord better than an ox or bullock . . ."* And in *I Samuel 15:22 we see, ". . . Hath the Lord as great delight in burnt offerings and sacrifices, as in obeying the voice of the Lord? Behold, to obey is better than sacrifice . . ."*

In summary, we learn that although blood sacrifice is Biblically based it is not essential. Repentance, with righteous conduct, is fully capable of being the means for forgiveness by God of intentional and unintentional sins. Loss of the Temple has removed sacrifice, but not removed forgiveness of sins in Judaism. Jesus is not a substitute blood sacrifice for atonement.

MAN CONDEMNED TO SIN.

Isaiah 64:6, "But we are all as an unclean thing, and all our righteousnesses are as filthy rags . . ."

Psalm 14:3 (Psalm 53:3), ". . . they are all together become filthy: there is none that doeth good, no, not one."

Ecclesiastes 7:20, "For there is not a just man upon earth, that doeth good, and sinneth not."

I Kings 8:46, "If they sin against thee (for there is no man that sinneth not,) . . ." (SEE Romans 5:12,18-19).

COMMENT: Good deeds and righteousness cannot overcome man's sinful nature. Jesus' vicarious atonement is necessary for God's forgiveness of man's sin, claims Christianity.

REBUTTAL: Yes, we all sin, for no human is sinless. This is the nature of man, but not his hopeless condition. In Judaism, we are not condemned by original sin, only hampered by human nature. However, God has presented man with the means by which he can overcome transgression. This is the holy act of personal repentance, on which we have elaborated in the previous section. "Blood Offering Needed." God has given us the ability to choose between good and evil. Read *Deuteronomy 30:11-12,14-15, "For this commandment which I command thee this day, it is not hidden from thee, neither is it far off. It is not in heaven, that thou shouldest say, Who shall go up for us to heaven, and bring it unto us, that we may hear it, and do it? But the word is very nigh unto thee, in thy mouth, and in thy heart, that thou mayest do it. See, I have set before thee this day life and good, and death and evil;"* So assuredly, we see that by choosing good we will live, which means eternally. With repentance, so that God forgives us our trespasses, and choosing good, man is freed from the unhappy state of sinfulness.

REGRET FOR PIERCING JESUS.

Zechariah 12:10, "And I will pour upon the house of David, and upon the inhabitants of Jerusalem, the spirit of grace and of supplications: and they shall look upon me whom they have pierced, and they shall mourn for him, as one mourneth for his only son . . ."

COMMENT: This supposedly alludes to Jews regretting having killed Jesus.

REBUTTAL: First, it must be remembered that the Romans were in charge of piercing and killing Jesus. The Jews did not crucify him. Second, the New Testament does not depict Jews as then mourning, nor is there any indication of Jerusalem's people having a special spirit of grace and supplications at the time of Jesus' death. If the passage is supposed to show that Jews in the future, say at the present time, will mourn, then it is true. However, instead of mourning for Jesus of Christianity, we pour out mourning for the real victims of Jesus' crucifixion who are the Jewish people. We have suffered blame and great harm throughout the Christian times because of his crucifixion by the

Romans who considered him a political danger.

Now, let's explain this verse. It is part of the description of the terrible wars in the latter times and the siege of Jerusalem. God intervenes on behalf of Israel and defeats the Gentiles at that time. But, many Jews will have died. The piercing of God's own people will be what is mourned by those surviving. The following translation from the Hebrew appears awkward, but it is correct and understandable, ". . . *they (Israel) shall look upon me (God who has a unique relationship to his servants) whom they (Israel's enemies) have pierced, and they (Israel) shall mourn for him (the part of God's servant which has been destroyed. . . .*" The point here is that by piercing God's people, Israel's enemies will have hurt God as well.

Also, note that the verse's "me" and "him" cannot refer in the same sentence to Jesus. John understood this and in *John 19:37* abridged the Scripture so that it fits his desires in, *"And again another scripture saith, They shall look on him whom they pierced."* Furthermore, there is no prophetical reference to Jesus as God's only begotten Son in this verse. The phrase, "as one mourns for an only son," is used to signify extreme sorrow, nothing more. *Amos 8:10* shows this same expression of extreme anguish, *". . . and I will make it as the mourning of an only son, and the end thereof as a bitter day."*

70 WEEKS, MESSIAH DIES.

Daniel 9:24-26, "Seventy weeks are determined . . . from . . . the commandment to . . . build Jerusalem unto the Messiah the Prince shall be seven weeks, and threescore and two weeks: . . . And after threescore and two weeks shall the Messiah be cut off, . . . and the people . . . shall destroy the city and the sanctuary . . ."
COMMENT: The date for Jesus' death is prophesied from this, they say.
REBUTTAL: The dates authenticating Jesus as the Messiah are based on translation errors and Biblical misunderstanding. The original Hebrew reads, "Seventy weeks are decreed . . . (STOP) from the going forth of the words to restore and to build Jerusalem unto one anointed, a prince, shall be seven weeks; (STOP) and for threescore and two weeks, it shall be built again. After the threescore and two weeks shall an anointed be cut off, . . . and the people . . . shall destroy the city and the sanctuary; . . ." We shall examine what happens when we use the accurate translation. Pay close attention to the explanation. For calculation of the dates, it is essential to know that "weeks" actually means time periods times seven years.

Christianity ignores punctuation separation between the seven "weeks" and the sixty-two "weeks." They do this in order to make the time fit Jesus in their calculations. It is clear in the original Hebrew that the time periods are separate, and it would be meaningless to separate the time periods if they belong together. They are not to be added together, and that is why they are not stated as a full sixty-nine "weeks" by Daniel. The separation of the seven "weeks" from the sixty-two "weeks" becomes understandable when properly analyzed.

"One anointed" is to come in seven "weeks," as written, not in sixty-nine "weeks," as joined. Then, after sixty-two "weeks" of the upbuilding of Jerusalem, another one anointed will die and Jerusalem's Temple will be destroyed. To support this explanation of the two different time periods look at verse 26, where it speaks of only the sixty-two "weeks," using the definite article "the" which emphasizes the second time period as separate. Any counting of the years to Jesus is proved miscomputed using the erroneous connection of the two periods of time.

The second major error of Christianity is the fanciful use of *Nehemiah 2:1,7-8* as the counting base towards Jesus. If it were correct, we would have added 483 years (which is sixty-nine "weeks" times seven) to 455 B.C.E. (although 445 B.C.E. possibly is the date that should be used for Nehemiah) and arrive at 33 C.E., the year of Jesus' death. But, this is pure, compounded error, on which no legitimate claim can be based. First, we have already shown that the joining of the seven to the sixty-two "weeks" is fallacious and deceiving. And second, Nehemiah's date of 455 B.C.E. cannot be utilized as a base date on which to add the incorrect 483 years.

Nehemiah's date was not a date of the "going forth of the word" or "commandment" for the rebuilding of Jerusalem and its sacredness. But, Christianity had to grasp at a solution to prove themselves. Adding 483 years to 586 B.C.E. (the First Temple's destruction date) lands them no where near 33 C.E. There are 103 years between. So, they searched the Scriptures for a suitable date to fit and found Nehemiah's date.

In Nehemiah, we have something quite different than the "commandment" to rebuild Jerusalem's sacredness. King Artaxerxes made no special decree as Daniel's verse requires. He gave Nehemiah letters, only permission documents. Read Nehemiah, "*. . . in the twentieth year of Artaxerxes the king (455 B.C.E.) . . . I said unto the king . . . let letters be given me to the governors beyond the river, that they may convey me over . . . And a letter . . . that he may give me timber to make beams for the gates of the palace . . . and for the wall of the city, and for the house that I shall enter into. And the king granted me, . . .*" You plainly see that Nehemiah is only getting letters of communication for safe passage and wants timber to be used for the gate and walls and other general house building. The purpose was to make Jerusalem safer and less in disrepair. Others also were repairing Jerusalem's walls which were in need of repair, as can be seen in *Nehemiah* chapter *3.* No holy "commandment" or "going forth of the words" is given or received. What we do have here is a love of the Holy City and a desire to fix its damaged areas.

These substantial obstacles surely disprove Christianity's counting of the years. Yet, even were we to use Nehemiah's date, a descrepancy is found in their counting. Note that the Jewish calendar has an extra month every three years, which adds five years to the "cut off" date. Instead of sixty-nine times seven or 483 years, we have 488 years. Therefore, the "cut off" date is 38 C.E., not 33 C.E. as it must be for Christianity. Hence, even using their compounded errors for counting, they are not correct.

And more fault is found. What happened to the last of the supposed sixty-nine "weeks" plus one, totaling seventy? Christianity has no answer based on the Scriptures. It is an enigma. But, as it affects the counting to the "cut off" date, it should be part of their consideration and another seven years should be added to their counting, arriving at 45 C.E. This extra "week" cannot be advanced to a second coming, for it deals with the supposed first coming's "cut off."

Recall that Daniel says that after sixty-two "weeks" an anointed one will die and the city and sanctuary will be destroyed. Certainly Jesus' death in 33 C.E. and the Second Temple's destruction in 70 C.E. did not occur at the same time. Almost four decades intervened. Once again, we see troubles here for Christianity using Daniel's passage in reference to Jesus. This, in combination with all the other mistakes we have exposed in this matter, proves that there is no prophesy concerning Jesus in this Scripture.

Who, then, is the anointed one of the first seven "weeks" presented in Daniel? If you believe Bible writing, you know it is Cyrus the King of Persia. Here is verification. *Isaiah 45:1* states, *"Thus saith the Lord to his anointed, to Cyrus . . ."* Notice that here "moshiach" is translated "anointed" properly. However, in Daniel this same Hebrew word is translated "Messiah." The term "anointed" is found elsewhere in the Hebrew Bible denoting kingly or priestly authority. The Hebrew term "moshiach," which is translated "anointed," is found, for example, in connection with Aaron in *Exodus 30:30,* and Saul in *I Samuel 10:1,* and David in *Psalm 23:5.* It is not used as a proper name anywhere. Christianity uses the word "Messiah" to turn the meaning as they require, with no language substantiation whatsoever and with obvious misleading consequences.

Pursuing our discovery of Cyrus as the anointed one, we read in *Isaiah 45:13, "I have raised him (Cyrus) up in righteousness, . . . he shall build my city . . ."* Continue with *Ezra 1:1-2, "Now in the first year of Cyrus king of Persia (537 B.C.E.), that the word of the Lord by the mouth of Jeremiah might be fulfilled,* . . . *Cyrus* . . . *made a proc-lamation* . . . *The Lord God* . . . *hath charged me to build him an house at Jerusalem* . . ." Also, this is found in *Ezra 6:3.* Let's proceed to Jeremiah that Ezra mentions Cyrus fulfilled. See *Jeremiah 29:10,* "*. . . after seventy years are accomplished at Babylon I will visit you,* . . . *causing you to return to this place (Jerusalem)."* Also read *Jeremiah 30:18, "Thus saith the Lord; Behold, I will bring again the cap-tivity (return) of Jacob's tents,* . . . *and the city shall be builded* . . ."

It is history that Cyrus did allow the Jewish people to return to their native land, with their sacred vessels, to build the Second Tem-ple. In the quotations, we have found the "commandment" or "going forth of the words." The time is 586 B.C.E. when the First Temple was destroyed and the Hebrew people were led into exile in Babylon for seventy years. God's word, through Jeremiah, made promise that the Jews would return to Jerusalem after seventy years in Babylon and made commandment to build Jerusalem in 516 B.C.E.

Now look at this Biblical match:—Cyrus is our anointed one. He issued a proclamation in 537 B.C.E., the first year of his reign. This proclamation, from the anointed one, did come seven "weeks," forty-nine years, after the commandment to build Jerusalem. The command-ment was in 586 B.C.E., the year of the Jewish people's exile into Babylon. The forty-nine years added to 586 B.C.E. is exactly 537 B.C.E. There is no manipulation here. It's a perfect fit, of course, because it is just Biblical word fulfilled. As you plainly see, with cor-rect identification of the anointed one as Cyrus, Christianity's counting is shown to be without foundation. We need go no further.

18

Proof-Texts—No Violence, No Deceit

Isaiah 53:9, ". . . he hath done no violence, neither was any deceit in his mouth."

COMMENT: Christianity claims Jesus is the perfect man.

REBUTTAL: Although the interpretation is in error that Isaiah's verse refers to a man, for it really is about the nation of Israel, we will go along with this idea in order to show that Jesus did not fit the Scripture in any way. The New Testament exposes the fact that Jesus, indeed, used both violence and deceit! This chapter presents evidence of his lack of perfection not in disrespect, but to reveal the human nature he possessed. These verses contrast sharply with others showing the Jesus of love, whom we do admire.

NOT PEACE, BUT SWORD.

Matthew 10:34-36 (Luke 12:49,51-53), "Think not that I am come to send peace on earth: I came not to send peace, but a sword (fire), For I am come to set a man at variance against his father, and the daughter against her mother, and the daughter in law against her mother in law. And a man's foes shall be they of his own household."

COMMENT: This concept of people against one another is taken from *Micah 7:6*, where the situation is seen properly as evil and not desirable. Micah's following verse gives the comfort that, *"Therefore I will look unto the Lord . . ."* Jesus, in contrast, says a sword and dissension are his goals.

ADVOCATED THE SWORD.

Luke 22:36, "Then said he unto them, But now, he that hath a purse, let him take it, and likewise his script: and he that hath no

sword, let him sell his garment, and buy one."
COMMENT: It is in clear language. Jesus said his followers should buy swords. The conflict with the famous quote from *Matthew 5:39 (Luke 6:29)* is irreconcilable. Read, *". . . resist not evil: but whosoever shall smite thee on thy right cheek, turn to him the other also."* But then again, Jesus did not follow his own advice about turning the other cheek, for in *John 18:22-23*, after he was struck by an officer, he asked why he had been struck and challenged it.

PERMITTED THE SWORD'S USE.

Luke 22:49-50 (Matthew 26:51) (Mark 14:47) (John 18:10), ". . . they which were about him . . . said unto him, Lord, shall we smite with the sword? And one of them smote the servant of the high priest, and cut off his right ear."
COMMENT: Thus, after telling his followers to buy swords, Jesus allowed this to occur. In effect, he was responsible for the violent act against a human being. He does not even rebuke his follower who committed the bloody act of cutting off a man's ear, but instead directs his rebuke to the others, not his followers. Only in Luke's Gospel does Jesus heal the ear. The other three Gospels mention nothing about Jesus healing the ear, which makes Luke's story doubtful. John's version identifies the follower who actually did the violent act as Simon Peter. Jesus is shown at odds with Peter, for, if we are to believe Luke, he restored the mutilated ear Peter caused. And in addition Jesus, after allowing the smoting, tells Peter that he had done enough and his sword should be put away. In other words, Jesus did not prevent the use of the sword on a human being. He just stopped its further use after the maiming of the servant had occurred. In Mark nothing is said about putting away the sword, and in Luke it is to be stopped at that time, with no reason given. In John Jesus said it should be stopped because it was meant to be thus, thereby emphasizing Christology. But, in Matthew we read that he said it should be stopped because using instruments of death can cause your own death, very down to earth advice completely lacking in morality.

SLAY HIS ENEMIES.

Luke 19:27, "But those mine enemies, which would not that I should reign over them, bring hither, and slay them before me."
COMMENT: Read these words of Jesus again. They are stunning. Christianity might wish they weren't in the New Testament, because they contradict the vision of Jesus as the man of peace, and love, and goodness. But, the Christian Inquisition as well as the Hitlerian hoards found the verse very comfortable as religious teaching. Apparently, Jesus asked for the killing of those who do not accept him as their ruler. Christianity, of course, must explain these words which seem to

be defenseless in light of humanity's rights on all levels of approach, material as well as spiritual. These words are irreconcilable with the very popular quote from *Luke 6:27 (Matthew 5:44)*, "*. . . Love your enemies, do good to them which hate you.*" The verse under discussion is shocking and out of joint when visualizing Jesus, the Christian embodiment of love. Yet, they are Jesus' words in the New Testament. And they say what they say, which is that Jesus asked for the violent death of those opposing him.

VIOLENCE IN THE TEMPLE.

John 2:14-16 (Matthew 21:12) (Mark 11:15-16) (Luke 19:45), "And (Jesus) found in the temple those that sold oxen and sheep and doves, and the changers of money sitting: And when he made a scourge of small cords, he drove them all out of the temple, and the sheep, and the oxen; and poured out the changers' money, and overthrew the tables; And said unto them that sold doves, Take these things hence; make not my Father's house an house of merchandise."

COMMENT: You should realize that the merchandise and money changing were all connected to the activities in the Temple. But, we can all agree that the goings-on were abusive of the holy area of the Temple. Yet, we can wonder whether Jesus needed to use a whip and such violence to correct the situation. With his power of persuasion, a sermon would have been appropriate to convince the merchants to move down the street. This is what a man who taught the ways of peace and love should have done, don't you think?

FIG TREE WITHERED.

Matthew 21:19,21 (Mark 11:13-14), "And when he saw a fig tree in the way, he came to it, and found nothing thereon, but leaves only (for the time of the figs was not yet), and said unto it, Let no fruit grow on thee (No man eat fruit of thee) henceforward for ever. . . . And presently the fig tree withered away. . . . If ye have faith, . . . ye shall (also do)."

COMMENT: Isn't a fig tree a creation of God? Why would the Son of God destroy, rather than assist, it? If he so wanted, as God the Son of Christianity, Jesus supposedly could have miraculously made figs appear. Instead, he curses it and it dies. Moreover, he says that faith would make others able to do the same thing. Christianity interprets this as an allegory, with the fig tree representing fruitless Judaism being cursed and dying. We need not go into the allegorical explanation in order to point out that it depicts a violent decree, which results in destruction of the fig tree. And if it were to be allegorically interpreted, so much the worse. For now violence is directed against a whole people. With this kind of ideology as its background, Christianity has been cursing Jews with hatred, persecution, terror, and murder throughout the centuries, culminating in the horrors of the planned destruction of the "fig tree" in the ovens of Auschwitz.

DROWNING OF SWINE.

Matthew 8:31-32 (Mark 5:12-13) (Luke 8:32-33), "So the devils besought him, saying, If thou cast us out, suffer us to go away into the herd of swine. And he said unto them, Go. And when they were come out, they went into the herd of swine: and, behold, the whole herd of swine ran violently down a steep place into the sea, and perished in the waters."

COMMENT: Why did Jesus cause the suffering and death of these harmless animals? Jesus allegedly was able to cast out devils from humans and had no need to allow them to go into the swine. This was supposed to be a real happening, so giving it an allegorical significance does not change the fact that Jesus caused violence here, albeit to hapless animals only.

HATE OF FAMILY TAUGHT.

Luke 14:26, "If any man come to me, and hate not his father, and mother, and wife, and children, and brethren, and sisters, yea, and his own life also, he cannot be my disciple."

COMMENT: It's hard to believe Jesus said this as reported in the New Testament. This verse is in direct contrast to his belief in the Hebrew Scripture's commandment of God as recorded in *Matthew 15:4 (Mark 7:10), "For God commanded, saying, Honor thy father and mother: and, He that curseth father or mother, let him die the death."*

ABANDONMENT OF RESPONSIBILITY TO FAMILY TAUGHT.

Matthew 19:29 (Mark 10:29-30) (Luke 18:29-30), "And every one that hath forsaken houses, or brethren, or sisters, or father, or mother, or wife, or children, . . . shall inherit everlasting life."

COMMENT: Does anyone believe that abandonment of family responsibility and desertion of ones relatives is worthy of anything but contempt? Where is the righteousness and morality in this teaching? It must be understood that much mental and material suffering most likely would result to the loved ones who are "forsaken." Certainly, religious commitment should not be tied to such cruel actions in order to obtain reward by God.

DISTRUST OF FAMILY TAUGHT.

Luke 21:16 (Mark 13:12), "And ye shall be betrayed both by parents; and brethren, and kinfolks, and friends; and some of you shall they cause to be put to death."

COMMENT: What very terrible thing was Jesus teaching his followers that would make a mother have her own son put to death? Think of it.

NO HUMAN SYMPATHY.

Luke 9:59-62 (Matthew 8:21-22), "*. . . Follow me. But he said, Lord, suffer me first to go and bury my father. Jesus said unto him, Let the dead bury their dead: . . . let me first go bid them farewell, which are home at my house. And Jesus said . . . (no) . . .*"

COMMENT: Jesus would not allow a son to attend his father's funeral. Again, Jesus teaches the breaking of the commandment of honoring father and mother. He even denies permission for a simple goodbye to relatives at home. Picture the situation. Instead of love, we find coldness of heart by Jesus. Is this the Jesus of love that Christianity propounds is theirs?

NO LOVE OR FORGIVENESS.

Mark 11:25-26 (Matthew 6:14-15) (Matthew 18:35), "*And when ye stand praying, forgive, if ye have ought against any; that your Father also . . . may forgive you . . .*"

COMMENT: The above verse is totally Judaic, showing the beauty of forgiveness. It can be said to exemplify Jesus' wisdom and religious excellence. Yet, we now present verses which are completely antithetical to this, which Jesus is quoted as saying.

1—*Matthew 13:41-42,* "*. . . them that do iniquity; . . . cast them into a furnace of fire: there shall be wailing and gnashing of teeth.*"

2—*Matthew 18:6-7 (Mark 9:42) (Luke 17:1-2),* "*But whoso shall offend one of these little ones which believe in me, it were better for him that a millstone were hanged about his neck, and that he were drowned in the depth of the sea. Woe unto the world because of offences! for it must needs be that offences come; but woe to that man by whom the offence cometh!*"

3—*Matthew 23:33,* "*Ye serpents, ye generation of vipers, how can ye escape the damnation of hell?*"

4—*Matthew 8:12,* "*But the children of the kingdom shall be cast out into outer darkness: there shall be weeping and gnashing of teeth.*"

5—*Matthew 25:41,* "*. . . Depart from me, ye cursed, into everlasting fire . . .*"

6—*John 15:6,* "*If a man abide not in me, he is cast forth as a branch, and is withered; and men gather them, and cast them into the fire, and they are burned.*"

7—*Mark 13:9,* "*. . . they shall deliver you up to councils; and in the synagogues ye shall be beaten . . .*"

8—*Mark 6:11 (Matthew 10:14-15) (Matthew 11:24),* "*And whosoever shall not receive you, nor hear you, . . . It shall be more tolerable for Sodom and Gomorrha in the day of judgment, than for that city.*"

9—*John 17:9,* "*I pray for them (believers): I pray not for the world, but for them which thou hast given me . . .*"

10—*Mark 16:16, "He that believeth and is baptized shall be saved; but he that believeth not shall be damned."*

SPOKE OPENLY OR NOT.

John 18:20-21, ". . . I spake openly to the world; I ever taught in the synagogue, and in the temple, . . . and in secret have I said nothing. Why asketh thou me? ask them which heard me, what I have said unto them: behold, they know what I said."

COMMENT: The New Testament verses presented here will contradict this, for neither the people who listened to him nor his disciples understood Christianity's Jesus.

1—*Mark 4:11-12 (Matthew 13:11,13-14) (Luke 8:10), "And he said unto them, Unto you it is given to know the mystery of the kingdom of God: but unto them that are without, all these things are done in parables: That seeing they may see, and not perceive; and hearing they may hear, and not understand . . ." (SEE: Isaiah 6:9).*

COMMENT: From this we learn that the people are spoken to in parables to confuse them, not to help them understand. Jesus admitted this. But, he also said that his disciples are spoken to so that they understand the kingdom of God. Do they? According to what is written in the New Testament, we have previously shown that they do not know Christianity's kingdom.

2—*Luke 9:45, Luke 18:34 (Mark 9:32), "But they (disciples) understood not this saying, and it was hid from them, that they perceived it not: and they feared to ask him of that saying. And they understood none of these things: and this saying was hid from them, neither knew they the things which were spoken."*

COMMENT: Therefore, the people and the disciples both were not enlightened by whatever Jesus supposedly taught. And Jesus said that he was telling secrets of the world to them. Read the following and ask why he would allegedly tell secrets of the world in a manner no one would understand. Why speak anything if the secrets are still to remain hidden? It appears that this is just one of the forced fulfillments of the New Testament, which in this case creates bewilderment.

3—*Matthew 13:34-35, "All these things spake Jesus unto the multitude in parables; and without a parable spake he not unto them: That it might be fulfilled which was spoken by the prophet, saying, I will open my mouth in parables; I will utter things which have been kept secret from the foundation of the world." (SEE Psalm 78:2).*

COMMENT: Moreover, if he spoke openly, why did he repeatedly tell people to keep secrets about himself? Jesus asked that his miracles not be publicized. More importantly, he asked that his supposed stature as the Messiah not be made known. Let's present verses which show that Jesus did not speak openly, indeed, that he supposedly did have secrets.

4—*Matthew 9:30, ". . . See that no man know it."*

5—*Mark 1:44, ". . . See thou say nothing to any man . . ."*

6—*Matthew 16:20 (Mark 8:29-30) (Luke 9:20-21), "Then charged he his disciples that they should tell no man that he was Jesus the Christ."*

7—*Matthew 17:5,9, ". . . a voice out of the cloud, which said, This is my beloved Son . . . Tell the vision to no man . . ."*

8—*Mark 3:12, "And he straitly charged them that they should not make him known."*

COMMENT: Jesus said, ". . . behold, they know what I said." Yet, not only is what he said not understood, but who he was is not understood as well. Apparently, Jesus was so secretive that there was great confusion even about who he was.

9—*Matthew 16:13-14 (Mark 8:27-28) (Luke 9:18-19), ". . . Whom do men say that I the Son of man am? And they said, Some say that thou art John the Baptist: some Elijah, and others, Jeremiah, or one of the prophets."*

LAID HOLD ON OR NOT.

Matthew 26:55, ". . . I sat daily with you teaching in the temple, and ye laid no hold on me."

COMMENT: On several occasions Jesus was reported to have caused outrage while teaching and was assailed by the people who believed he was a blasphemer. Therefore, they did lay hold on him.

1—*John 5:16, "And therefore . . . the Jews . . . sought to slay him . . ."*

2—*John 8:59, "Then took they up stones to cast at him: but Jesus hid himself, and went out of the temple . . ."*

3—*John 10:31, "Then the Jews took up stones again to stone him."*

OTHER WORLD KINGDOM OR THIS WORLD.

John 18:36, "Jesus answered (Pilate), My kingdom is not of this world: if my kingdom were of this world, then would my servants fight, that I should not be delivered . . ."

COMMENT: His kingdom, which is God's kingdom, was of this world, because his disciples expected his return to an earthly rule. Read *Matthew 16:28, Matthew 24:34 (Mark 13:30) (Luke 21:32) Acts 1:6-7, "Verily I say unto you, There be some standing here, which shall not taste of death, till they see the Son of man coming in his kingdom. . . . This generation shall not pass till all these things be fulfilled. . . . they asked of him, saying, Lord, wilt thou at this time restore again the kingdom to Israel?"* In spite of what Christianity has made of the kingdom of God, Jesus' teachings to the multitudes were Judaic and of this world. However, another conflict exists here. He said, if his kingdom were of this world, his servants would fight so that he could escape. Well, his disciples did fight with swords, as discussed earlier in this chapter. Consequently, again we know that his kingdom was of this world, which he denied and yet, in effect, also affirmed.

IN PARADISE TODAY OR NOT.

Luke 23:43, "(to criminal) Verily I say unto thee, Today shalt thou be with me in paradise."
COMMENT: If this were true, then the story of Jesus' resurrection, the rising after three days, would be false and the basis of Christianity found in error. Christianity must choose between the two, because they conflict.

JOHN THE BAPTIST IS ELIJAH THE PROPHET OR NOT.

Matthew 17:12-13 (Mark 9:13), "But I say unto you, That Elijah is come already, . . . Then the disciples understood that he spake unto them of John the Baptist."
COMMENT: John the Baptist himself denied being Elijah, and he would not lie about it if he were Elijah. In this book's chapter, "Proof-Texts—General Messiah," this is discussed. For instance, in *John 1:21* he is asked, ". . . Art thou Elijah? And he saith, I am not. . . ." We must conclude that Jesus was deluded or deceptive in asserting John the Baptist was Elijah.

DESTROY THE TEMPLE CONFUSION.

John 2:18-21 (Mark 14:58), ". . . What sign showest thou . . . ? Jesus answered . . . Destroy this temple, and in three days I will raise it up. . . . Forty and six years was this temple in building, and wilt thou rear it up in three days? But he spake of the temple of his body."
COMMENT: Jesus deliberately confused people by the double meaning of the word "temple." He meant to mislead, and he did.

AGREE WITH ADVERSARY TRICKERY.

Matthew 5:25 (Luke 12:58), "Agree with thine adversary quickly, . . . lest at anytime the adversary deliver thee . . . and thou be cast into prison."
COMMENT: This is Jesus' advocacy of trickery in order to escape possible trouble. What happened to honor and honesty?

IT SHALL BE DONE OR NOT.

Matthew 7:7-8 (Luke 11:9-10), ". . . Ask, and it shall be given you; seek, and ye shall find; knock, and it shall be opened unto you. For every one that asketh receiveth . . ."
Matthew 21:22 (Mark 11:24), "And all things, whatsoever ye shall ask in prayer, believing, ye shall receive."
John 15:16 (John 16:23), ". . . ask of the Father in my name, he may (will) give it you."
COMMENT: All prayers may be answered in a spiritual sense, but only

some are answered in the material sense as implied in these verses. And surely, the Christian's prayers are not answered in any material manner differently from the prayers of the non-Christian, whether the prayers be in Jesus' name or otherwise. Prayers are not answered as Jesus said they "shall be," because spiritual belief does not create events, only deep comfort. Many prayers remain unanswered in the sense wished, although surely some prayers are answered to the heart's content, for Christians as well as non-Christians.

John 14:12, ". . . He that believeth on me, the works that I do shall he do also . . ."

COMMENT: Either Christians do not believe in Jesus or his words are false, for we do not see the multitudes of Christians doing what Jesus was able to do.

Matthew 17:20 (Matthew 21:21) (Mark 11:23) (Mark 9:23) (Luke 17:6), ". . . If ye have faith . . . ye shall say unto this mountain, Remove hence to yonder place (be thou cast into the sea); and it shall remove; and nothing shall be impossible unto you."

COMMENT: This we consider figurative speech, for any other interpretation is absurd. It is great as a psychological boost and spiritual uplift, but in the world many things remain impossible for human beings, as we all know.

Matthew 18:19, ". . . if two of you shall agree on earth as touching any thing that they shall ask, it shall be done for them of my Father . . ."

COMMENT: It just is not true that the prayers of two are any more effective than a single person's prayer. Also, notice that once again the Father in heaven is the one with the power of granting petitions.

Mark 10:29-30, ". . . There is no man that hath left house, or brethren . . . for my sake, . . . But he shall receive an hundredfold now in this time, houses, and brethren, . . . and lands, . . . and in the world to come eternal life."

COMMENT: We know not of the afterlife reward, but we do know that these promises were not kept on earth as stated in the material sense.

SIGNS OF A BELIEVER IN JESUS.

Mark 16:17-18, "And these signs shall follow them that believe; In my name shall they cast out devils; they shall speak with new tongues; They shall take up serpents; and if they drink any deadly thing, it shall not hurt them; they shall lay hands on the sick, and they shall recover."

Matthew 7:22-23, ". . . Lord, Lord . . . have we not . . . in thy name cast out devils? and in thy name done many wonderful works? And then will I profess unto them, I never knew you; depart from me, ye that work iniquity."

COMMENT: Jesus said his followers would be able to do these things, inferring all and at all times. He asserted that those who believe will have these signs. Yet, the masses of Christians do not have these signs. Taken to its strange conclusion, we could assume that there are no Christians who believe as Jesus required. It is of interest to know that even having these signs and using Jesus' name does not automatically make a person beloved by Jesus. Such a person may even be evil, in Jesus' own estimation.

PAUL'S DECEIT.

Before we conclude this chapter, we feel that we should demonstrate the unreliability of the man who actually formulated the break away from Judaism by the early Church. Paul was the leader in the denial of Judaism's place with God. We have shown that Paul contradicted Jesus in important religious matters and made himself greater than his master. Now see who he is, by his own words. He admitted using trickery and deception to gain his ends. We can wonder whether his missionary effort was flawed with fiction throughout as well.

I Corinthians 9:20, "And unto the Jews I became as a Jew, that I might gain the Jews; to them that are under the law, (I became) as under the law, that I might gain them that are under the law;"

II Corinthians 12:16, ". . . nevertheless, being crafty, I caught you with guile."

Further exposing Paul, his story of his conversion on the road to Damascus has flaws which reveal its lack of trustworthiness. In one place, men are said to have heard the voice of Jesus, while in another place they are said to have heard nothing. And they saw the light, yet were not blinded as he was.

Acts 9:7, "And the men which journeyed with him stood speechless, hearing a voice, but seeing no man."

Acts 22:9, "And they that were with me saw indeed the light, and were afraid; but they heard not the voice of him that spake to me."

This double presentation of this fateful event for Paul throws doubt on the entire scene, as contradiction must. All could have been Paul's inner mental turmoil, having no substance in reality. Except for commenting that Jews who turn on their own people in self-hate are not unknown, we need not examine Paul's "fit," whether physical, spiritual, imagined, or contrived. However, by his own words, he would do anything to capture converts. Why wouldn't Paul concoct a story of a light and a voice as part of his plan to use craftiness?

As a final exposure of Paul's dishonesty, Paul, who denounced circumcision, had his disciple circumcised. Read *Acts 16:3, "Him (Timotheus) would Paul have to go forth with him; and took and circumcised him because of the Jews . . ."*

19

Proof-Texts—Suffering Servant

Isaiah 53 ALL (Including Isaiah 52:13-15 introduction). "He is despised and rejected of men; . . . But he was wounded for our transgressions, . . . with his stripes we are healed. . . . The Lord hath laid on him the iniquity of us all. . . . when thou shalt make his soul an offering for sin, . . . for he shall justify many; . . . made intercesssion for the transgressors."

COMMENT: This selected summary is considered by Christianity to be about the voluntary suffering servant of God, Jesus Christ, who was rejected by his own people, was wounded for their transgressions, bore the iniquity of many, made his soul an offering for sin, makes intercession for transgressors, and justifies and saves believers. This is the ultimate proof-text from the Hebrew Scriptures which is used to validate Jesus being the Messiah. Isaiah chapter 53 is certainly a formidable chapter for Christianity in its claim for Jesus Christ.

REBUTTAL: Christianity's claim is entirely wrong. Isaiah's prophesy is not about Jesus Christ, but is actually about the nation of Israel. It is not about the Hebrew Messiah, but about the Chosen Hebrew People. We shall prove that all matters in Isaiah chapter 53 concerning the suffering servant are fulfilled by Biblical Israel, not Jesus! Christianity cleverly misappropriates these verses, because their interpretation of Isaiah chapter 53 is very important for them in showing the supposed Biblical basis of Jesus being the Messiah. The vagueness and literary style of Isaiah here make misinterpretation easy for Christianity. They have taken great satisfaction in these verses, as in no other Hebrew Scripture, for the words presumably could be interpreted as the foreshadowing of Jesus' suffering and vicarious atonement. Jesus' death, occurring before the fulfillment of Messianic expectations, has been a stumbling block for Christianity, no matter how surely they have advanced the message of the second coming. They have had to find substantiation for their Christ's death and the non-occurrence of Messianic expectations, while pressing forward their concept of a return of Jesus to earth. In this book's chapter, "Jesus Was Not the Hebrew Messiah . . . ," we have shown the fallacy of a second coming. Now we shall lay bare the fallacy of believing Isaiah chapter 53 is about Jesus.

Christianity is on very troublesome ground when using this as a proof-text. Their interpretation is defective in many substantial ways and lacks validity when analyzed correctly by using Scriptural evidence. The Hebrew Bible itself is our source of proof. Christianity must accomplish the following if their explanation of the Hebrew Bible's verses is to be made as responsible as Judaism's.

1—HEBREW SCRIPTURE EVIDENCE. Christianity's interpretation must be shown to have substantiation from the Hebrew Bible. Any leap of faith is out of place here. There must be evidence for the belief of their concept.

2—COMPLETE VALIDATION. We must be given complete validation, not a partial pick-and-choose verse selection. All verses must suit their concept perfectly.

3—SPECIFICITY. All verses must be revealed fitting for Jesus, and no other. There must be specificity, so that no future suffering Messiah, or person, or group of people (such as those who suffered and died in the Holocaust) could fit.

4—HEBREW MESSIAH EXPECTATION. It must be established that the suffering servant is the expected Hebrew Messiah, and no other. Any acceptance of a Christologic Messiah must be based on evidence, in context, from the Hebrew Bible, not from the New Testament.

5—POSITIVE PROOF. Christianity's explanation must be positive proof of Jesus being the suffering servant, not negative ideology concerning the nation of Israel having lost its place as God's servant, the Chosen People. The denial of Israel's place with God does not automatically confirm Jesus as a substitute.

6—NATURAL BIBLICAL INTERPRETATION. Nothing presented should be forced. It must be seen correct because it falls into place naturally and fully. The interpretation must be smoothly and logically applicable to the Hebrew Scriptures.

With all this substantiation in mind, we proceed to unfold that the suffering servant of the Lord is totally and satisfactorily explained within Judaism, using Scriptural evidence, as the people of the nation of Israel. The serious troubles of the Christologic version will be clarified. Contrast will be made of the natural and complete explanation of Judaism to the flawed, forced, and fragmentary one of Christianity, which is self-serving and lacking in any Hebrew Biblical foundation.

Let us begin by discussing the humanization. In Isaiah here, the humanized "he" is utilized by the prophet with poetic license to express the uniqueness of the people of Israel as the servant of God. Israel (Jacob) is "he" expressed as a singular human servant. To prove this, we give you a sampling of other Biblical verses by Isaiah which express the nation of Israel in human terms, in servant terms.

1—*Isaiah 41:8-9, "But thou, Israel, art my servant, Jacob whom I have chosen, the seed of Abraham my friend . . . Thou art my servant; I have chosen thee, and not cast thee away."*

2—*Isaiah 43:10, "Ye are my witnesses, saith the Lord, and my servant whom I have chosen . . ."*

3—*Isaiah 44:1-2, ". . . hear, O Jacob my servant; and Israel, whom I have chosen: . . . Fear not, O Jacob, my servant . . ."*

4—*Isaiah 44:21, "Remember these, O Jacob and Israel; for thou art my servant: I have formed thee; thou art my servant . . ."*

5—*Isaiah 45:4, "For Jacob my servant's sake, and Israel mine elect . . ."*

6—*Isaiah 48:20, ". . . say ye, The Lord hath redeemed his servant Jacob."*

7—*Isaiah 49:3, ". . . (The Lord) said unto me, Thou art my servant, O Israel, in whom I will be glorified."*

Having just established that the people of Israel, the Jewish people, are the servant of God, let's proceed to verses which describe Israel as a suffering nation, the suffering "he" of Isaiah chapter 53. This is simple to do, because it is basic Hebrew Scripture revelation. God has afflicted the Hebrew people in order to bring them back to righteousness. By Judaism's light, the whole world is to turn to the God of Israel. The prophets have spoken of the troubles of Israel in terms of sickness and wounds. Captivity is Israel's sickness, while redemption is its healing.

1—*Jeremiah 30:10,12,15-17, "Therefore fear thou not, O my servant Jacob, saith the Lord; . . . Thy bruise is incurable, and thy wound is grievous. Why criest thou for thine affliction? . . . and they that spoil thee shall be a spoil, . . . For I will restore health unto thee, and I will heal thee of thy wounds . . ."*

2—*Jeremiah 33:6, "Behold, I will bring it health and cure, and I will cure them (Judah and Israel)."*

3—*Lamentations 2:13, ". . . for thy breech is great like the sea: who can heal thee (daughter of Jerusalem and Zion)?"*

4—*Hosea 6:1, ". . . (the Lord) will heal us; he hath smitten, and he will bind us up."*

5—*Nahum 1:12, ". . . Though I have afflicted thee, I will afflict thee no more."*

6—*Zephaniah 3:19*, *"Behold, at that time I will undo all that afflict thee: and I will save her that halteth . . ."*

Now let's continue by offering the following quotations of Isaiah himself. These are explicit verifications that it is the Israel nation which is depicted as the suffering and sick body. Although Christianity has taken hold of ambiguity it found in Isaiah chapter 53, fortunately Isaiah elsewhere clearly states that the affliction belongs to the Jewish people.

1—*Isaiah 1:4-6*, *"Ah sinful nation, . . . Why should ye be stricken any more? . . . the whole head is sick, and the whole heart faint. From the sole of the foot even unto the head there is no soundness in it; but wounds, and bruises, and putrifying sores: they have not been closed, neither bound up, neither mollified with ointment."*

2—*Isaiah 30:26*, *". . . in the day that the Lord bindeth up the breach of his people, and healeth the stroke of their wound."*

Scriptural presentation of the Messiah is as the servant of God. Elsewhere Isaiah describes the Messiah as God's servant, as do others. However, he is never a suffering servant. He is an exalted, powerful, and successful ruler in God's kingdom. Nowhere is the Messiah portrayed as afflicted, which is why Christianity has grasped Isaiah chapter 53 in desperate attachment. Concerning the grandure of the Hebrew Messiah, we present these verses.

1—*Isaiah 9:6*, *". . . and the government shall be upon his shoulder . . ."*

2—*Isaiah 11:10*, *". . . root of Jesse . . . to it shall the Gentiles seek: and his rest shall be glorious."*

3—*Isaiah 19:20*, *". . . (the Lord) will send them a savior, and a great one, and he shall deliver them."*

4—*Isaiah 55:4*, *"Behold, I have given him for a . . . leader and commander to the people."*

5—*Isaiah 50:10*, *". . . obeyeth the voice of his (God's) servant . . ."*

6—*Zechariah 9:9-10*, *". . . and his dominion shall be from sea to sea, and from the river even to the ends of the earth."*

So we see that the Messiah is to have an earthly kingdom to rule, which he shall lead successfully and gloriously. We have previously expounded this in this book's chapter, "The Hebrew Messiah." No inglorious death or second coming is ever written in the Hebrew Bible concerning the Messiah. There is absolutely no reason to believe that Isaiah chapter 53 speaks of the servant of God who is the Messiah. No evidence is found linking the suffering servant to the Davidic king, who will govern a redeemed Israel in peace, plenty and perfection.

In summary, we have just illustrated that Israel is Biblically described as a personification in the form of a servant. We have presented verses to prove that Israel is described as suffering and afflicted. And we have shown that the Hebrew Scriptures depict the

Messiah as successful and powerful, never afflicted. Now, we shall examine each verse of Isaiah 52:13-53:12 to expose Christianity's erroneous interpretation.

ISAIAH 52:13, "Behold, my servant shall deal prudently, he shall be exalted and extolled, and be very high."
COMMENT: After its affliction, Israel will be this exalted servant in the Messianic times. Here is the Scriptural verification of this interpretation.

1—*Genesis 12:2, "And I will make of thee a great nation, and I will bless thee, and make thy name great; . . ."*

2—*Zephaniah 3:19, ". . . I will get them praise and fame in every land where they have been put to shame . . ."*

3—*Malachi 3:12, "And all nations shall call you blessed: for ye shall be a delightsome land, saith the Lord of hosts."*

4—*Isaiah 61:6,9, "But ye shall be named the Priests of the Lord: men shall call you the Ministers of our God: . . . the seed which the Lord hath blessed."*

As recounted in the New Testament, Jesus was not this exalted servant. He was arrested and put to death in a humiliating and wretched fashion by the Romans. Yet, the Messiah is to be exalted on earth, as is Israel. This Messiah is to deal prudently, as is Israel. The original Hebrew even is translated, "Behold, My servant shall prosper, . . ." Whether this is about the nation of Israel, as a collective people, or the Hebrew Messiah, as God's representative leader of the Chosen People, is not as important as the clear fact that it does not refer to Christianity's Jesus, who did not have earthly success. He had no chance to deal prudently, as he had no land to rule. He received execution, not exaltation. No "other-wordly" interpretation can properly be accepted here, as no reference to heavenly prudent dealing or heavenly extolling is put forward in the context of Isaiah's writing.

ISAIAH 52:14-15, "As many were astonished at thee; his visage was marred more than any man, and his form more than the sons of men: . . . the kings shall shut their mouths at him: for that which had not been told them shall they see . . ."
COMMENT: The marred visage is Israel's. In Messianic times the world's nations, the Gentiles and their kings, will come to the light of Judaism and be amazed at its beauty. They will marvel at how in former days Israel was considered deformed and ill-favored, despised and more contemptuously treated than any other people. For in the Messianic Era a miraculous reversal will occur, which will find the

Gentiles following Judaism's light in utter admiration of the Jews. Gentiles will not be able to explain their former lack of esteem for Israel and will be astounded at the transformation of their regard for the Jewish people from the lowest to the highest respect. This is what is conveyed here.

ISAIAH 53:1-2, "Who hath believed our report? . . . For he shall grow up before him as a tender plant, . . . he hath no form nor comeliness . . ."
COMMENT: Israel is pictured as a tender plant, fragile and lacking in outward beauty, which has not shown its eventual magnificent appearance. Jesus is not this image, with no form or comeliness. He had a body, and thus a form. He is not described anywhere in the New Testament as deformed or lacking in attractiveness. If anything, we know he had dynamic magnetism. He had charisma which, together with the miracles he performed, drew people to him and his message of repentance. The multitudes gathered to see and hear him from all over the Holy Land and were captivated by him. Furthermore, we know he was not ugly or deformed from *Luke 2:52, "And Jesus increased in wisdom and stature, and in favor with God and man."*

ISAIAH 53:3, "He is despised and rejected of men; a man of sorrows, and acquainted with grief: and we hid as it were our faces from him; he was despised, and we esteemed him not."
COMMENT: This is one of those very general verses that could fit anyone, including those of us who feel down in the dumps at times. More appropriately it could fit our martyred six million. Whenever a verse like this appears, we can make a connection to the six million of God's human beings who were most cruelly murdered in Hitler's Holocaust just because they were Jews. But, in truth, Isaiah is describing all of the people of Israel and we should interpret it thus. Doesn't every word, sadly, describe the Jew? Are we not despised and rejected, in sorrow and grief?

Let's present evidence which contradicts Christianity's use of this verse for Jesus. First, the verse utilizes the past tense, which doesn't fit the time of Jesus. After all, Isaiah was being read by people who lived many hundreds of years before Jesus. Yet, they read the past and present tenses here, not the future. The reason, of course, is that the verse is about Israel, not Jesus.

A second point is that Jesus was not generally despised and rejected. Although it is true that some Jews believed he was a blasphemer who led people away from God's laws, many others followed him throughout his ministry. Those opposed to Jesus were shocked at his sacrilegious talk about his power of God. Lacking any Christologic background, the Jews who left him were displaying their deep devotion to God. Read these.

1—*John 5:16,18, ". . . because he had done these things on the sabbath day. . . . also . . . making himself equal with God."*

2—*John 10:33 (Mark 14:64), "For a good work we stone thee not; but for blasphemy; and because that thou, being a man, makest thyself God."*

But, it is just as true that Jews continued to follow him in great numbers. The people who followed him believed him a holy man who performed miracles with God's help. He performed miracles in order to attract Jews to his message from the heart of Judaism, that people should repent their sins for entrance into the kingdom of God. He had popularity and was esteemed even among the Jewish rulers for his teaching of repentance, not for any Christology. See these verses.

1—*Mark 3:7-8 (Matthew 4:25) (Luke 6:17), ". . . and a great multitude from Galilee followed him, and from Judea, And from Jerusalem, . . . and from beyond Jordan; and they about Tyre and Sidon . . ."*

2—*Luke 5:15, "But so much the more went there a fame abroad of him: and great multitudes came together to hear, and to be healed . . ."*

3—*Matthew 21:46, ". . . they feared the multitude, because they took him for a prophet."*

4—*Mark 12:37, ". . . And the common people heard him gladly."*

5—*Luke 8:4, "And when much people were gathered together, and were come to him out of every city . . ."*

6—*John 12:42, "Nevertheless among the chief rulers also many believed on him . . ."*

Another point to be made is that to have sorrow and grief is a universal feeling, which has no specificity as a pointer to Jesus. In fact, we have explained that the misery is Israel's. The Christians who have allowed such unhappiness to befall the Jewish people befit the verse, ". . . we hid . . . our faces from him; . . ."

Last, Jesus is proved to have had tremendous acceptance by the growth and success of Christianity. How could this verse be about a man who was so greatly respected that a religion developed about him that calls him God?

ISAIAH: 53:4-6, "Surely he hath borne our griefs, and carried our sorrows; yet we did esteem him stricken, smitten of God and afflicted. But he was wounded for our transgressions, he was bruised for our iniquities: the chastisement of our peace was upon him; and with his stripes we are healed. All we like sheep have gone astray; we have turned every one to his own way; and the Lord hath laid on him the iniquity of us all."

COMMENT: First, recognize that the three verses are about something already accomplished. For about eight hundred years, until Jesus' time, Jews were reading of Isaiah's suffering servant who had been wounded, not one who will be wounded. No ambiguity existed. It was not a prophesy of someone who "shall be," but who "was." Note that in *Isaiah 52:6,10* we read, *"in that day . . . all the ends of the earth shall see the salvation of our God,"* signifying the Messianic future. But, in Isaiah here, we read that the wounding for transgressions had already occurred and the stripes for healing were at that time in process. The full healing, of course, is to occur at the time of redemption, at which time the sorrows will cease.

Keep in mind that Isaiah is using terms of affliction, such as wounds, bruises, and stripes purely figuratively. They describe Israel's sufferings in exile. These are not literal terms, as we have previously revealed. The prophets have used this kind of expression for Israel's miseries. Christianity would like to have this as a literal understanding, but we will add further evidence of how misfitting it would be to read Isaiah in the strict sense of his words. Let's go to a nearby verse, *Isaiah 51:23.* It reads, *"But I will put it (God's fury) into the hand of them that afflict thee; which have said to thy (Israel's) soul, Bow down, that we may go over: and thou hast laid thy body as the ground, and as the street, to them that went over."* Stop and ask. Was Jesus walked over literally as he was supposedly wounded literally? Certainly not. Therefore, we can reasonably ask if Israel was walked over figuratively, as the nation was wounded figuratively. The reply is surely "yes" for Israel. The verses fit Israel perfectly.

Understand that Isaiah is writing of the Gentiles' eventual appreciation of the fact that Israel has been bearing the burden of the world's transgressions. In the glorious Messianic times, the Gentiles will come to know that Israel has been specially selected by God to carry the profound responsibility of the Torah in order to combat mankind's wickedness. God put the "griefs" and "sorrows" of all humankind on His servant, Israel. The Jewish people's troubles will be known in Messianic days to have been of a special spiritual nature. The exile and tribulations will be seen by all as done for Israel's improvement, not rejection, and for its strengthening in righteousness, not punishment. The Gentiles will remember when they thought Israel's suffering was due to God's desire as we read, ". . . we did esteem him stricken, smitten of God, . . ." This seems to be exactly what Christianity has claimed, doesn't it? Yet, Israel as the light to the nations will be their salvation as we read, ". . . with his stripes we are healed."

The Gentiles will not only come to realize that Israel was given a holy mission by God and was exiled for a purpose, but they will admit that much of the tribulation Israel received belonged to the Gentiles themselves for their own wrongdoing. We read this in, "But he was wounded for our transgressions, . . ." Let's explain an important translation correction here. "Wounded for" should be rendered "wounded because of," or "wounded due to," or "wounded as a result of" our transgressions. A similar correction applies to "bruised for." The proper verbage clearly shows that Israel's troubles were the result of the misconduct of others.

Furthermore, the Gentiles will confess culpability in the horrendous suffering of Israel. They will comprehend that they obtained worldly welfare for themselves by using the Jewish people as their scapegoat. They added "stripes" to God's suffering servant in exile. We read of this also in *Zechariah 1:15, "And I (God) am very sore displeased with the heathen that are at ease: for I was but a little displeased (with Israel), and they (the heathen) helped forward the affliction (of Israel)."*

At the redemption, God will punish the Gentiles for this evil. See *Isaiah 61:6, ". . . ye shall eat the riches of the Gentiles, and in their glory shall ye boast yourselves."* But, also at the redemption Gentiles will be converted to the God of Israel and be freed of their transgressions. As written in *Jeremiah 16:19, ". . . the Gentiles shall come unto thee from the ends of the earth, and shall say, Surely our fathers have inherited lies, vanity, and things wherein there is no profit."* And we read in *Genesis 12:3, "I will bless them that bless thee, . . . and in thee shall all families of the earth be blessed."* Eventually, in the Messianic times, Israel will being all mankind to the greatness of God and His Torah. This book's chapter, "Scriptural Messianic Expectations," tells about this.

One other observation is of importance here. Verse 6 completely contradicts Christianity's claim that the suffering servant voluntarily suffered. It is written, ". . . and the Lord hath laid on him the iniquity of us all." Consequently, we know the burden was given as God desired, not as requested by the servant. He was not a voluntary sacrifice as Christianity has it. Moreover, even more plainly we know that the suffering servant is not God the Son of the Trinity, for we read, ". . . the Lord laid on him . . . ," which surely means God gave to an entity other than Himself.

ISAIAH 53:7 (SEE "Proof-Texts—Crucifixion Related" under "Openeth Not His Mouth" for an examination of this verse previously given).

ISAIAH 53:8, "He was taken from prison and from judgment: and who shall declare his generation? For he was cut off out of the land of the living: for the transgression of my people was he stricken."

COMMENT: Again, note the past tense throughout, which was used many hundreds of years before Jesus lived. Now we will explain the correct translation of the words which Christianity makes "from prison." It is properly rendered "by oppression and judgment he was taken away . . ." Thus we see that by human cruelty and decree the Israel nation was taken away.

The exile will be such a great misfortune that human expression of it will be inadequate. The people cut out of the land of the living, the Holy Land, will be like a nation which died. The phrase, "he was cut out of the land of the living," is a metaphorical expression meaning the nation of Israel in its exile. *Ezekiel 37:11* has a similar expression, *". . . these bones are the whole house of Israel: . . . we are cut off. . . ."*

The correct translation and interpretation of the last sentence should be "Because of (due to) (as a result of) the transgression of my people (humanity) was he (Israel) stricken." The Gentile nations will comprehend they were responsible for the strokes given to the suffering servant, Israel. In other words, although Israel accepts its exile as God's punishment, which is at the same time God's means of cleansing, much of the horrors of the exile will be recognized by mankind as due to the Gentiles' own wickedness. In these following ways the Gentiles are responsible for the suffering of God's Chosen People.

1—ISRAEL CARRIES THE BURDEN OF THE TORAH. Israel has been carrying the burden of the world's sinfulness, chosen by God to receive the Torah. The Jewish people have been shouldering the burden of being a light to the Gentiles.

2—ISRAEL SUFFERS FOR THE GENTILES' SINS. Much of Israel's afflictions should have been for the Gentiles themselves. Israel has been hurt due to the transgression of the Gentiles and is suffering because of the sins of mankind.

3—ISRAEL IS MISTREATED BY THE GENTILES. Israel has been severely mistreated by the Gentiles in exile. The wicked treatment has been the cause of much of the suffering of the servant of the Lord.

Note this important point:—In this verse by Isaiah, there is absolutely no indication, explicit or implicit, that the suffering servant atoned for the sins of others. He suffered as a result of the sins of others. Nothing is written about shouldering the transgressions of others in order to make vicarious atonement, even in the Christian translation.

ISAIAH 53:9, (SEE "Proof-Texts—Crucifixion Related" under

"Grave With the Wicked, Numbered With Transgressors" for an examination of this verse previously given).

ISAIAH 53:10, "Yet it pleased the Lord to bruise him; he hath put him to grief: when thou shalt make his soul an offering for sin, he shall see his seed, he shall prolong his days, and the pleasure of the Lord shall prosper in his hand."

COMMENT: God has given his servant Israel punishments not for sin as such, but for eventual improvement in righteousness. The chastisement is not a penalty, but a benefit. Israel has been exiled as a learning experience. We can liken this to hard times making people spiritually stronger. Read the words of *Malachi 3:3-4, ". . . and he shall purify the sons of Levi, and purge them as gold and silver, that they may offer unto the Lord an offering in righteousness. Then shall the offering of Judah and Jerusalem be pleasant unto the Lord, as in the days of old . . ."* In Messianic times Israel's spiritual strength will be rewarded.

How can Christianity apply the first sentence of this verse to Jesus? Jesus, who is God the Son in the Trinity, cannot be bruised by other parts of the Trinity. God cannot grieve God in any logical manner. Moreover, why would God hurt God? And why would the Lord be pleased to do so? Do you see how senseless all this is? There is no way this can apply to Jesus of Christianity. If they want to claim this for Jesus, they must admit Jesus is not God.

The words, "make his soul an offering for sin," have nothing to do with vicarious atonement. What they do mean is that the servant's soul, burdened with responsibility for the world's righteousness, will make itself holy and acceptable to God in perfect repentance. Israel will be a light to the nations in its righteousness. A restitution of the unblemished soul given to Israel by God is, in fact, Israel's "offering for sin" to God. There is nothing here of Christologic sin offering, rather there is only Judaism's repentance and atonement.

Isaiah has fortunately made it clear that Christianity's conclusion that it is Jesus' soul being offered for sin is fallacious. Isaiah's words tie the phrase to prophesies which Jesus did not fulfill. Regard the word "when," for it binds the sin offering to occurrences of abundant physical offspring and length of life? Did Jesus have children? Did Jesus have length of life? Certainly not. However, observe how fitting it is to assume that it is Israel which will make the sin offering, see many offspring, and prolong its days. This prophesy is about Israel, and we present other verses from the Hebrew Scriptures supporting this interpretation.

1—*Deuteronomy 28:11, "And the Lord shall make thee (Israel) plenteous in goods, in the fruit of thy body . . ."*

2—*Jeremiah 23:3, "And I will gather the remnant of my flock out of the countries whither I have driven them, . . . and they shall be fruitful and increase."*

3—*Isaiah 65:20, "There shall be no more thence an infant of days, nor an old man that hath not filled his days: for the child shall die an hundred years old . . ."*

4—*Zechariah 8:4, ". . . and every man with his staff in his hand for very age."*

Understand that the Biblical word for "seed" as found here always has the meaning of physical descendants, not figurative ones. Christianity would like the Hebrew word to have general significance, so that perhaps disciples or the Christian community could fit the "seed" designation. They are not entitled to such an interpretation, for it must be literal, not symbolic, children. By the way, "abundant" is understood to belong in the phrase "see his seed." This is the way in Biblical language usage, which may omit an understood term.

Concerning the lengthening of life, as promised here, it cannot be likened to eternal life in regard to Jesus, for in Christianity Jesus already is immortal. He is part of God eternal in the Trinity. Therefore, his life cannot be extended or prolonged as mentioned in this verse. The last sentence is an acknowledgement that God's purpose will be successfully performed by the Chosen People.

ISAIAH 53:11, "He shall see the travail of his soul, and shall be satisfied: by his knowledge shall my righteous servant justify many; for he shall bear their iniquities."

COMMENT: We have already exposed the serious errors incurred when trying to fit Jesus as the subject of *Isaiah 52:13—53:10.* Don't you think this verse will also be shown to be about Israel, rather than Jesus? This verse has a vagueness which lends itself to use by Christianity, but we will show that it is to be interpreted completely within Judaism.

God will see Israel's soul undergoing its difficult turn to pure repentance in exile and be happy at what occurs. If this sentence were about Jesus, it would have the soul of God, as God the Son, in agony. Could God have an agonized soul? And could God be satisfied with His own soul in travail? Isn't God perfect, making this impossible? By asking questions like these we reveal the nonsense of Christianity's view of this verse, and others like it.

Let's continue by explaining how by Israel's knowledge many shall be justified before the Lord. Israel, as God's Chosen People, has been given the Torah. We possess the knowledge of what God requires of mankind by knowing the Torah, the Hebrew Bible and its teachings. In Messianic times, all nations shall be brought to God through Judaism's light and shall be made righteous and just through Israel, God's servant. Here is the Scriptural evidence of this correct interpretation.

1—*Isaiah 2:3 (Micah 4:2), "And many people shall . . . go up to the mountain of the Lord, . . . and he will teach us of his ways, and we will walk in his paths: for out of Zion shall go forth the law, and the word of the Lord from Jerusalem."*

2—*Isaiah 49:3,6, ". . . Thou art my servant, O Israel, in whom I will be glorified. . . . I will also give thee for a light to the Gentiles, that thou mayest be my salvation unto the end of the earth."*

3—*Isaiah 56:6-7, "Also the sons of the stranger, that join themselves to the Lord, to serve him, and to love the name of the Lord, to be his servants, every one that keepeth the sabbath from polluting it, and taketh hold of my covenant; Even them will I bring to my holy mountain, and make them joyful in my house of prayer: their burnt offerings and their sacrifices shall be accepted upon mine altar; for mine house shall be called an house of prayer for all people."*

The verse says, "by his knowledge shall my righteous servant justify many." This cannot be about Jesus, because we have shown that in all of Jesus' ministry he never imparted knowledge of his supposed vicarious atonement to the multitudes of his followers. Jesus' teaching was of personal repentance for acceptance into the kingdom of God. No one, including his disciples, knew why he supposedly had to die. Not only didn't he impart knowledge of Christology to the people, but the few words he did impart to his disciples they did not comprehend. See this book's chapters, "Jesus Was Not the Hebrew Messiah . . . ," under "Jesus' Disciples Do Not . . . Understand" and also, "Proof-Texts-General Messiah," under "Resurrection . . ." for pertinent comments. Even though Christianity would like to reverse the meaning and have knowledge "of" him, rather than "by" him, justify, it is not written so.

Christianity says that faith in Jesus' sacrificial death and resurrection justifies and offers salvation. Read *Romans 10:9, "That if thou shalt confess with thy mouth the Lord Jesus, and shalt believe in thine heart that God hath raised him from the dead, thou shalt be saved."* Paul said that. Christianity believes what Paul said. We are not challenging Christianity's belief. We are, however, challenging the use of Isaiah chapter 53 to verify their belief.

Now ask how God could be called a righteous servant or a servant of himself at all. He cannot be credited with virtue, when He is virtue. He cannot, with reasonableness, be a servant of Himself either. We can inquire how a part of the Trinity can work for another part and still be one essence. The conundrum is not a "mystery" as Christianity replies to that which makes no sense. It is a flawed concept, which no one outside of Christianity need accept and those within Christianity should stop to ponder.

Finally, we'll discuss, ". . . shall . . . justify . . . shall bear their iniquities." Taken out of context this phrase is perfect for Christianity. It seems to lend credibility to their assertion that Jesus took the sins of mankind upon himself and atoned for them vicariously. This is the all-important message of Christianity, and they want this verse to confirm their claim. Taken out of context this can mean whatever they want it to mean. But, it exists in association with all of what Isaiah has been saying in chapter 53, and must be interpreted in this connection.

We have already commented on Isaiah 53:5 where it says, ". . . he was bruised for our iniquities," in the past tense. Learn now that the translation here, from the original Hebrew, is "did justify" and "did bear," in the past tense also. This certainly eliminates Jesus, in any capacity, who lived so many hundred of years after Isaiah.

Well, if the verse is not about Jesus, what does the last phrase mean? We have already revealed its meaning. First, Israel by being given the Torah has been shouldering the burden of the world's sinfulness. Second, Israel has been hurt due to the transgressions of the Gentiles. And third, Israel has had evil treatment by the Gentiles in exile. Thus Israel bears iniquities. Nevertheless, even if we were to read the phrase in the future tense, as the Christian translation erroneously has it, it still would be very comfortably explained within Judaism. We would understand that in the Messianic Era God's Chosen People will still be carrying the burden of mankind's iniquity, however in a spiritual sense only. The nation of Israel will still be a light to the Gentiles and be the teacher of God's Torah to the Gentiles who will have turned to Judaism and Judaism's God.

ISAIAH 53:12, "*Therefore will I divide him a portion with the great, and he shall divide the spoil with the strong; because he hath poured out his soul unto death: and he was numbered with the transgressors; and he bare the sin of many, and made intercession for the transgressors.*" (SEE "Proof-Texts—Crucifixion Related" under "Grave With the Wicked, Numbered With Transgressors").

COMMENT: Note the past tense for all he had done and the future tense for the rewards. Once again the grammatical fact eliminates Jesus as the subject. But, let's continue with the verse. That Israel will have "a portion with the great," meaning great honor, is shown in many Biblical passages. Turn back to our comments on Isaiah 52:13 for illustrating verses.

Also, we see that in the Messianic Era Israel will take "the spoil" of her former enemies. Here are some other verses to that effect.

Jeremiah 30:16, "*. . . they that spoil thee shall be a spoil, . . .*"
Zephaniah 2:9, "*. . . the residue of my people shall spoil them,*"

and the remnant of my people shall possess them."

The concepts of receiving honor and dividing spoils cannot be relevant to Jesus. Can God the Father give God the Son honor? Add to this impossibility the notion that the honor would be shared by others with great background. Jesus is unique in Christianity, therefore making this flawed as a reference to Jesus in any manner. Also, it makes no sense for God to give Jesus spoil of his enemies, spoil that would be shared with others. It just does not apply to Christology. However, the concerpts fit the nation of Israel perfectly. Israel will have honor and its enemies' spoils in the Messianic times as written in many verses. Sharing honor and spoils with the great and strong is simply literary style meaning Israel will be a great and strong servant.

Continuing our analysis, we recognize that in the Christian viewpoint Jesus "poured out his soul unto death." However, many more millions of all people have done just the same. The phrase is vague and not specific. It means nothing special about Jesus and only Jesus. Christianity has not one iota of justification that this should be interpreted in a Christologic sense. On the other hand, it very properly slides into the metaphoric symbolics which is seen over and over referring to the nation of Israel in its tribulation in exile.

"Numbered with transgressors" is discussed elsewhere, as indicated at the start. It simply means that Israel in exile is treated as sinful. Of course, the Gentile oppressors are themselves at fault. "He bare the sin of many" has been discussed here already in its triple significance:—Torah burden, Gentile transgression suffering, and Gentile mistreatment.

Now let's get to ". . . made intercession for the transgressors." This certainly sounds Christologic. We have come through all of Isaiah here in this chapter demonstrating that it belongs to Judaism completely. This does too. We simply ask what is so special about intercession? It just means asking help for someone else, praying in behalf of another. We all do it when we pray to God to help someone we love. In this case, it is the people of Israel who are interceding for the sinners who surround them in their exile. Read *Jeremiah 29:7* for verification of this, *"And seek the peace of the city whither I have caused you to be carried away captives, and pray unto the Lord for it: for in the peace thereof shall ye have peace."*

Intercession has no meaning of vicarious atonement in this Biblical verse. We do not have expressed an idea that intercession is connected to offering oneself as a sacrifice. Christianity reads into it whatever they wish, but the words give no confirmation of their belief. Yet, we take this one step forward in asking with whom would Jesus be making intercession? In Christianity, he is one in the Godhead with the Father. Does he intercede for the sinner to himself? God is God and cannot intercede to himself. If he makes intercession to God, then he is not God in the Trinity Godhead. No matter how we stretch our minds, the words cannot accomplish what Christianity would have them do, in any rational manner. It is not a mystery of Christology, but sheer irrationality. Christianity answers that those who are without Christian faith cannot appreciate the mystery. Non-Christianity replies that those with Christian faith have allowed mysteries to replace God-given reason. Judaism's advocate replies that Christian faith has replaced Biblical revelation.

Indeed, in the New Testament itself, Jesus is shown not to be an intercessor in Christologic terms. Read *Luke 23:34*, *"Then said Jesus, Father, forgive them; for they know not what they do."* First, his role is depicted as mediator between God and people, thus showing that he is not God. Second, he asks God to bestow forgiveness, as an intercessor would do, thus showing that forgiveness is not his to bestow. We learn quite a lot from this verse in Luke, all of which contradicts Christianity's concept of Jesus being God incarnate and offering forgiveness of sin. We need not mention his releasing Jews from punishment, except to say that Christians should do what Jesus asked and stop persecuting Jews.

In commenting on all of Isaiah 52:13- 53:12, we offer the words of Jesus in *Matthew 27:46 (Mark 15:34)*, *". . . My God, my God, why hast thou forsaken me?"* Also, we give *Matthew 26:39 (Mark 14:35-36) (Luke 22:42)*, *". . . O my Father, if it be possible, let this cup pass from me: nevertheless not as I will, but as thou wilt."* Both these quotes are Scriptural evidence from the New Testament that Jesus, as God the Son, was not a voluntary self-sacrifice for mankind's transgressions. These verses are implicit contradictions of Christology as well as the Trinity.

Returning to Isaiah under examination, we bring to light an important missing element. Have you noticed that nothing at all is intimated about the alleged resurrection of Jesus which is so essential to Christianity? It is entirely missing. Yet, without a resurrection the sacrificial death would be of no consequence, even as Paul wrote. The whole of Isaiah here could be considered valueless for Christianity without mention of a resurrection. Of course, nothing like this exists because Isaiah is not about Jesus, but about the nation of Israel.

It's time to summarize our findings. Isaiah is completely out of joint when considered to be about Jesus Christ, while on the other hand, it is smoothly and fully interpreted when considered to be about Israel, as Judaism teaches! Christianity has no justification from the Hebrew writings to interpret Isaiah as a proof-text. Many contradictions and incompatabilities to Christianity exist. The few phrases which supposedly might fit their beliefs lack any Christologic verification and are faulted in various ways. As we have shown, most parts of the verses do not fit Jesus properly. Therefore, any selected part, out of context, cannot be claimed to be about Jesus. Specificity is lacking. Usage of the past tense makes pointing to Jesus absurd. Moreover, nowhere in the Hebrew Scriptures is the Messiah expected to suffer. Read this book's chapters on "The Hebrew Messiah" and "Scriptural Messianic Expectations" to learn why Judaism is certain Jesus is not the Hebrew Messiah prophesied.

One last word is offered here about the irony of interpreting Jesus as the suffering servant of God, rather than the people of Israel, who are the true suffering servants as we have demonstrated. Because Christianity has misappropriated the chapter of Isaiah for Jesus, the nation of Israel is even further afflicted. What sorrowful irony!

20

Proof-Texts—
Judaism's Covenant

UNTIL SHILOH COME.

Genesis 49:10, "The sceptre shall not depart from Judah, nor a lawgiver from between his feet, until Shiloh come; . . ."

COMMENT: Shiloh is seen to be Jesus the Messiah, who has taken the royal scepter from the Jews.

REBUTTAL: History shows that the Jewish tribe of Judah did not have a king and scepter after the fall of the First Temple. Jesus lived many hundreds of years later, and therefore this verse does not refer to him. In fact, if taken in this light, it is impossible for it to allude to anyone at all. Actually, the verse has an entirely different meaning. It is generally considered a blessing of Jacob upon the tribe of Judah, where Judah is given the blessing of supremacy over the other tribes. Even though other tribes may rule, it is Judah which is given perpetual right to the scepter of authority.

The phrase, "until Shiloh come," does not mean that the authority over the scepter will end at the coming of the Messiah, but will continue. "Until" is not a limiting term here, but a point of reference and emphasis. A similar use of "until" is found in *Genesis 28:15, ". . . for I will not leave thee, until I have done that which I have spoken to thee of."* God is promising to do something, not saying he will leave after doing it. This same thrust is found in our subject verse where Judah is to have the scepter even after the Messiah comes.

CURSE OF THE LAW.

Deuteronomy 27:26, "Cursed be he that confirmeth not all the words of this law to do them . . ." (SEE Galatians 3:10).

COMMENT: This was used by Paul who taught that those who abide by the law are under a curse. Paul contended that neglecting even one law makes it as if all were broken, and therefore sinfulness is inevitable. This is Christianity's argument for the necessity of Jesus Christ's vicarious atonement for man's sin. Man cannot free himself from sin by the law of Moses, only by faith in the vicarious atonement, they say. REBUTTAL: By this interpretation, Paul was able to free the early Church from its Hebraic obligations. However, he was wrong in calling the law ineffectual. Certainly, God knows He created man with imperfections. He expects people to follow his commandments with all their power, even though the effort and results are imperfect. Read *Deuteronomy 30:6, "to love the Lord thy God with all thine heart, and all thy soul . . ."* Thus we learn that it is fulfilling the laws with our full effort which is required, not perfection. God wants us to observe all the laws, because He doesn't want us to pick and choose among His perfect laws. Read *Psalm 19:7, "The law of the Lord is perfect . . ."*

Furthermore, regard the word "confirmeth." "Confirmeth" signifies to give approval to the words of the law, nothing more. It means that Jews should uphold the validity and efficacy of all the laws. Of course, when one understands that the laws are good, are God's desire, one should do them. But, it is the supporting of the observance of the law of Moses which is required, not the obeying of each and every ordinance totally and perfectly.

Regarding the word "all," the original Hebrew does not include it. Yet, the very next sentence does include the word "all" in, "And all the people . . ." *Jeremiah 11:3* has a similar message. The Christian text in that case does not use the word "all." Read, ". . . *Cursed be the man that obeyeth not the words of this covenant."* The emphasis is obviously on the listening to God's word, not scrupulously attending to all details. The Hebrew even reads "heareth," rather than "obeyeth."

Let's return to the thought that God knows He created man with faults. Man, having weakness, does err. His efforts are hampered by his human nature. God knows this. Therefore, at the same time God created laws for man, He created the means by which man can correct his imperfect nature. In Judaism "repentance" overcomes human failings. We return to God through sincere regret for our lack of complete righteousness. Through repentance, prayer, and good deeds we establish our place as God's children. Through personal atonement (at-one-ment) we offer amends. Read *Hosea 14:1-2* for example, *"O Israel, return unto the Lord thy God; for thou hast fallen by thy iniquity. Take with you words, and turn to the Lord: say unto him, Take away all iniquity, and receive us graciously . . ."* Also read *Job 33:27-28, "He looked upon men, and if any say, I have sinned, and perverted that which was right, and it profited me not; He will deliver his soul from going into the pit, and his life shall see the light."* For more, refer to this book's chapter, "God and His Chosen People," under "God Forgives Sinners Who Repent . . ." Hence, there is no curse in the law, as Paul taught in his rebellion against Judaism's obligations to God, but instead a bonding to God. The law is a supreme blessing for Jews and mankind, for it teaches righteousness and leads us in God's pathways.

Think of this:—If you believe there is a curse in the law, then you believe God makes mistakes, or is hardhearted, or perhaps is even powerless. This is how it goes. In the view of Christianity, man was born with original sin, which condemns man to hell. This is a cruel concept, don't you think? But, God tried to correct this by giving the laws at Sinai. He blundered. The laws to overcome sin did not work properly, as people could not do them all perfectly. So, God is seen as fallible. Otherwise, God is seen as continuing the cruelty of original sin, knowing He made ineffectual laws. Thus, God is seen as hardhearted. Yet, if not fallible or cruel, then we could assume God is powerless to create proper, effective laws. Take your choice of these impossibilities. In any case, man was still damned according to Christianity. Then God, really wanting to allow man to have victory over sin, initiated a new method. He "killed" himself in the semblance of His sacrificed Son and merely asked for belief that this occurrence was a vicarious atonement which frees man of all sin. This belief in the resurrection is all that is needed to obtain eternal salvation in Christianity's view, not any good conduct or following of laws.

The trouble with the above scenario is that God is not capable of error, as He is all-knowing, all-good, and all-powerful. Consequently, it is impossible not because of the Christian concept of vicarious atonement alone, but more basically because of the very nature of God. He does not change His mind. See *Numbers 23:19, "God is not a man, that he should lie: neither . . . repent: hath he said, and shall he not do it? . . ."* Also, God's works are perfect. Read *Deuteronomy 32:4, ". . . his work is perfect: . . . a God . . . without iniquity . . ."* The law of Moses is God's law and following it gives righteousness as God intended.

SACRED DAYS AND DUTIES ARE ABOLISHED.

Isaiah 1:13-14, "Bring no more vain oblations; incense is an abomination unto me; the new moons and sabbaths, the calling of assemblies, I cannot away with; it is iniquity . . . Your new moons and your appointed feasts my soul hateth: . . ."

COMMENT: Christianity uses this to sanction the discarding of Judaism's sacred holidays and obligations.

REBUTTAL: Isaiah's verse must be read in context of the entire chapter in which God rebukes the people of Israel for doing evil. It is the people's sinfulness which makes the sacred days and duties unacceptable to God. Their unrighteousness is being chastised, not the holidays and rituals. See *Isaiah 1:16,* *"Wash you, make you clean; put away the evil of your doings . . ."* Isaiah certainly does not mean that God voids the sacred holidays, sabbaths, and duties. This is demonstrated when he says that all mankind will join with the people of Israel and be observant of the sacred days in the Messianic times. Observe *Isaiah 66:23,* *". . . from one new moon to another, and from one sabbath to another, shall all flesh come to worship before me, saith the Lord."*

JUDAISM'S HOLIDAYS END.

Hosea 2:11, *"I will also cause all her mirth to cease, her feast days, her new moons, and her sabbaths, and all her solemn feasts."*
COMMENT: This also is said to mean the ending of Judaism's sacred days.
REBUTTAL: Because of the exile of the Hebrew nation, lamentation instead of joy accompanies the celebration of the sacred days along with all other bitter things. The affliction of the exile will have negative affects on the celebrations. This can be clearly seen in the context of the Hosea chapter, which speaks of the emptiness of the exile. But, God who has given the exile will also give the reward. Read *Hosea 2:23,* *". . . and I will have mercy upon her that had not obtained mercy; and I will say to them which were not my people, Thou art my people; and they shall say, Thou art my God."*

TEMPLE RUINED, HOLIDAYS END.

Lamentations 2:6, *"And he hath violently taken away his tabernacle, as if it were of a garden: he hath destroyed his places of the assembly: the Lord hath caused the solemn feasts and sabbaths to be forgotten in Zion . . ."*
COMMENT: Again here, Judaism's holy Temple, assembly places, and holidays are depicted as ended, in Christianity's view.
REBUTTAL: Because of idolatry in sacred places, God's anger has caused the Temple's ruin. Due to iniquity, Israel's celebrations of the holidays are not as they should be. This passage from Lamentations is among all the "sorrow" passages describing Israel in misery due to God's punishment for unrighteousness. Dreadful misfortunes occur. The punishments, however, are for strengthening in righteousness, not eternal desertion by God. The "sorrow" is to be followed by the "promise." The eternal validity of God's word is sure. The hope of repentance renewing the former fullness of the Temple and observances is expressed in *Lamentations 5:21,* *"Turn thou us unto thee, O Lord, and we shall be turned, renew our days as of old."*

In addition to *Isaiah 66:23* which testifies to the eternal truth of the law, and holy days, and observances, we present these which show they are not to end even in the Messianic times. This book's chapters,

"God and His Chosen People" and "Scriptural Messianic Expectations," give further pertinent information.

Deuteronomy 11:1, "Therefore thou shalt love the Lord thy God, and keep his charge, and his statutes, and his judgments, and his commandments, alway."

Deuteronomy 12:28, "Observe and hear all these words which I command thee, that it may go well with thee, and with thy children after thee for ever . . ."

Deuteronomy 29:29, ". . . those things which are revealed belong unto us and to our children for ever, that we may do all the words of this law."

Isaiah 56:6-7, "Also the . . . stranger . . . every one that keepeth the sabbath from polluting it, and taketh hold of my covenant; . . . their burnt offerings and their sacrifices shall be accepted upon mine altar."

Isaiah 59:21, ". . . my words which I have put in thy mouth, shall not depart out of thy mouth, nor out of the mouth of thy seed . . . from henceforth and for ever."

Zechariah 14:16, "And it shall come to pass, that every one that is left of all the nations . . . shall even go up from year to year to worship the King, the Lord of hosts, and to keep the feast of tabernacles."

Exodus 12:17—Indicates the Passover feast is forever.

Exodus 31:16—Indicates the Sabbath (seventh day) is forever.

Leviticus 23:27,31—Indicates the Day of Atonement (Yom Kippur) is forever.

Numbers 15:38-39—Indicates fringes on garment borders (tsitsit) are forever.

GOD ABANDONED JEWS.

Leviticus 26:38-39, "And ye shall perish among the heathen, and the land of your enemies shall eat you up. And they that are left of you shall pine away in their iniquity . . ."

REPLY—*Leviticus 26:44, "And yet . . . I will not cast them away, . . . to destroy them utterly, and to break my covenant with them: for I am the Lord their God."*

Jeremiah 30:12, "For thus saith the Lord, Thy bruise is incurable, and thy wound is grievous."

REPLY—*Jeremiah 30:17, "For I will restore health unto thee, and I will heal thee of thy wounds, saith the Lord . . ."*

Amos 9:8, "Behold, the eyes of the Lord God are upon the sinful kingdom, and I will destroy it from off the face of the earth . . ."

REPLY—*Amos 9:8—continuing, ". . . saving that I will not utterly destroy the house of Jacob, saith the Lord."*

COMMENT: Passages like the above are used to show that God

chastised the Jews who are sinful and left them.

REBUTTAL: The passages of chastisement are accompanied by passages which show that God will remain with Israel always and have compassion. Truly, the Lord chastises whom He loves.

GOD IS ANGRY FOREVER.

Jeremiah 17:4, ". . . mine anger, which shall burn for ever."

COMMENT: Israel has God's perpetual anger.

REBUTTAL: The Hebrew word "forever" used here is utilized in three different ways in the Bible. One way, it means unlimited time. Another way fits man's lifetime. See *I Samuel 1:22, ". . . and there abide for ever."* And a third way is given in relation to an unknown end. See *Isaiah 32:14, ". . . the forts and towers shall be for dens for ever, . . . Until the spirit be poured upon us from on high."* The third way is the way the word "forever" is used in Jeremiah. We know this because God's anger is repeatedly said to end and consolation given for the time of redemption. For example read *Jeremiah 32:42, "For thus saith the Lord; Like as I have brought all this great evil upon this people, so will I bring upon them all the good that I have promised them."*

Other examples of the consolation verses are presented in the discussion before this one. Also see this book's chapter, "Scriptural Messianic Expectations," for more quotations of the "promise."

ISRAEL IS CONDEMNED FOREVER.

Amos 5:2, "The virgin of Israel is fallen; she shall no more rise; she is forsaken upon her land; there is none to raise her up."

COMMENT: Christianity says this means Israel is never to be released from its tribulations.

REBUTTAL: There are two replies of substance. First, the consolation is given at the end of *Amos 9:15, "And I will plant them upon their land, and they shall no more be pulled up out of their land which I have given them, saith the Lord thy God."* The second answer is that Amos, two verses following, announces that God has given to Israel the means to overcome its destruction. *Amos 5:4 reads, ". . . Seek ye me, and ye shall live:"*

ISRAEL'S REDEMPTION IS CONDITIONAL.

Jeremiah 18:7, "At what instant I shall speak concerning a nation, . . . to pluck up, and to pull down, and to destroy it;"

COMMENT: This supposedly means that God's promises of redemption and blessings are conditional on Israel's behavior. And as all are sinful, there will be no redemption for the nation of Israel, in the belief of Christianity.

REBUTTAL: It is true that man is sinful.

Ecclesiastes 7:20, "For there is not a just man upon earth that doeth good, and sinneth not."

Isaiah 64:6, "But we are all as an unclean thing, and all our righteousnesses are as filthy rags."

But, it is just as true that God has given man the means of overcoming transgression, through repentance and personal atonement. God guides us in His paths by holy laws. When we fall short of His straight path, He asks for our heart's repentance. Through His great mercy He accepts our turning to Him as if we were completely pure. There is a full circle leading from God to man and back again to God.

1—EFFICACY OF REPENTANCE.

Deuteronomy 30:2-3, "(Thou) . . . shalt return unto the Lord thy God, and shalt obey his voice . . . with all thine heart, and with all thy soul; That then the Lord thy God will turn thy captivity, and have compassion upon thee . . ."

Isaiah 55:7, "Let the wicked forsake his way, . . . and let him return unto the Lord, and he will have mercy upon him; . . . he will abundantly pardon."

2—REDEMPTION GIVEN FREELY TO SHOW GOD'S MIGHT.

Ezekiel 36:9,11, "For, behold, I am for you, and I will turn unto you, . . . and ye shall know that I am the Lord."

Ezekiel 36:23, " . . . and the heathen shall know that I am the Lord, saith the Lord God, when I shall be sanctified in you before their eyes."

3—REDEMPTION FOR GOD'S SAKE, NOT MAN'S BEHAVIOR.

Isaiah 48:9,11, "For my name's sake will I defer mine anger, and for my praise will I refrain for thee, that I cut thee not off. For mine own sake, even mine own sake, will I do it . . ."

Ezekiel 36:22, " . . . Thus saith the Lord God; I do not this for your sakes, O house of Israel, but for mine holy name's sake . . ."

4—REDEMPTION FOR RIGHTEOUSNESS TO SHINE.

Isaiah 62:1, "For Zion's sake . . . I will not rest, until the righteousness thereof go forth as brightness . . ."

CONSOLATION WAS FOR FIRST EXILE ONLY.

Deuteronomy 28:15(-68), "But it shall come to pass, if thou wilt not harken unto the voice of the Lord thy God . . . all these curses shall come upon thee . . ."

COMMENT: Christianity uses this to show that the consolation was given only when the First Temple's destruction and exile occurred, as there is no consolation following. They claim there is no consolation given when the Second Temple was destroyed.

REBUTTAL: The fact is that the consolation is given, but in reverse order. Read *Deuteronomy 28:1-2(-14)*, *"And it shall come to pass, if thou shalt harken diligently unto the voice of the Lord thy God . . . God will set thee on high above the nations of the earth! And all these blessings shall come on thee . . ."* The blessings are then listed. Moreover, the return from Babylon and the building of the Second Temple did not fulfill the redemption promises by God. So, evidently all passages of consolation refer to our present state, which is in expectation of the Messianic Era. This book's chapter, "Scriptural Messianic Expectations," gives full details.

ARK AND COVENANT ENDED.
   Jeremiah 3:16, *". . . in those days, saith the Lord, they shall say no more, The ark of the covenant of the Lord . . . neither shall they visit it; neither shall that be done anymore."*
COMMENT: This is supposed to tell that the laws of Moses and the covenant will cease.
REBUTTAL: The ark was the place the tables of the covenant were kept. See *I Kings 8:9*, *"There was nothing in the ark save two tables of stone, which Moses put there . . ."* What is to happen, as reported here, is that the formality around the convenant will no longer be needed in the Messianic times. All of Jerusalem will be filled with sanctity, not just the ark of the covenant in the Temple. Read *Joel 3:17*, *". . . then shall Jerusalem be holy, and there shall no strangers pass through her any more."* Our subject verse alludes to the latter days when all nations will follow the God of Israel and the laws will be in the inward parts of man.

NEW COVENANT.
   Jeremiah 31:31, *"Behold, the days come, saith the Lord, that I will make a new covenant with the house of Israel and . . . Judah:"* (SEE *Hebrews 8:7-13*).
COMMENT: This verse is used by Christianity to indicate that Jews have lost the covenant, the laws are abrogated, and Christianity is the new Israel. Paul quotes it.
REBUTTAL: Reading this in context we learn that it is not a new agreement, but a new manner of giving it being promised. Contrary to the laws being abolished, they will be made part of the very nature of man. The same convenant, not another, will be made stronger in profound soul-penetrating dynamics. Also, notice that it will be the same people of Israel and Judah who have the covenant. The following writes of it directly after our subject verse.
   Jeremiah 31:33, *". . . I will put my law in their inward parts, and write it in their hearts . . ."*
There is no transfer of binding to another people, but the same nation of Israel will be given more intimacy with God.

Jeremiah 31:33, ". . . and (I) will be their God, and they shall be my people."
The Jewish people will be so familiar with God that no instruction in the knowledge of God will be needed.

Jeremiah 31:34, "And they shall teach no more every man his neighbor (brother), . . . for they shall all know me . . ."
The covenant will be unbreakable by the Jews, because it will be more deeply ingrained. Moreover, the people are blamed for the breaking of the covenant, not God. God is not going to break or change the former covenant with Israel. He hasn't made an imperfect covenant, but one which will be of new qualities in the superb days of Messianic fulfillment.

Jeremiah 31:32, "Not according to the covenant that I made with their fathers . . . which . . . they brake . . ."
Finally, let's put into perspective the impossibility of a replacement covenant by reading the following.

Deuteronomy 4:2, "Ye shall not add unto the word which I command you, neither shall ye diminish ought from it, that ye may keep the commandments of the Lord your God which I command you."

Isaiah 40:8, "The grass withereth, the flower fadeth: but the word of our God shall stand for ever."

EVERLASTING LIFE.

Daniel 12:2, "And many of them that sleep in the dust of the earth shall awake, some to everlasting life, and some to shame and everlasting contempt." (SEE John 5:28-29 (Matthew 25:46)).
COMMENT: Eternal life is obtained through Christianity, they believe.
REBUTTAL: John seems to parallel Daniel's verse, which is Hebrew Scripture revealing that eternal life is obtained in Judaism. Daniel, you note, says nothing of Christologic belief. Read carefully and you see that John also says nothing of Christologics. It says, ". . . the hour is coming, in which all that are in the graves shall hear his (Son of God's) voice, And shall come forth; they that have done good, unto the resurrection of life; and they that have done evil, unto the resurrection of damnation." Analyze this as if it were not in the New Testament. It is doing good which earns everlasting life at the time of resurrection. In this John is clearly Judaic.

Put aside that John believes Jesus, rather than God the Father, will be calling the dead from their graves. Christianity can believe this, if they wish. But, apart from this the verse is a complete validation of Judaism's teaching that the good are rewarded and the evil are punished in the hereafter. This verse by John is devoid of any teaching that vicarious atonement offers everlasting life. Nothing, absolutely nothing, is said about "believing" offering salvation. We have demonstrated in this book that in listening to Jesus we hear Judaism's message. Repentance, returning to God's holy laws, is what he taught. Vicarious atonement belief was not his message. Refer to this book's chapter, "Jesus Was Not the Messiah . . . ," under "Jesus Preached Repentance . . ." for details. Look at what Jesus said in *John 5:24*, *". . . He that heareth my word (repentance) and believeth in him (God) that sent me (gave me inspiration), hath everlasting life . . ."* Amazingly, here is Judaism's message of how to obtain eternal reward in heaven.

21

Which—What—New Testament Contradictions

This chapter is organized to display the contradictions within the New Testament. The conflicting verses selected are representative of the many which can be found. We will offer no comments about the verses, because the confusion and disarray are self-evident. The layers of opinion are seen in clear contrast. We are not inquiring about the existence of truth in the midst of the strikingly incompatable passages. It is Christianity's New Testament and Christianity's dilemma. They must explain it for themselves.

Read each presentation very carefully, so that the opposing statements are fully comprehended. Some pairs of verses have religious significance, others just have differing meanings. Some passages have relevance to Judaism, while others do not. If you are of Jewish heritage, ask yourself this:—If one verse presents the vindication of Judaism and the other does not, shouldn't you accept the validity of the Judaically oriented passage which nullifies the Christologic one? Both are in the New Testament, yet one is of what we know is true while the other is of what we know not. Christianity, remember, accepts our Holy Bible as truth. So should you. And so should you recognize as true the layers of Judaism's confirmation within the pages of the New Testament!

Can Christianity's Scripture, so lacking in harmony and coherence, so flawed in contrary statements, be considered other than unreliable as the word of God to the non-Christian? Can the basis of conversion to Christianity rest in a book having so much confusion? These paired passages highlight the absence of justification for conversion to the Christian religion by any Jew who uses his God-given intelligence. If anything, the New Testament's contradictions make

Judaism's authentic interpretation of the Hebrew Scriptures even more certain for us. Let's now read these astonishingly opposing verses.

1—John 20:28, "And Thomas answered and said unto him, My Lord and my God."
OR . . . *Matthew 19:17 (Mark 10:18) (Luke 18:19), ". . . Why callest thou me good? there is none good but one, that is, God . . ."*

2—John 10:30, "I and my Father are one."
OR . . . *John 6:38, "For I came down from heaven, not to do mine own will, but the will of him that sent me."*
   John 14:28, ". . . for my Father is greater than I."

3—Colossians 1:15, "(his dear Son) Who is the image of the invisible God . . ."
OR . . . *I John 4:12, "No man hath seen God at any time. . . ."*

4—Matthew 11:27 (Luke 10:22) (John 7:28-29) (John 17:25), ". . . neither knoweth any man the Father, save the Son, and he to whomsoever the Son will reveal him."
OR . . . *Matthew 5:8, "Blessed are the pure in heart: for they shall see God."*
   Acts 3:18, "But those things, which God before had showed by the mouth of all his prophets . . ."

5—Colossians 1:13, ". . . and hath translated us into the kingdom of his dear Son:"
OR . . . *Matthew 6:9-10 (Luke 11:2), ". . . Our Father . . . Thy kingdom come . . ."*

6—Philippians 2:10, "That at the name of Jesus every knee should bow, of things in heaven, and things in earth, and things under the earth;"
OR . . . *Romans 14:11, "For it is written, As I live, saith the Lord, every knee shall bow to me, and every tongue shall confess to God."*

7—Matthew 28:17, "And when they saw him, they worshipped him: but some doubted."
OR . . . *Matthew 4:10 (Luke 4:8), ". . . Thou shalt worship the Lord thy God, and him only . . ."*

8—John 16:15, "All things that the Father hath are mine . . ."
OR . . . *Mark 13:32, "But of that day and that hour knoweth no man, . . . neither the Son, but the Father."*

9—John 14:13-14, "And whatsoever ye shall ask in my name, that will I do, that the Father may be glorified in the Son. If ye shall ask any thing in my name, I will do it."
OR . . . *Matthew 26:39 (Mark 14:36) (Luke 22:42), ". . . O my Father, if it be possible, let this cup pass from me: nevertheless not as I will, but as thou wilt."*

10—John 18:20, ". . . I spake openly to the world . . . and in secret have I said nothing."
OR . . . *Mark 8:30, "And he (Jesus) charged them that they should tell no man of him."*

11—Matthew 28:18, ". . . All power is given unto me in heaven and in earth."
OR . . . *Matthew 20:23 (Mark 10:40), ". . . but to sit on my right hand, and on my left, is not mine to give, but it shall be given to them for whom it is prepared of my Father."*

12—Matthew 11:27 (Luke 10:22) (John 3:35) (John 13:3), "All things are delivered unto me of my Father . . ."
OR . . . *Matthew 18:35, "So likewise shall my heavenly Father do also unto you . . ."*

13—Matthew 9:6 (Mark 2:10) (Luke 5:24), "But that ye may know that the Son of man hath power on earth to forgive sins . . ."
OR . . . *Luke 23:34, ". . . Father, forgive them. . . ."*
   Matthew 6:14 (Mark 11:25), "For if ye forgive men their trespasses, your heavenly Father will also forgive you:"

14—John 9:39, ". . . For judgment I am come into this world . . ."
OR . . . *John 12:47, "And if any man hear my words, and believe not, I judge him not: for I came not to judge the world . . ."*

15—John 5:22, "For the Father judgeth no man, but hath committed all judgment unto the Son:"
OR . . . *I Peter 1:17, "And if ye call on the Father, who without respect of persons judgeth according to every man's work . . ."*

16—I John 5:18, "We know that whosoever is born of God sinneth not; but he that is begotten of God keepeth himself, and that wicked one toucheth him not."
OR . . . *Galatians 5:19-21, "Now the works of the flesh are manifest, which are these; Adultery, fornication, uncleanness, lasciviousness, Idolatry, witchcraft, hatred, varience, emulations, wrath, strife, sedi-*

tions, heresies, Envyings, murders, drunkenness, revellings, and such like: . . . they which do such things shall not inherit the kingdom of God."

17—Matthew 10:34 (Luke 12:51), "Think not that I am come to send peace on earth: I came not to send peace, but a sword."
OR . . . *Matthew 26:52, ". . . Put up again the sword into his place: for all they that take the sword shall perish with the sword."*
Matthew 5:9, "Blessed are the peacemakers: for they shall be called the children of God."

18—Matthew 10:35-36 (Mark 13:12) (Luke 12:52-53), "For I am come to set a man at varience against his father, and the daughter against her mother, And a man's foes shall be they of his own household."
OR . . . *Matthew 15:4 (Mark 7:10), "For God commanded, saying, Honor thy father and mother: and, He that curseth father or mother, let him die the death."*

19—I Corinthians 5:11,13, "But . . . if any man that is called a brother be a fornicator, or covetous, or an idolator, or a railer, or a drunkard, or an extortioner; with such an one know not to eat . . . put away from among yourselves that wicked person."
OR . . . *Matthew 9:10 (Mark 2:15) (Luke 5:30) (Luke 7:34) (Luke 15:1-2), ". . . many publicans and sinners came and sat down with him and his disciples."*

20—Matthew 15:11 (Mark 7:15,18), "Not that which goeth into the mouth defileth a man . . ."
OR . . . *Acts 15:29(20), ". . . abstain from meats offered to idols, and from blood, and from things strangled . . ."*
James 4:11, ". . . but if thou judge the law, thou art not a doer of the law, but a judge."

21—Matthew 6:19, Matthew 19:24 (Mark 10:23-25) (Luke 18:24-25), "Lay not up for yourselves treasures upon earth, . . . It is easier for a camel to go through the eye of a needle, than for a rich man to enter into the kingdom of God."
OR . . . *Matthew 25:29 (Mark 4:25) (Luke 8:18), "For unto every one that hath (talents—money) shall be given, and he shall have abundance: but from him that hath not shall be taken away even that which he hath."*

22—Luke 11:23 (Matthew 12:30), "He that is not with me is against me . . ."
OR . . . *Luke 9:50 (Mark 9:40), ". . . he that is not against us is for us."*

23—Matthew 28:19 (Luke 24:47), "Go ye therefore, and teach all nations . . ."
OR . . . *Matthew 10:5-6 (Matthew 15:24), ". . . Go not into the way of the Gentiles, . . . go rather to the lost sheep of the house of Israel."*

24—Matthew 16:12, " . . . he bade them . . . beware . . . of the doctrine of the Pharisees . . ."
OR . . . *Matthew 23:2-3, "Saying, The scribes and the Pharisees sit in Moses' seat: All therefore whatsoever they bid you observe, that observe and do . . ."*

25—Matthew 8:12, "But the children of the kingdom shall be cast out into outer darkness: there shall be weeping and gnashing of teeth."
OR . . . *Romans 11:1-2,28, "I say then, Hath God cast away his people? God forbid. . . . God hath not cast away his people which he foreknew . . . As concerning the gospel, they are enemies for your sakes: but as touching the election, they are beloved for the fathers' sakes."*

26—Matthew 27:25, "Then answered all the people, and said, His blood be on us, and on our children."
OR . . . *Acts 3:17, ". . . I wot that through ignorance ye did it, as did also your rulers."*
I Timothy 1:13, "(I, Paul) Who was before . . . a persecutor . . . obtained mercy, because I did it ignorantly in unbelief."

27—Matthew 23:35, "That upon you may come all the righteous blood shed upon the earth . . ."
OR . . . *Luke 23:34, ". . . Father, forgive them; for they know not what they do. . . ."*

28—Mark 6:11, "And whosoever shall not receive you, nor hear you, . . . It shall be more tolerable for Sodom and Gomorrha in the day of judgment, than for that city."
OR . . . *I John 3:15, "Whosoever hateth his brother is a murderer; and ye know that no murderer hath eternal life abiding in him."*
Matthew 5:44 (Luke 6:27), "But I say unto you, . . . Love your enemies . . ."

29—II John (1)10, "If there come any unto you, and bring not this doctrine, receive him not into your house, neither bid him God speed:"
OR . . . *Galatians 6:10, ". . . let us do good unto all men . . ."*

30—II Corinthians 6:14, "Be ye not unequally yoked together with unbelievers: for what fellowship hath righteousness with unrighteousness? . . ."
OR . . . *Matthew 5:47, "And if ye salute your brethren only, what do ye more than others? do not even the publicans so?"*

31—Matthew 23:33 (Luke 3:7), "(scribes and Pharisees) Ye serpents, ye generation of vipers, how can ye escape the damnation of hell?"
OR . . . *Matthew 5:20, ". . . except your righteousness shall exceed the righteousness of the scribes and Pharisees, ye shall in no case enter into the kingdom of heaven."*

32—Matthew 10:33, "But whosoever shall deny me before men, him will I also deny before my Father which is in heaven."
I Corinthians 16:22, "If any man love not the Lord Jesus Christ, let him be Anathema . . ."
John 17:9, ". . . I pray not for the world, but for them which thou hast given me . . ."
OR . . . *I John 4:8, "He that loveth not knoweth not God; for God is love."*

33—John 14:6, ". . . no man cometh unto the Father, but by me."
OR . . . *Matthew 6:6, ". . . when thou prayest, enter into thy closet, and when thou hast shut thy door, pray to thy Father which is in secret; and thy Father which seeth in secret shall reward thee openly."*

34—John 16:23, ". . . Whatsoever ye shall ask the Father in my name, he will give it you."
OR . . . *James 5:16, ". . . The effectual fervent prayer of a righteous man availeth much."*

35—John 3:18, "He that believeth on him is not condemned: but he that believeth not is condemned already, because he hath not believed in the name of the only begotten Son of God."
OR . . . *Luke 9:56, "For the Son of man is not come to destroy men's lives, but to save them."*

36—John 3:15, "That whosoever believeth in him should not perish, but have eternal life."
OR . . . *Matthew 7:21 (Luke 6:46), "Not every one that saith unto me, Lord, Lord, shall enter into the kingdom of heaven; but he that doeth the will of my Father which is in heaven."*

37—John 6:47, ". . . He that believeth on me hath everlasting life."
OR . . . *John 5:24, ". . . He that heareth my word, and believeth on him that sent me, hath everlasting life . . ."*

38—John 14:1, ". . . ye believe in God, believe also in me."
OR . . . *Romans 14:12, "So then every one of us shall give account of himself to God."*

39—Mark 16:16, "He that believeth and is baptized shall be saved; but he that believeth not shall be damned."
OR . . . *John 5:29, "(all) . . . shall come forth; they that have done good, unto the resurrection of life; and they that have done evil, unto . . . damnation."*

40—John 4:42, ". . . this is indeed the Christ, the Savior of the world."
Philippians 3:20, ". . . we look for the Savior, the Lord Jesus Christ."
OR . . . *Luke 1:47, "And my spirit hath rejoiced in God my Savior."*
I Timothy 1:1, ". . . by the commandment of God our Savior . . ."
Jude (1)25, "To the only wise God our Savior . . ."

41—Romans 10:9, "That if thou shalt confess with thy mouth the Lord Jesus, and shalt believe in thine heart that God hath raised him from the dead, thou shalt be saved."
OR . . . *James 4:12, "There is one lawgiver, who is able to save and to destroy . . ."*

42—Galatians 3:12, "And the law is not of faith . . ."
OR . . . *Hebrews 11:6, "But without faith it is impossible to please him: for he that cometh to God must believe that he is, and that he is a rewarder of them that diligently seek him."*

43—Romans 3:28, "Therefore we conclude that a man is justified by faith without deeds of the law."
OR . . . *Romans 2:6,10 (Matthew 16:27) (Revelation 22:12), "Who will render to every man according to his deeds . . . to every man that worketh good, to the Jew first, and also to the Gentile:"*
Galatians 6:7, "Be not deceived: God is not mocked: for whatsoever a man soweth, that shall he also reap."
James 2:17-18,24, "Even so faith, if it hath not works, is dead, being alone. . . . I will show thee my faith by my works. Ye see then how that by works a man is justified, and not by faith only."

44—Galatians 3:11, "But that no man is justified by the law in the sight of God, it is evident . . ."
OR . . . *Galatians 3:12, ". . . but, The man that doeth them (the law of Moses) shall live in them."*

45—Galatians 3:13, "Christ hath redeemed us from the curse of the law . . ."
OR . . . *Romans 2:13, "For not the hearers of the law are just before God, but the doers of the law shall be justified."*

46—Acts 13:39, "And by him all that believe are justified from all things, from which ye could not be justified by the law of Moses."
OR . . . *Romans 7:12,14, "Wherefore the law is holy, and the commandment holy, and just, and good. For we know that the law is spiritual . . ."*

47—John 3:36 (John 8:23-24), ". . . and he that believeth not the Son shall not see life; but the wrath of God . . . (ye shall die in your sins)."
OR . . . *I John 5:3, "For this is the love of God, that we keep his commandments: and his commandments are not grievous."*

48—Matthew 12:8, "For the Son of man is Lord even of the sabbath day (to keep the Sabbath is one of the ten commandments)."
OR . . . *Matthew 5:19, ". . . whosoever shall do (the commandments) . . . shall be called great in the kingdom of heaven."*

49—John 14:15, "If ye love me, keep my commandments."
OR . . . *Matthew 19:16-17 (Mark 10:17-19) (Luke 18:18-20), ". . . Good Master, what good thing shall I do, that I may have eternal life? . . . if thou wilt enter into life, keep the commandments (law of Moses)."*

50—Acts 16:30-31, ". . . Sirs, what must I do to be saved? And they said, Believe on the Lord Jesus Christ, and thou shalt be saved, and thy house."
OR . . . *Luke 10:25-28, ". . . Master, what shall I do to inherit eternal life? He said unto him, What is written in the law? how readest thou? And he answering said, Thou shalt love the Lord thy God with all thy heart, and with all thy soul, and with all thy strength, and with all thy mind; and thy neighbor as thyself. And he said unto him, Thou hast answered right: this do, and thou shalt live."*

22

Epilogue

The unprepared Jew is caught off guard when approached by the Christian missionary. The missionary is well able to quote chapter and verse from our own Scriptures, and this is startling to the person being so accosted. His barage of quotes might leave the listener with the impression that the missionary is a knowledgeable religious individual. We wrote this book with a deep desire to fill the gap which exists in the religious education of such a Jewish person, who may succumb to this impression and be at a loss to know Judaism's reply. This book, prayerfully, will be all that is necessary for this Jew, maybe you, to see through the many basic flaws of the missionary's arguments. With this book, you become armed with factual defenses. These can be added to your residual store of Jewish learning and feeling. Your instinctive confidence in and appreciation for your heritage should make all the pieces fall in place. The missionary has no chance of advancing his cause and converting the Jew who knows Christianity's errors. If the information presented in this writing effort is studied and utilized for response by the rational person, the missionary has met defeat!

You can be certain that any verses not covered are just as readily explained properly within Judaism. We may add that if any presentation in this book is found imperfect, keep in mind that these pages need not be perfect in order to demolish the missionary's assault on Judaism. The evidence we have gathered, organized, and clearly presented is overwhelming in all respects. We have given our best explanations. There may be other ways to explain some subjects, but they also would be in confirmation of Judaism's eternal validity.

The missionary has a burning need to convert you, for he needs self-confirmation based on Judaism's destruction. When this misguided person meets with solid, sensible rejoinders, such as are pointed out in the pages of this book, he probably will not admit he is wrong or give up. He probably will not be swayed by your proof of Judaism's eternal value and truth, as written in the Hebrew Scriptures. Chances are he will just continue to throw quotes at you, even though the previous ones were not successful. You must understand that the missionary is a person whose power of rational reasoning likely has long since been disengaged. He bombards you with verse after verse, misinterpreting them all. He is driven by his own need to convince you that Jesus is the Messiah and Christianity is the successor to Judaism. Note that rarely is mention made of Jesus being God incarnate in Christianity, for the missionary knows that this would be an enormous turn-off to any Jew, even an uneducated one.

When you expose the Biblical errors he is making in his mission to the Jew, he will not flinch, because he cannot open his mind to Judaism's truth and at the same time keep his world together. The missionary cannot emotionally accept Judaism's position and counter-claims, because if he did his entire religious survival might collapse. The missionary's view is that Christianity's unique salvation through belief in Jesus Christ rests on the supposition of Judaism's demise. His illogical thrusts are psychologically necessary for him. He must keep himself in the pictured outstretched arms of his beloved Savior. Jesus is his comfort, warm and restful. Judaism's Biblical truth cannot be allowed to interfere with his found relationship with the Son of God. His indoctrination into Christianity's missionary nature, whether he be former Jew or Gentile, makes him impervious to reasonable persuasion.

Don't be frustrated if you fail to convince the missionary of Judaism's role in the plan of God. Although it would be wonderful to convince the former Jew, who is now a Christian missionary, to return to his Judaism, don't count on it. The missionary's mental well-being is supported by his belief. His mind is closed to disturbing intrusions. As a Jew for Judaism, you should be content that you are well informed of God's Scriptural truth. Your knowledge has saved you, and thus Judaism wins. Moreover, your knowledge can be used in your life's encounters to present to other Jews the traps of the Christian missionary. Indeed, you can now consider yourself Judaism's missionary to the Jew!

Let's now look at the tactics used by the missionary and how to respond to them. First, don't allow him irrationality. Make him give logical reasoning for everything he says. Analyze his claims one at a time. Make him answer your questions point by point. And do utilize the rebuttals you have learned, for your questions and your refutations are your strength. Explain to him Judaism's understanding. We have shown all manner of fallacies of their proof-texts. You can be completely sure that nothing, absolutely nothing, he puts forward is going to be valid proof of his Christian viewpoint. Look up all he presents. His erroneous claims can be put in their place with Judaism's proper replies.

The missionary will call you a sinner, a nonbeliever with a stiff-neck who is headed for damnation and hell. Reply to his accusation with the verses we have shown which establish the Jew's rightful place in heaven following the Torah and doing God's commandments with our full heart.

He will offer a prayer for your soul's conversion and your salvation, with your heart opening to accept the Christian Christ. Counter this emotional situation with a prayer for his heart and mind to open to the eternal affection of the God of Israel for His Chosen People. Conclude with the words, "Shema Israel, Adonai Eloheynu, Adonai Echod," Judaism's everlasting clout.

The Christian missionary will say that the faith of Christianity is a mystery, which only those called to love Jesus are able to know. You, a nonbeliever, can never comprehend this mystery. But, if you will only believe in Jesus, all doubt will end. Answer that the mystery of faith must be based on Hebrew Biblical revelation and that belief in Jesus and vicarious atonement are not spoken of in Hebrew Scripture. Assert that if God meant for us to accept Him in mystery, He would not have said that He is the God who took His Chosen People out of Egypt, has given them his Covenant, and has set them to be a light to the nations. It is quite clear, Biblically, that God has given Jews the opportunity of doing good and earning eternal life. And what God gives He does not take away, for God's word is not a lie, or untrustworthy, or changed. The mystery of faith is not meant to violate God's Biblical evidence. Faith is not given by God to circumvent the Scriptures but to rest on them, and proper understanding of the word of God is the only foundation for the mystery of faith! Jewish faith encompasses the mind and heart together, both God's creations. Any other description of faith is a deception.

He will say that by belief in Jesus your life will be changed. You will be transformed, be born anew, and have peace. Reply to this that by giving yourself to the God of Israel, by accepting the yoke of His Torah, you convert your life in the only way God accepts for His Jewish people. By becoming a baal teshuvah and committing yourself to fulfill God's desires, you do what pleases Him and offers salvation.

Now, let's offer a word about the warmth of outreach of the missionary. He loves you. Jesus loves you. The world is full of love for you the potential convert. Just come to the Church which awaits you lovingly. Think, Jew. This is the "love trap." It has nothing but psychological escape to offer in the guise of religion. Every religious "cult" has drawn people to it by this same love magnet. They have been just as attractive to people as Christianity has been. Jews have deserted their heritage for both. Are "cults" in possession of religious truth? Are "cults" of God? In agreement, both Judaism and Christianity reply, "no." Therefore, we know that the magnet of love is without religious value.

And what about the individual trying to tear you away from your heritage? Isn't he asking you to break the commandment of honoring father and mother? The missionary does not care what he leaves in the wake of his attempt to capture the soul of a son or daughter. Great unhappiness and mental anguish result because of apostasy. If this is the peace Christianity offers, it seems to be only for the convert, not for his family which is left in torment. Is this what your moral judgment says is right and good?

Furthermore, look at what God says of those who lead Jews away from Judaism. He plainly announced that they should be killed. Yes, killed. So the missionary, especially the former Jew, who leads Jews to Christianity, is to be put to death by God's command. Read *Deuteronomy 13:6-10, "If thy brother . . . entice thee . . . saying, Let us go and serve other gods, . . . Namely, of the gods of the people which are round about you, . . . Thou shalt not consent unto him, nor harken unto him; . . . But thou shalt surely kill him; thine hand shall be first . . . and afterwards the hand of all the people. And thou shalt stone him with stones, that he die; because he hath sought to thrust thee away from the Lord thy God, which brought thee out of the land of Egypt . . ."*

We have an idea for you to utilize whenever the name of Jesus Christ is aimed at you, which can be very intimidating at times. Do the following to balance your equilibrium. Substitute the name of "God" for the name of Christianity's "Jesus Christ." See how comfortably it fits? Missionaries speak of Jesus in close relationship, but this relationship really belongs to God, the Father of us all!

1—Put "God" in your life.

2—"God" loves you.

3—"God" saves.

4—Open your heart to "God."

Judaism's truth is firmly established. Unfortunately however, there is an area of appeal the missionary uses which has nothing to do with rational analysis and Biblical evidence. The missionary concentrates on emotional faith, which is his way of escaping Biblical demands. He says that faith is a spiritual gift. Consequently, nonbelievers who do not have this gift of faith do not understand Christianity's truth. This is the circular reasoning which missionaries advance to end all criticism and overcome all errors of interpretation. There is glaring illogic in this. Let's illustrate the subterfuge of this type of thought from the words of the New Testament itself.

John 8:42,47, "*. . . If God were your Father, ye would love me: for I proceeded forth and came from God; neither came I of myself, but he sent me. He that is of God heareth God's words: ye therefore hear them not, because ye are not of God.*"

I John 4:6, "*We are of God: he that knoweth God heareth us; he that is not of God heareth not us. Hereby know we the spirit of truth, and the spirit of error.*"

Read these verses again, for they blow the mind with irrationality and self-righteousness. An instant analysis of this is that "as we are right, all those who don't believe us are wrong." The stuff of proof and reason, is it not? Yet, the reply of Judaism to this circular reasoning for Christian faith is presented in the New Testament as well.

John 9:29, "*We know that God spake unto Moses: as for this fellow (Jesus), we know not from whence he is.*"

In spite of this lack of proper proof, converts are won away from Judaism to Christianity. "Believe and be saved" and "Jesus loves you" have gained more converts to Christianity than any so-called prooftext. Psychological need for comfort and instant immortality is a very powerful force. It is a force which has propelled Christianity to its success in the world. Christianity offers a supposed cure-all for the world's trials in easy to take form.

Well, we have shown that Judaism "saves," so there is no need to enter unknown realms, realms which may be the road to damnation for the apostate. And as for Jesus Christ "loving you," he doesn't. We have uncovered Christianity's Jesus of hate. And this hate is meant for every innocent Jew who ever lived. Just read *Matthew 8:12*, "*But the children of the kingdom shall be cast out into outer darkness: there shall be weeping and gnashing of teeth.*" Jesus "loves?"

In some Christian theology "belief" is all that is necessary for obtaining eternal reward in heaven. It flows from verses such as *Romans 10:9*, "*That if thou shalt confess with thy mouth the Lord Jesus, and shalt believe in thine heart that God hath raised him from the dead, thou shalt be saved.*" Moreover, Christianity also relegates all nonbelievers to hell. This is derived from verses such as *Mark 16:16*, "*He that believeth and is baptized shall be saved; but he that believeth not shall be damned.*" This is the new message of Christian salvation. Paul made clear that works are not part of the requirements for Christian salvation in *Romans 3:28*, "*. . . a man is justified by faith without the deeds of the law.*" This is fundamental Christianity about belief, and only belief, offering salvation. We leave it for them to expound, with any kind of liberalism they might add in order to allow non-Christians into God's scheme of the world.

Let's extend this thought about Christianity's message of salvation to Adolf Hitler and the six million Jewish martyrs of the Nazi Holocaust. Picture this:—If Hitler "believed," he is enjoying heaven's reward for believers, yet the six million Jewish human beings he so demonically tortured and murdered are in hell as nonbelievers. Is this your concept of the goodness of God? Is this your concept of heaven, filled with believers such as Hitler? We need not delve into Christian theology to discover the ungodly error inherent in "belief" salvation, which allows evil to triumph on God's earth. God would not permit unrighteousness to take the place of righteousness in His plan for eternal salvation. Good conduct must enter the salvation road. And once righteousness is seen as God's will, Judaism's law of Moses, which is Biblically commanded by God, is found to be a sure path to eternity at His side!

We suggest that you visualize the following whenever you are accosted by the missionary oozing love and prayers for your soul. Jesus died on the Roman cross as well as in the ovens of the Holocaust's concentration camps. Imprint on your heart the emaciated, tormented body of just one of the millions of Jewish human beings who suffered extreme torture which was our lot. Picture Jesus as this Jew, for Jesus the Jew died with us in the Holocaust, as every spiritual Jew has died. We are all one in this the greatest of human tragedies. And as all Jews have spiritually suffered Christian persecution, ironically, so has Jesus the Jew.

If you are attracted to Jesus, admire him as the dedicated Jewish man described in the New Testament. If you need this feeling of attachment, use him as the symbol of the sacredness of Judaism, for that is what he taught. If you succumb to the heart-to-heart appeal of the missionary, let it be from your heart to the heart of Jesus' Father, your Father in heaven. Lean on God as Jesus did, for even Jesus said we should pray to "our Father." So, if you must, grab Jesus' Jewish hand and travel with him on Judaism's road, which we have shown was his road, and leave Jesus Christ to the Christians!

If there were truth in Christianity being based on Judaism's Bible, a person seeking religious fulfillment might be compelled to believe and convert. Tradition could be tossed aside. Obligation to one's people could be denied. Family bonds could be broken. Indeed, the horrors perpetrated in the name of Christianity on helpless Jews throughout the centuries could be excused as bad human conduct, even though inspired by the writings in the New Testament. However, it must be understood that a person who looks to Christianity as a religion of truth must have Biblical verification of this truth. Conversion could not be excused on any other grounds, because apostasy is not only against one's heritage, but against God Himself who brought forth the Jew. In this book, we have given abundant proof of the fallacy of Christianity's claim that its teachings are based on the Hebrew Scriptures. There is no justification for conversion to Christianity, because the Hebrew Scriptures do not speak of Jesus Christ!

Conversion in order to marry outside of Judaism, to find financial success, or to obtain social acceptance is rejected on any level. We cannot offer a judgment of God's reaction to Jews who through the centuries were forced to convert or face misery, torture, and death. We believe that God has a special understanding of this. However, in this book we are directing our attention to conversion through religious commitment, not any other reason.

The Jewish convert to Christianity must fear for his soul's fate. It is his wandering soul which is in jeopardy of eternal damnation, having rebuffed God and abandoned His pathway of the Torah's fulfillment. This book has shown that God and Jesus are separate entities, even in the New Testament. Although Christianity claims that Jesus is not "other gods," there is no verification of their claim in the Hebrew Bible. Therefore, the apostate, who has converted to Christianity, has turned to "other gods." Now see what God says about turning to other gods in *Deuteronomy 30:17-18 (Deuteronomy 8:19-20)* which reads, *"But if thine heart turn away (from the Lord thy God), . . . and worship other gods, and serve them; I denounce unto you this day, that ye shall surely perish . . ."* Speaking to the people of Israel, which is you Jewish reader, God announced His desire for unswerving devotion to Himself alone. The consequence of apostasy is to "perish." Thus it is written in the Scriptures.

We ended our chapter, "Personal Salvation Through Judaism," with the following, which bears repeating here:—"Perhaps you know in your innermost parts that Judaism is of God, but you're afraid of return. You're afraid of losing the guarantee of salvation, afraid of damnation falling on you, afraid of being wrong, and afraid of the unknown. Well, you should be in fear. But, your fear should be of your forsaking the God of your fathers for who knows what. Your abandonment will lie heavy on your soul when you die, if you die a willing apostate."

It would be beneficial for you to remember the multitude of Jewish martyrs throughout the Christian Era who chose death rather than conversion. Our holy martyrs refused to leave Judaism because they knew the Scriptures and knew God's Torah was their road to heaven, as it is ours! Our pious sages, who rejected apostasy, are our shining beacons. Let their strength and heroism enter into your understanding of God's religious plan for His Chosen People. They held firm to Judaism because it is the revealed word of God, not merely because they felt a loyalty to people and tradition. They suffered and gave their lives for the God of Israel, who is your God too, with whom you should never part. Our pious forefathers surely have their place in heaven, for this is what the Hebrew Bible indicates. Devoted Jews hope for this glorious reward for the righteous in the next world. So should you.

All Jews are part of a linkage of Jewish existence from our ancestors, beginning with the patriarch Abraham nearly four thousand years ago. The chain will stretch into the Messianic times. How electrifying! The born Jew has a sacred responsibility to God to remain steadfast to the Torah, to carry on the traditions of Judaism's heritage, and to teach his children the ways of Judaism. This is God's Biblical command.

God gave His Torah to His Chosen People as a responsibility, as well as an honor. The Torah is our yoke, as well as our springboard to heaven. God wants us to be a light to the nations. Why we were selected for His immutable Covenant is only for God to know. But, the nation of Israel was chosen, and we are His servants eternally. We dare not disengage from God by leaving His Torah. We cannot guiltlessly desert our pathway to Him, for it is, conversely, His pathway to us!

Being a religious Jew makes you a child of your Father in heaven, in direct contact with Him in all your prayers and in all you do during your entire day, entire year, and entire life. Every experience is more meaningful, because God is at your side. The world is a purposeful abode. The Torah is your road to righteousness and spiritual awakening, with eternal life your expectation. The Scriptures are God's holy communication with man, in which we find that Judaism is His religious plan for all the world.

Why are Jews being lost to Judaism? What has gone wrong? It is perhaps because Judaism has been lacking a spiritual spark for the modern generation. Its truth, offered in a vacuum of emotional feeling has not made for religious contentment. Truth and religious emotion should be found together. Picture the Lubavich's type of religious commitment and fervor and you realize what Judaism is and the heights to which it rises. Judaism never lost it, and the religious ardor is there for you to take up into your heart and soul.

Let's put it plainly. Judaism can and should be filled with the spirituality which lights up your life. Yet, your religious background may be the biggest turn-off to Judaism there is. If your Bar (Bat) Mitzvah was lacking in emotional excitement, you missed Judaism's holy breath. If you learned your Hebrew prayers without knowing the meaning of the words, you were denied religious gratification. Did you learn the law of Moses with God in the forefront of each Torah commandment? Did you have a holy man, who inspired you, as your rabbi? Did you have devotional services devoid of distracting noise and filled with communication with the forever? Did you have Bible

instead of bingo? In short, have you experienced the spiritual uplift of
Judaism? You have a right to want Judaism's soul-stirrings, for without
spirituality religion is unfulfilling. With it, the world is turned around.

The blandness of Jewish experience has lost us many Jewish
souls. But, the insipid, negative aspects of a person's Jewish background are not what Judaism is all about. They really are Judaism's
negation, preventing the Jew from contacting God and His pathway.
When we pray, we should feel we are speaking to God and touching
Him through the ages. We should find a holiness which encompasses
us in the synagogue. We should find eternity. Only those who have not
experienced the spiritual vibrations within Judaism would seek holiness outside of Judaism. That you have had a sterile Jewish life does
not mean Judaism lacks deep religious beauty and fulfillment. Our religion does possess exquisiteness. Seek it. The wavering Jew, maybe
you, should return and get your "religious high" in Judaism's home
where you belong!

Come, immerse yourself in Judaism. Find your Jewish heart. Let
bloom your Jewish faith. Say "thank God," and mean it. Start your
baal teshuvah, your return to Judaism, with the heart-warming experience of daily prayer, If you prefer, pray at home at first. Open your
soul to the beauty and benefits of prayer to God. It need not be in
Hebrew, so long as you understand the words. Then look for a synagogue which bursts with enthusiasm during services. Find a rabbi who
leads his congregation in vibrant worship.

You can become as deeply excited with Judaism as you may have
been with Christianity, wavering Jew. The reverence for the Hebrew
Scriptures, which you perhaps discovered in Christianity, will help you
appreciate your own Judaism! This may be the one good result of your
seeking holiness outside of Judaism. Christianity knows that the
Hebrew Bible is of God. Now you, the Jewish seeker of holiness,
know the sacred nature of your own Book of God. It's your Bible.
Read it with your Jewish eyes, mind, and heart. Learn that the God of
Israel is the one God of all the world. Your dedication to religious life
will grow all the more as you turn to Him and His Torah, with the
knowledge that God is your only Savior.

Now let's give some practical advice. Begin your return to Judaism by fulfilling some special areas of observance you feel are meaningful. For example:—Have a mezuzah on your front doorpost, and
touch it on leaving and returning home, to contact God as you come
and go. Wear a "chai" or Star of David to affirm your Jewish heart.
Say a blessing before eating bread (Baruch Atah Adonai Eloheynu
Melech ha-olom ha-motsee le-chem min ha-aretz). Light Sabbath candles Friday night with a prayer (Baruch Atah Adonai Eloheynu Melech
ha-olom asher kideshanu bemitzvatov vitzivanu le-hadlik ner shel

Shabbat). Drink wine with a kiddish prayer (Baruch Atah Adonai Elo-heynu Melech ha-olom boray pree ha-gefen). Pray the Shema on aris-ing and going to bed each day (*Deuteronomy 6:4-9, Deuteronomy 11:13-21, Numbers 15:37-41*). Use the Jewish prayer book daily. Look for the kosher symbol on food packages. Participate in Torah study. Read good books on Judaism. And most important get enlightenment from religious Jews who know the eternal God of Judaism.

You need not keep the Sabbath entirely at first, but start with what you can do comfortably. You need not be entirely kosher, but do what you can and stick to it. Your observance need not be total or perfect, but should be done with your full heart. Select the basics to you and do them to satisfy your level of dedication. As you grow in understanding, so will you grow in your desire to expand your observance. God will accept your return, if done with your full heart, and mind, and love.

Another suggestion that is a must for you is that you experience Shabbatons. They are the most rewarding of activities for people who wish to feel the vibrations of God and catch the fervor of believing. You will sense exultation. You will sing and dance, pray and learn, react and feel the tremendous warmth of your religion. Your soul will truly be refreshed, and you will be turned-on to Judaism as you may never have thought possible. Chances are that you will wonder why you were never advised to attend a Shabbaton before. You will wonder why it was not made part of your Bar (Bat) Mitzvah experience. If these happenings were made available to all young Jewish people, they likely never would seek spirituality elsewhere. Call some Jewish orga-nizations for the Shabbatons they organize or know about. Among oth-ers, you should contact the Lubavitch, the National Conference of Synagogue Youth, the Union of Orthodox Jewish Congregations of America, and Young Israel.

One last personal word is offered here concerning the writing of this book. Our initial fear of the undertaking faded when in a close to mysteri-ous way the book seemed to take shape by itself. As we approached one subject, the next seemed to flow from it. The answers we found were solid, substantial, and satisfying. What we found was even more than we had hoped to gather for the upholding of the eternal nature of Judaism's truth. We discovered Jesus the Jew in the New Testament, with his God the God of Israel and the law of Moses called effective for salvation. We discovered the treasure of eternity in the Hebrew Scriptures, with God and the Chosen People in a special holy relationship. We were amazed at how the answers fell in place for all the so-called proof-texts and even more surprised at the vindication of Judaism within the pages of the Christian Book. From trepidation at perhaps finding hints of the validity of Christianity based on the Hebrew Bible, we arrived at Judaism's com-plete confirmation. We found certainty in the legitimacy of our beliefs.

We saw that the Hebrew Messiah and the Christian Christ have nothing in common and that the Messianic expectations are unfulfilled. We observed that the Lord God of Israel is the one God alone, even in the New Testament. At every turn in our investigation and every level of thought, Judaism's holiness emerged. We thank God who gave us the opportunity to write this book and seems to have had His hand upon ours in this undertaking.

Baruch Ha-Shem.

The following prayer is given here, at the conclusion of this book, so that you can see the immense beauty of Jewish prayer, the hopes envisioned, and the supreme heights to which Judaism soars.

SHEMONEH ESREH PRAYER.

"When I proclaim the name of the Lord, give glory to our God! O Lord, open thou my lips, that my mouth may declare thy praise. Blessed art thou, Lord our God and God of our fathers, God of Abraham, God of Isaac and God of Jacob; great, mighty, and revered God, sublime God, who bestowest lovingkindness, and art Master of all things; who rememberest the good deeds of our fathers, and who wilt graciously bring a redeemer to their children's children for the sake of thy name.

O King, Supporter, Savior and Shield. Blessed art thou, O Lord, Shield of Abraham. Thou, O Lord, art mighty forever; thou revivest the dead; thou art powerful to save. Thou sustainest the living with kindness, and revivest the dead with great mercy; thou supportest all who fall, and healest the sick; thou settest the captives free, and keepest faith with those who sleep in the dust. Who is like thee, Lord of power? Who resembles thee, O King? Thou bringest death and restorest life, and causest salvation to flourish. Thou art faithful to revive the dead. Blessed art thou, O Lord, who revivest the dead. Amen."

JEREMIAH		EZEKIEL		DANIEL	
14:8	174	18:21	70,197	9:24-26	199
16:19	99,221	18:21,27	78	12:1-2	71
17:4	236	18:22	71	12:2	239
18:7	236	18:23	71	12:13	71
22:30	157	18:24	70		
23:3	92,223	18:26	70	HOSEA	
23:4-6	87	18:27	70	1:7	141
23:5-6	147	18:28	70	1:10	50,111,145
29:7	227	18:30	70	2:11	234
29:10	202	18:31	70	2:18	94,95
30:7-11,17	91	18:32	71	2:19	78
30:9	86	20:11	71	2:23	79,234
30:10	64	20:13	71	3:4-5	91,101,195
30:10,12,15-17	215	20:44	79	3:5	104
30:12	235	28:25	100	5:15	175
30:16	95,226	33:11,19	102	6:1	215
30:17	235	33:19	78,197	11:1	167
30:18	202	34:13	92	13:4	64,136,174
30:22	77	34:23-24	86,111	14:1-2	232
31:4,13	93	34:25	94	14:1-2,4	102,197
31:9	145	36:9,11	237		
31:15	167	36:22	237	JOEL	
31:31	238	36:23	237	1:8	159
31:31,33-34	97	36:25	97	2:1,10,32	103
31:32	239	36:26	98	2:24,26	93
31:33	238,239	36:27	98	2:27-28	101
31:34	20,76,156,239	37:5-7,10-14	71	3:14,16	103
32:40	98	37:11	222	3:17	238
32:42	91,236	37:12	192	3:18	102
33:6	215	37:23	97	3:19-20	95
33:8	76	37:24-25	86	3:20-21	101
33:14,16	87	37:25	190		
33:15	85	37:26	100	AMOS	
33:16	148	37:26-28	101	5:2	236
36:3	102,197	37:27-28	78	5:4	236
46:27	94	38:8	104	8:10	91,199
50:20	97	38:8,11	94	9:8	235
		38:18-23	103	9:8,14-15	91
LAMENTATIONS		39:4,6,11,13	104	9:11	101
2:6	234	39:9	94	9:15	236
2:13	215	39:29	101		
3:30	23	43:7	100,152	JONAH	
5:21	234	47:12	102	3:10	197
EZEKIEL		DANIEL		MICAH	
18:4	70	2:28	104	4:2	98,152,225
18:9	70,78	2:44	19,84,95	4:3-4	94
18:13	69	7:13-14	83,170,174	4:7	19,101
18:17	70	7:18	84	5:1	189
18:18	70	7:26-27	171	5:2	165
18:19	70	7:27	84	5:3	165
18:20	70,156	9:18-19	79	5:5	165